A Vagabond's

Being further reminiscences of

troubadour in many lands

A. Safroni-Middleton

Alpha Editions

This edition published in 2024

ISBN : 9789362099013

Design and Setting By
Alpha Editions
www.alphaedis.com
Email - info@alphaedis.com

As per information held with us this book is in Public Domain. This book is a reproduction of an important historical work. Alpha Editions uses the best technology to reproduce historical work in the same manner it was first published to preserve its original nature. Any marks or number seen are left intentionally to preserve its true form.

Contents

FOREWORD .... - 1 -
CHAPTER I .... - 4 -
CHAPTER II .... - 9 -
CHAPTER III .... - 12 -
CHAPTER IV .... - 19 -
CHAPTER V .... - 27 -
CHAPTER VI .... - 34 -
CHAPTER VII .... - 46 -
CHAPTER VIII .... - 58 -
CHAPTER IX .... - 69 -
CHAPTER X .... - 80 -
CHAPTER XI .... - 95 -
CHAPTER XII .... - 103 -
CHAPTER XIII .... - 116 -
CHAPTER XIV .... - 130 -
CHAPTER XV .... - 138 -
CHAPTER XVI .... - 144 -
CHAPTER XVII .... - 162 -
CHAPTER XVIII .... - 168 -
CHAPTER XIX .... - 176 -
CHAPTER XX .... - 185 -
CHAPTER XXI .... - 192 -
CHAPTER XXII .... - 201 -
CHAPTER XXIII .... - 213 -
CHAPTER XXIV .... - 223 -
CHAPTER XXV .... - 235 -

CHAPTER XXVI ....- 240 -
CHAPTER XXVII ....- 251 -

FOREWORD

"The path to hell is paved with good intentions."

LOOKING reflectively over this second instalment of my autobiography, I perceive that I am such a genuine vagabond that I have even travelled along in my reminiscences without caring for the material niceties of recognised literary method; so I have gone back over the whole track and tried earnestly to polish my efforts.

It seems quite unnecessary for vagabonds to wear (metaphorically speaking) old trousers with fringed ends to the legs, penniless pockets, dusty boots, an unshaven face and dirty collar, or to give vent to the devil-may-care utterances and all the ungrammatical "politeness" of the phraseology of the grog shanty and bush hotels, when they attempt to live over again on paper the tale of their wandering life. I cannot reform the world into a population of convivial beachcombers, nor would I if I could, out of consideration for future vagabonds, who naturally want the outer spaces of the world for their special province. Neither can I make you believe I could have done better in a literary sense if I had taken more trouble with my book. But I can to some extent reform myself, and at least strive to compete with the literary aristocrats on the slopes of their own cultivated ground. I am sure they will make good company if I succeed, and they will have been my best friends. Yes, I half believe in jumping out of bed on a cold night to hold a candle to the devil! I know that sometimes while you stand shivering you discover that he's really not such a bad fellow, and the candlelight is likely to give you a glimpse of some faint resemblance in his wrinkled face, some far-off expression of that beautiful old life that he lived ere he sinned, became respectable and fell—banished from heaven.

Life is a terrible contradiction; we are dead because we are born alive. Our very creed is based on the sad fact that the cemetery tablets record the dates of the true beginning of life everlasting. The thundering city is a necropolis wherein multitudes of wandering corpses breathe, with inert souls and thoughts that are like night bats flitting through the sepulchres of our death, with dead eyes and dead mouths that open to cough and even sometimes laugh! My book of reminiscences is (to me at least) like those silent, moss-grey tablets of immortality; but even more wonderful and true (as far as I know), for, while I am dead, I can see my long ago. I can lift the stone slab from the grave in the silent night and gaze on the dead boy's face, and in a way make the dead eyes laugh and the voiceless mouth mutter and sing in a hollow voice old, far-away songs of love, romance and its comrade, grief. Yes, you and I can see such things. Oh, how ineffably sad to some of us!

You may wonder what all this has to do with the preface to a book of reminiscences. It has a lot to do with the matter, because I am a born vagabond, and the world is incorrigibly respectable!

There are about one hundred pages missing from this book—pages that should have told of the inevitable details of stern existence: those things that all men who are vagabonds experience, such as the stomach-rumbles of hunger, monstrous hopes and misgivings, hospitals and illnesses, and cold nights sleeping out under the coco-palms and gum-trees when the wind suddenly shifts to a shivering quarter. Evil thoughts, heartaches, the tenderest wishes, passionate drums, longings, and memories in the night of a woman's eyes, the fall before great temptation, atheistical thoughts, curses and religious remorses you will look for in vain. For, after all, I am not brave enough to tell the truth! I might have done so if I had had the friendly, courageous publisher who would not cut them out of the original manuscript. But where is the publisher who would let me hide behind his influential bulk as he risked all and published the truth? Yes, those things which would make the reader recognise the truth by his own responsive thrills.

Well, I will risk my reputation on the opinions of those critics who will be able to read the hundred pages I have left out. For real scallawags do not always leave the worst out only. Moreover, I may be lucky enough to find sympathy, for even critics are sometimes at heart genuine vagabonds, and they may realise that I have turned into the light of other days, the stars, the blue tropical skies, moonlit seas by coral reefs and palm-clad isles, and into the heart of intense dreams, to paint faithfully all that I tell.

Before my North American experiences, which I have recorded in the opening chapters of this book, I had shipped before the mast of a sailing ship, the S——p, at Sydney, N.S.W., intending to go with her round the Horn, and so home to England. But, being unable to tolerate the bullying chief mate and the offal-flavoured fo'c'sle food, I left the boat at 'Frisco and again shipped on an American tramp that was chartered for trading purposes to go cruising in the South Seas, where once more I had many ups and downs, and settled for a few months in the Fiji group and elsewhere. My reminiscences, and many of the incidents of that time, I have told in the second part of the present volume, which opens with "The Charity Organization of the South Seas."

My South Sea Island legends and fairy tales have never been told elsewhere. I have written them as nearly as possible in the manner in which they were told me by the Samoan children and natives who were my friends. The mythology of the South Seas is unfortunately becoming almost completely forgotten by the natives, who now live under such different conditions, and seem only interested in the creeds, legends and mythology of the Western world.

These experiences of mine are written from memory, and I have as nearly as possible kept them in the order that I lived them; and if they seem far-flung for one as young as I was, let me assure you that hundreds of English boys have had my experiences and could tell this tale.

I am from a family of rovers. My uncles were travellers and explorers. My brothers out of the spirit of adventure all went to sea, and achieved success on sea and land through perseverance. My grandfather in his boyhood went to sea. (I believe he was born at sea. His mother was a lady of the Italian Court, noted for her beauty and an accomplished musician.) He was a direct descendant of Charles, the second Earl of Middleton, whose estates were eventually confiscated by creditors—an evil destiny that has survived right down to the present, it having cropped up in the author's own affairs.

I hope to follow this volume with another one, wherein I shall tell of my life when I settled for a while among civilised peoples and became respectable, and my serious troubles commenced.

I have to thank Messrs Boosey & Company, of London, for permission to use certain extracts from my military band Entr'actes, Marches, etc., which they have published.

A. S.-M.

CHAPTER I

In Boston—Song-composing—Looking for a Publisher—How I secured him—I visit Providence—I play in the Military Band—Hard up

IN those old days of my youth an atmosphere of romance gathered from old novels and dreams still sparkled in my head. I am going to tell of the adventures that followed directly on my boyhood, when before the mast I had crossed the seas with eyes athirst for romance, looking for the wonderful, the beautiful in distant lands, in men and in women, and for that opportunity to perform those mighty, world-thrilling deeds that, alas, I have not even yet performed!

After much wandering in search of wealth and fame, following desperate trouble owing to schemes that failed in Australia and the South Sea Islands, I at length caught typhoid fever in San Francisco. With many misgivings I recovered. At last I found myself sitting in a top attic in North America. It was a humble little room, the atmosphere and surroundings the very thing to feed the fire of my aspiring mind, to force one to do better. Its one windowpane was broken; the furniture consisted of an old table, a box chair, a candlestick and my extemporised bed on the floor! I was in Boston, "the Hub of the Universe"! My sea-chest and best suit were in pawn in San Francisco. My money had almost all gone, and my latest grand passion had faded. I had been practising the violin furiously day and night, for I hoped to become the world's greatest violinist. Yet at heart I still felt triumphant. The world seemed especially mine! One thing only existence lacked—a kindred spirit to stand shoulder to shoulder by my side on some quest for glorious violence, adventurous thrills, voyaging across the uncharted seas of imagination. O too brief, splendid madness of youth!

Far below, outside my window, over the city's stone-slabbed streets, rattled vehicles, and the hurried, endless battalions of Yankee citizens passed by, seeking fortune or the grave. Gold seemed the incentive to all thrills; human passion, hope and ambition seemed congealed into a mechanical state of steam, electric locomotion, and all that the almighty silver dollars would clink against. I also seemed to have frozen and become a part of the machine which is called civilisation. The songs of sails aloft, the noise of forest winds and soundings across deep waters, had faded from my dreams into a wail of selfishness. Imagination is the soul of the Universe, and grief is its Bible; but, alas, I felt a gross craving for food.

So my ambition to outrival Paganini on the violin had subsided from its state of enthusiastic fire and had left in my heart a dull callousness. One intense wish survived: to get a sound pair of boots and a new suit! Winter snows were only just melting, and much privation had considerably thinned me. I had done many things which I feel remain best untold. Necessity had inspired me with many original and desperate schemes, the latest of which was a determination to compose songs. Music hall hits come, have their day, are whistled and sung by the élite and by the street-arab, and suddenly I thought, why should not I supply the public with those rotten melodies? I would do it on original lines and give the American public something new. Did they not hail as brand-new old melodies that Wellington's soldiers sung at Waterloo and antiquated strains brought over by the passengers of the *Mayflower* with one bar reversed and the title altered.

I would jump from my bed at night and, throwing off my "blanket," which consisted of half-a-dozen old overcoats which my landlady had lent me, write down inspired strains and next day put them to suitable words, words with those sentimental and lascivious suggestions in them that suit the public taste—for the artist in me had sorrowed and become temporarily gross. I sought money more than the applause of musical critics. Boston publishers became familiar with my handwriting. I had about fifty rejected manuscripts with specially printed forms, notices that offered me "their appreciation of my favours, and the editor's sincere compliments, and by the same post with many regrets they were returning the MSS." At length I thought my name was getting too well known: I was obliged to seek a *nom de plume*. With characteristic family cautiousness I hit on a name that was already famous in New York musical circles. My youthful innocence had almost passed, and I vaguely felt that to compete with the world I must deliberately stain myself with its contagion. Often my heart bristled with schemes as multitudinous as quills on a hedgehog's hide.

I had composed an attractive melody and had placed suitable words to it, but, notwithstanding my famous *nom de plume*, "Muller," I had had my manuscripts returned, torn in the post, the editor's marks indelibly damaging it, and too often a dark stain across the first page that looked suspiciously like editorial tobacco juice.

Things began to look serious. I became, if possible, even thinner. My landlady's politeness became gross; she thumped the door for rent. I was starving and only had a cake of common yellow soap. With the superhuman energy and pluck of aspiring youth I tried again, imitated the latest hit and sent the manuscript to "D—— & Co.," of Boston, a small publishing firm in a side street off 6th Avenue. I signed it with my *nom de plume*; the initials differed by one letter from those of the original owner—I thought this necessary to save legal trouble.

I waited three days. The post brought me no letter, so I wrote to the publisher and said:

"Dear Sirs,—I am an Englishman on tour, and a member of the Carl Rosa Opera Company's orchestra. I may have to leave Boston at any moment, so, much against my wish, I must worry you for speedy consideration of my manuscript song, *Dreams of Eldorado*, which I can get publicly performed in London town when I arrive back."

Two days later, to my great delight, I received a letter asking me to call on D—— & Co. *re* my manuscript. The very thought of my song reaching engraving and print thrilled me; that I should be published in America at another man's expense seemed impossible! A Vanderbilt-like feeling pervaded my being. I pawned my violin, paid my landlady a week's rent and gave the little blue-eyed daughter twenty-five cents to buy sweets with. I could have sung with joy. Next morning at ten-thirty I was to be at the publisher's office. By night the reaction set in. I became suspicious. Suppose it was all a ruse! For had I not borrowed a famous name? A thousand thoughts haunted me; my musical ability seemed nil. I had no talent. I hummed my melodies over; they seemed ridiculously tuneless. There was no doubt about it: the Boston publishers had seen through my scheme, had held a solemn council, and most probably would be waiting in that office to pounce upon me and charge me with my duplicity, and then God knows what they might do. On the floor all night the old overcoats moved and moved as I restlessly turned in my bed. I was numbed with awful suspicions and possible contingencies. I rose haggard and wretched, and against all my usual instincts sought a saloon and drank twenty-five cents' worth of rum. With renewed courage I prepared to risk all. At ten o'clock I walked past a brass-plated door with D—— & Co. on it. Three times I passed it and then, walking crabwise, I went in. A little man with a skull-cap on got up and welcomed me. I hurriedly glanced round; the ambushed publishers of my imagination faded as the girl typewriter yawned and clicked away. My erstwhile gloom blossomed to monstrous hopes. Negotiations commenced. "What did I usually ask for my work?" he demanded. I blushed and hastily wiped my nose. "Will fifty dollars do?" I answered. I eventually got five dollars for the song as a preliminary payment on royalties to come. Such royalties! One cent on each copy sold after the first ten thousand advertisement copies had been given away and the second one thousand had repaid the actual expenses of the publication and engraving. Afterwards, too, I found out that to engrave a song of four plates cost the publisher five dollars. I trembled as I clutched the green five-dollar bill. "Will he alter his mind?" was my chief thought. "Does he think I am the great Muller?" The publisher broke in on my thoughts. "Place your name there," he said, and I signed the imposing agreement, four times the length of my manuscript song.

Readjusting his skull-cap and wiping his spectacles, he began to examine my signature. The weather was cold, but I started to perspire. Was he comparing my signature with Muller's? It was an awful thought, and with a sickly farewell I bolted!

Hurrying down the main street, I longed to get out of sight with the dollars, but I heard a shout behind me; my assumed name was loudly called: I turned; my heart sank. I nearly fainted: the publisher was running after me. I clutched my money, determined to resist. The new greatness thrust upon me by the sale of my song still remained with me. I could not humiliate my pride and run, though I longed to do so. With his little skull-cap askew, he stood puffing in front of me! I gave one glance to warn him not to get too near my person, and heard him saying: "Oh, excuse me, Mr Muller, I suppose you will be in Boston long enough to correct the proof?"

In a dream I reached my room, packed up my brush and comb, got my violin out of pawn and left Boston for Providence, where my brother lived, who had left England years before. To my great regret I found, when I arrived, that he was away in California. No one seemed to know when he would return. I could not force my way into his bachelor rooms, and so I was once more on the rocks.

I became acquainted with a young Swede who was musical and played the clarionet. Together we fixed up a small orchestra, went out to play at dances and so just managed to exist. We hired a large room in a hall near the Hoyle Buildings in Westminster Street; made our own furniture out of meat tubs and our beds of old overcoats. My violin, with coats doubled on it, made an excellent pillow. With our heads side by side on it we slept as soundly as though we were in the Australian bush. I spent hours each day, and sometimes worked far into the night, practising my violin and reading the lives of great musicians and writers.

My brother, a crack violinist and a well-known journalist in the States, did not return for four or five months, and in the meantime our orchestra failed. My friend and I lived for a time on the free lunches of the grog saloons. North American saloon owners do not allow their customers to starve while they supply them with alcoholic poison, which is, however, fifty per cent. better than English spirit. For Americans are both humane and practical. They know that dead men do not buy rum, so the bars at luncheon hours steam with hot Frankforts, plates of cold meat, cheese and biscuits, provided without any charge to their customers. The honesty of Providence is illustrated by one fact alone—if you buy ten cents' worth of whisky they hand you a glass and the bottle, that you may help yourself. In London, Australia and the South Seas the grog-keeper would be ruined in a week if he ran his business on those lines! You seldom see a woman in a grog saloon, and never drunk in the streets.

Eventually I secured several jobs at concert halls. The pay was small, but, though other work was to be had, my temperament strongly objected to anything that needed muscular power. To tell the truth, I was ambitious. I longed to raise myself out of the ordinary ruck of things. However, when my Swedish friend got a job out at Pawtucket, digging post-holes, the high wages tempted me and I too started work there. Together we toiled for three weeks. Then once more I started composing, and had several pieces of dance music accepted in my own name. I arranged them as pianoforte solos, and one or two for the violin and piano.

When the weather got warm I sometimes went out to Fort Hill, on the Seekonk river. The prairie-land of Rhode Island survives in variegated patches of miles of beautiful scenery, with rushing rivers, and landscapes dotted by wooden homesteads that remind one of New Zealand and the Australian bush-land.

CHAPTER II

United States Military Music—The Roger Williams Park—Indians—Rhode Island Scenery and Amusements—Yankees—Experiences—A Miner from California

IN Providence I made friends with a military band conductor. He was a jolly customer, hard up but good-natured and humorous, a real American bandmaster of the old convivial school, kind at heart and fond of good whisky. His greatest virtue was a commonplace one: he would always pay you back anything he borrowed, but unfortunately he was hard up and could not do so. He had every excuse for this, for, as elsewhere, bandsmen, indeed musicians in general, were supposed to be able to live on melody and royalties that might arrive in some remote future. I worked for him, borrowed my comrade's clarionet and secured a position in the military band. It played in Roger Williams Park, performing on the usual holidays and on sunshiny evenings.

American conductors believe in vigour and fire when they perform, and sacrifice artistic pianissimo to force and go: on the march the bands lift you off your feet through the lilt of the music. The characteristic go-ahead of the Yankees is finely illustrated by the music they perform, and the military bands swing the population along as they march down the streets: men, women and children instinctively fall into line. A Pied-Piper-of-Hamelin fever seizes hold of the citizens; the whole population is suddenly on the march as the band goes by. I played in the band on the Fourth of July, a day celebrated by fireworks and gun-firing. Americans go mad on that date, wear masks and do other hideous things; it's a kind of Guy Fawkes celebration.

The Roger Williams Park is partly wild and partly cultivated, and artistically laid out with gardens and miniature landscapes that in summer-time are a paradise of flowers. Various kinds of tropical-looking trees abound, in scattered clumps that are haunted at sunset with bright, roving eyes: for springing from bough to bough jump swarms of big, wild, grey squirrels; their brush tails, a foot long, stick up as they jump. The children are their boon companions, and come miles with lumps of cake and bread to feed their tiny, soft playmates; for they are as tame as white mice, spring down from bough to bough and sneak a peanut off your hand, turn, brush your face with their tails and are gone! In a second they are sitting on a skyward twig nibbling away at your gift, safe against the blue sky. I found a nest of them at Pawtucket Falls, a wild, beautiful spot near Rhodes. As I was looking at the fluffy youngsters the mother arrived and, to my astonishment, chased me away.

At Pawtucket Falls, too, I met a group of travelling Indians, menagerie people I think, *en route* for somewhere. Fenimore Cooper and other Indian tales still interested me, so I talked to them and spoke to "Bull Face," a grave-looking chief, tawny and wrinkled with years, and clothed in a heavy brown blanket which swarmed with fleas. He spoke English as well as I did; but the South Sea Island breeds are far removed from the Indian tribes, both by blood and habit. I never sought his tribe again. I also saw Indians camping at Ochee Springs; real Indians they were, with squaws attending to their wants as they blinked their eyes and gazed scornfully on the onlookers. Smoking their calamets, dressed in tribal fashion, they inspired me with curiosity. I cannot say that the women were as handsome as I expected, for they had stolid, broad, reddish-brown faces and expectorated frequently as they sucked clay pipes. A pretty little papoose tugged at its mother's breast, and did not look unlike a South Sea Island baby, excepting that its forehead was high and receding, and it had an impertinent European look. The women carry their suckling babes in a basket on their back: when the babe finishes pulling at the breast it crawls into the basket behind and goes to sleep until the next meal. I saw the papooses of another tribe too; the children looked like little wrinkled old men, and you might have thought that they were small authors sitting on their bundles of unaccepted manuscript, so worried did they look.

Providence is a spacious city; English towns are in the shade compared to it, and seem overcrowded and gloomy. The streets are wide; terraced store buildings on each side tower to the skies. Piazzas shade the pavements and the citizens from scorching sunlight and rain. America has built her cities on the improved plans of the Old World, and so has an advantage over London and our provincial towns. Room to breathe in is the natural birthright of America. Extensive parks, rushing rivers, and relics of primeval scenery surround the city, and divide the suburbs for miles and miles.

No sign of poverty is betrayed by the well-dressed crowds that chatter cheerfully up and down the main streets; street-arabs are unknown. A Mile End woman of London town in rags, with bruised nose and eyes, walking down the street would create a sensation in Providence, and their weekly papers would devote an article to the distressing incident.

Brilliantly lit saloons shine in the evening streets, and regiments of laughing youths and girls hurry to the various depots, bound for the ferry-boats on moonlight trips down the rivers. The bars are closed on Sunday, but men trust men, and more sly rum is drunk on Sunday than weekdays. Niggers with ebony faces mingle with the white population, wearing white collars which support their ears: a shabby nigger has never been seen in Providence. If you shoot a nigger and do not kill him you are in danger of getting six months in the State prison for wasting shot and powder!

Many of the characters you meet in American cities remind you of Englishmen, but you can never really forget that you are in America. No true Yankee with self-respect allows you to quash his opinion. Nothing on earth can beat Providence, Boston, or any state you happen to be in. They will argue for ever; and if you at length say anything that has indisputable conviction in it, a true Yankee will squirt a stream of tobacco juice with the deliberate intention of not missing you.

Things of this kind worry you for a while, but you soon fall into their ways, and if you are smart can outrival them on their own ground; but you have got to be smart. To tell the truth, Americans have good reason to be proud of their states, and really have plenty to blow about.

Literary critics have hinted that Bret Harte discovered his characters in his own imagination. I can on oath dispute that fact. Grim Mr Billy Goat Whiskers, who fought in the North and South wars, draws his munificent pension, chews tobacco and dwells in Providence to-day. You do not meet him everywhere, but he is to be met.

In the grog saloons old miners from California told me their experiences, drew from their pockets photographs of gold nuggets and of gold claims that revealed small white dots in the far background—the tombstones of men who had thwarted them! They were innocent-looking enough, these men scarred with wounds, tropic heat and bad rum. They followed the various occupations that suited aged heroes. One old miner from Alaska suddenly arrived in Providence quite penniless. His name was Cargo. Walking down Z—— Street, he spied the name of Cargo over a sign-writer's shop, walked straight in, spat on the floor, called the "boss," and tried to make him believe he was the ancestor of the family of Cargo, and the rightful owner of the business. He was immovable. They expostulated with him; he would not go, so they gave him a job and thus saved legal proceedings in the High Courts of the state, and the expense of regiments of lawyers who would dispute the true owner's claim to his business.

Providence is full of reminiscent men who tell of adventures that are wide and wonderful.

If you are disinclined to go to the theatre you can always go into a bar and in peace and comfort sit within earshot of some grog-nosed hero of the old school, and find subject matter to outrival the romance of fiction. You must take good care not to let the old fellow know you are listening, otherwise he leaves facts alone and, with ill-concealed pride, makes your blood congeal with vivid descriptions of old days, murder and despair, or your mouth water for a breath of the fortunes that knocked around ere you were born.

CHAPTER III

I travel and sell Bug Powder—Seeking my Wages—Pork and Beans—Reminiscences of Sarasate—I strive to outrival Paganini—Practising the Violin—I am presented with a Round Robin—My Blasted Ambitions

AS the hot months came round my money gave out. Work was plentiful in the numerous factories that throb and thunder with machinery in Providence, but such work was not congenial to my temperament, and would ruin my fingers for violin-playing, as the post-digging job did. Nevertheless I should have availed myself of the opportunity had no alternative appealed to me. But my friend the conductor was a crank who was always producing some new scheme or invention that would assist him financially and augment his moderate musician's salary.

One night he came to my diggings beaming with enthusiasm over a plan to make us both rich. He had invented a new bug powder: our fortunes were made; all we had to do was to let the Providence public know the catastrophe that we had ready for these insects. Suburban houses in the States are generally made of wood that is specially suitable for the bug state. So the population of Rhode Island all have one secret; and on dark nights in hot weather candle gleams and shadowy figures can be seen dodging on the windows of the tenements, as restless folk in their nightshirts smash bugs on the wooden walls. I write from experience. They creep down the walls in regiments, and while you sleep eat your eyelids; if you wink they seek crevices, dart into your ears, and prepare for the next attack! Closing your toes together swiftly at night in bed, you can be sure that you have squashed three or four American bugs. I have carelessly glanced at skeletons which I thought were ancient dead bugs on the walls in the room of my new lodgings, and then at midnight I have lit the candle, and down the walls were marching battalions of old bug-skins! They had smelt me, and the regiments on the frontier of my bedstead were already full blown with my blood.

So it is obvious that a good insect powder would be a blessing in Providence.

Well, my Swedish friend and I threw our musical instruments aside, and started on the bug powder business, full of hope. I had several musical compositions that I was ambitious to publish on my own account. I felt that Providence bugs had presented the tide in my affairs which I should take at the flood.

With our pockets stuffed with a thousand bills, advertisements bearing testimonials from American presidents and English royalties who had stayed in America, my comrade and I tramped along with our hearts singing the excelsior song of happiness. We really lived in a paradise of ignorance and youth. "A rose by any other name would smell as sweet" is a true phrase, and happy, though selling bug powder, was equally true of us.

We marched, singing, on the dusty, white track to Narragansett. In the suburban gardens that led to the front doors grew gorgeous flowers. I can still dream that I smell their fragrance, and see the dancing blossoms in the brilliant sunshine. Strange things darted over us, hovered near the blooms and moaned like big humble bees. They were humming-birds, glittering and flashing their vivid colours, outrivalling the flowers with their brilliant feathery garment. The sky was blue as a girl's eyes, and nearly as beautiful. We delivered the thousand bills and spent the rest of the day by a river. Wild fowl swam across it, and fresh from the eggs, with frightened eyes gleaming, the little ones paddled behind them. For miles the country was strewn with trees and houses, many of them made of wood, and at these especially we left three or four bills and at length disposed of the lot.

When we called on my friend the conductor for a first instalment of twenty dollars for our services we found him out, but after several visits we caught him. He was pleased to hear that we had worked a full week and left five thousand advertisements, but he put off the payment of our wages and borrowed my last five dollars! We haunted him for days; he was seldom home. My comrade and I sweated for miles and miles, seeking him at his various musical engagements; but the man seemed gifted with second sight, for as we knocked at the front entrance he hurried off from the back and vanished. The bug business failed and he moved. Still we demanded our wages by post; for he had left no address, and we hoped that the postal authorities would forward our pleading request. At last we found him. The sound of martial music came down D—— Street: a military band was leading a funeral procession, of some old soldier I suppose. There at the head of the band he blew solo cornet. We dared not approach him, but in our excitement we waved our hands. He winked in a friendly way as he passed on, and the strains of Chopin's *Funeral March* faded with our hopes.

Eventually we caught him in a cul-de-sac, got ten dollars out of him and lived on pork and beans for a fortnight. Providence would be indeed stricken without pork and beans. As a rule they are not cooked, or rather baked, at home, but bought in jars, hot from the baker's oven, ten and twenty-five cents a jar. Crime is scarce in Providence, capital punishment abolished. If a citizen sat down to his meal and discovered no pork and beans, and slew the waiter, he would get off on extenuating circumstances. Well, to revert to the bug powder business, like all my commercial enterprises, it ceased on my receiving the ten dollars, and my employer the bandmaster told me, when I met him a month after, that I had made five dollars more out of the enterprise than he did.

This brings me to another friend, a Sioux Indian, who was married and lived in the next rooms to my own. His wife, a white woman, took in washing and kept him. I used to sit in the evening and listen to his opinion of the States. His whole soul hated the Yankees. I once praised the Americans and their cities. He was down on me in a flash. "I am the true American," he growled, "and the day will come when we shall get our country back." I did not argue the point with him; his old wife kept him, and he showed base ingratitude by his opinions. He was educated and well dressed, and revealed to me, by all his conversation, the same kind of spite for the foreigner that I had noticed in the South Seas. Notwithstanding that the States had been peopled by whites so long, still the Yankee was an interloper and the robber of his country. He was not a bad old Indian, and was a friend to me during my stay at his tenement.

Just before I took his rooms I went to Boston to hear H——, a celebrated violinist who was performing there; I was anxious to hear if he was as wonderful as the review notices made him. I do not think I have ever heard such fine playing equalled even. He played Mendelssohn's concerto, and swayed the legato strain out till it sang like a rivulet of silver song as the deeper notes mellowed to a golden strain as perfect in quality as the sunset lyre-bird of Australia. I have heard Sarasate, Ysaye, Joachim and many others, but no one with a better tone and intonation, except Sarasate, who played like some inspired magician off the concert stage. I heard him play at his villa in Biarritz, where I had the pleasure of receiving a gratuitous lesson from the celebrated *maestro*. "No, like this," he said, as I played one of his own compositions: then he lifted his violin to his chin, and looked out of the villa's latticed window as he played and rippled out a sparkling chain of diamond-pure notes and then literally swooned into the adagio.

I never had the courage to play that particular piece after.

After hearing that violin virtuoso at Boston I became enthusiastic and returned to Providence. The fever was on me. Again I determined to be the world's greatest violinist! I almost wept at my wasted life on sea and shore. What might I not have been now, thought I, had I been practising the violin all those thousands of days instead of making sailors and South Sea Island savages my comrades? I went to the music stores and purchased the American editions of Petrie's *Studies*, and Paganini's *Twenty-four Etudes-Caprices*.

In my room, over the old Indian's, I commenced. At daybreak I jumped each morning off my trestle bed and started practising. At first I tackled the Caprice which is double-stopping throughout. In a week I had got it off. I had long fingers, otherwise I should think it an impossibility. All day I bowed away. My furniture consisted of a music-stand, the *Etudes*, my bed and me!

When I look back and think of my wonderful perseverance, it seems almost incredible. True and wonderful is the energy and happiness that aspiration brings to youth! Day after day I worked away at the studies with almost demon-like fury. Soon my chin had a great scab on it where the violin rested as I ground out the double-stopping sweeps, arpeggios and staccatos. I became thin and haggard-looking. I greedily devoured the lives of great violinists, among them Paganini and Ole Bull; also, after long intervals, pork and beans, as the old Indian below-stairs cooked them. He soon looked upon me as a sad kind of madman. I would gulp down the beans, look at his old grandfather clock and rush upstairs, then once more grind away, determined to make up for lost years. I saw the mighty crowds at concerts TO BE, applauding my wonderful playing! I was a new Paganini. Ah! how I remember it all. Through excessive playing the corns on my finger-tips became so hard that I could not feel the strings! My nervous system was soon wrecked, and my brain became ethereal with dreams—music was the all in all of life. People who did not play the violin were insanely ignorant.

Inspired, I extemporised melodies as I bowed and toiled away during the night hours: the day was not sufficient. The doors of the next tenement would suddenly bang, and strange tappings sound on the walls. I opened the window at midnight. I thought my double-stopping assuredly entranced the neighbours. It was hot weather, their windows were open too. In my imagination I thought I was playing to crowded houses. I heard the applause. Do you think I exaggerate? Believe me, I could never write down the depth, the magnificence, of those enthusiastic dreams. Only those who have felt as I felt, and were once inspired with ambition as I was inspired, will know exactly all that I felt, and all that I dreamed.

One day ten solemn-looking American citizens appeared outside the door of the Indian's tenement; they wanted to see me. My name was called. I laid the violin down. I had no friends. Had my brother arrived? Strange thoughts flitted through my brain. Had people come as a special convoy to praise my extraordinarily fine playing? I opened the door and, white-faced and tremulous, I stared at a grey-bearded, solemn-looking old man who acted as spokesman. He presented me with a round robin. Fierce faces were looking over his shoulders! Two or three hundred signatures were there, the landlord's signature looked the boldest! I was either to stop playing the violin or give up the premises and move at once. This was a terrible blow to me. I should lose a day's practice if I had to tramp about looking for another room. I hated the world. Men were hard and mercenary. Only violinists and musicians had souls. I looked at my violin; it was my dear, abused comrade, and I clung to its reputation more than ever. No mother on earth ever leaned over her child with thoughts that outdid the tenderness of mine as I leaned over my tiny, responsive comrade, silent in its coffin-shaped bed. The dead child of my musical aspirations it seemed to me, for they were gone, and my mighty ambition lay a dead failure. Oh, you aspirants, you musicians and poets of this world, all you who love art for art's sake, for you, and you alone, I write this. You will understand; you are my brothers. I can wish you more success, but no greater happiness than the delirium, the ecstatic joy that was mine when I sought to become the world's greatest violinist.

I became melancholy: my incessant practice and irregular meals had, for the time being, destroyed my nerves. I thought of my schooldays and my life at sea, and longed for my boyhood's days in the Australian bush. I remembered the kingly stockman and his wife, and the surrounding bush loneliness; the leafy gum clumps and the parrots roosting in them; and the hours when I sat on the dead log by the scented wattles in the hollows and watched the fleets of cockatoos like tiny canoes fade away in the sunset. I heard in dreams the laughter of the romping bush children as I raced them down the scrub-covered slopes, and I longed for those ambitionless days to come again.

MEMORIES

I can still see the forest trees

All waving in the dusk,

As scents drift on the wandering breeze,

From wattle-blooms and musk;

And o'er the mountains far away

Where home the parrots flock,

Roams through the sunset's crimson ray

The drover with his stock.

The old bush homestead by the sea

Still stands, the front door swings

As on the tall, gaunt, dead gum-tree

The magpie sits and sings.

There, by the door, the stockman sits

And smokes; as on her rug

His pale wife sits just by and knits—

His beard three children tug!

And as I stand and, dreaming, gaze,
The years have taken wing,
And from my heart out of old days
Comes this sad song I sing.
That garden where those children ran,
Raced me, laughed, screamed with joy,
Is overgrown—and I, a man,
Have overgrown the boy.

I know the redwood's forest height
Of branches thrilled with words,
All laden with God's golden light—
Songs of soft, bright-winged birds—
Has blazed to ash in homestead fires
Of cities o'er the plains;
Of all those woods and sweet desires
This poem now remains.

Sweet Ellen, curled hair and brown eyes,
I loved her pretty ways;
And as I dream sad heart-mists rise
From those wild boyhood days.
My love was half a passion then,
That pure love God earth gave—
It comes in after years to men
For someone in a grave.

Their shanty where I sweetly slept
And heard the night-birds' screams—
As thro' the scrub the dingo crept—
Has rotted into dreams.

Now thro' the hills the echoes fly
Of hearts o'er shining rails—
The night express fast thundering by
That brings the English mails!

Yet often I go back again
To where the homestead stands;
I gaze in eyes thro' mists of pain
And clasp old shadow hands;
Kiss Ellen, Bertha and Lurline:
Those pretty children three
May some day read these lines of mine
And all remember me.

CHAPTER IV

My Brother's Return—Scenery—Old Providence—Robert Louis Stevenson—New York—At Sea—The Change

IN August that year I at last received a letter from my brother, telling me he had left California and would arrive in Providence in a few days. I was delighted, for I was then completely on the rocks, having spent all my earnings on buying a violin bow and a stock of music! My comrade the Swede promised to come with me to meet my relative at the station.

The next day we stood on the platform together at eleven o'clock. The telegram said 12.30 P.M., but we were young and eager. We rubbed our hands with joyful anticipation as we stood there anxiously watching. Our funds were low and my brother had performed a miracle—he was a poet and journalist, and had made money out of his profession. When the train steamed in and the saloon car door opened I recognised at a glance the characteristic contour of the family face, though I had not seen my brother since we were children. I rushed forward overjoyed, and the welcome of brotherhood smiled in his expression. Six feet in height, and correspondingly athletic in appearance, he was well able to carry his own portmanteau, but privations and thoughts of affluence from his exchequer inspired me. Impulsively I seized it!

Years of residence in the States seemed to have changed his original nationality and the accent of his speech. He stood smiling before me, a Yankee of the aristocratic type. His keen grey eyes stared at my shabby clothes: the situation was evident to him at a glance. In a store by the civic centre, with an entrance that looked like the south nave of the Crystal Palace, my comrade and I were measured for new suits. Words could not express my gratitude.

With this lightening of my financial cares I felt the dim delirium, the exuberance, the faint revival of my old romantic glamour return; the world seemed beautiful after all.

My Swedish friend was delighted too, and smiled from ear to ear. I can still see his tall, lanky figure, and his merry round blue eyes as he puffs and tootles away on his beloved clarionet. Ah, how happy we were, marching on, carelessly unfulfilling the great promise of youth while we were yet youthful! Yet what is the good of promise fulfilled when youth is gone, when the glamour has faded, and you look through the grim spectacles of reality at the rouged cheeks of blushing truth and beauty? Oh, to remould this scheme of life, and be born old! To travel with Time and grim experiences down the years towards cheerful, glorious youth, back, back to the innocence and beauty of childhood's dreams! To die full of hope and fond beliefs—and let the true believers travel the other way!

I know not where we went or why we went. I only know that my brother embraced the occasion and caught the vagabond fever; and that our valet, an old Turk (who kept swearing that he wasn't an Armenian), sang jovial songs that were musically reminiscent of his harem days as he stumbled and struggled behind us, carrying our bundles of fruit, new suits, bouquets of flowers, and my long-wanted expensive copyright *Etudes*, Petrie's *Violin Studies*, and all that sudden and unexpected affluence inspired us to buy.

I recall, too, how we were walking up the brilliantly lighted main street when a negro, who was anxiously watching for the editor of a Providence journal (that had criticised his lodging-house and the lady lodgers who kept such late hours), suddenly whipped out a revolver and fired. The editor had appeared at his door and received a bullet in his face, but he too had a revolver—probably he had been expecting the negro's compliments—and he fired back and blew all the negro's front teeth out. The next bullet from the negro's revolver went through the *Violin Studies* which I held by my side, and but for the fortunate ricochetting of the bullet I should not now be able to write my reminiscences! I think the negro recovered from his wound and the editor was severely reprimanded for not hitting a vital spot. For the sins of negroes are dwelt upon like the sins of the poor relation, and I must admit that negroes are sometimes almost as bad as white men. There were no moving pictures in those days to perpetuate the episode, but still it is flashed vividly before my mind's eye. I see the three races of good fellowship, my tall brother and myself, between us my lanky Swede comrade, and, just behind us, straight-nosed Turkey struggling along on bandy legs. Equipped with argosies of youthful dreams, pitching the moon and stars and sun from hand to hand, with rollicking song on our lips we fade away down the uncharted seas of Westminster Street, Providence!—to awaken on dim shores of cold daybreak as once more I kneel and take the sacrament before the grim, mock-eyed old priest—Reality! When I was twenty years and one month old—how long ago it seems!

We visited most of the fashionable places of interest, went almost everywhere, through the Open Sesame of my brother's liberality. And that is saying a good deal, for theatres and palatial halls of amusement abound. There's "The Gaiety," "The Colonial," "Hippodrome," "Sans Souci," "Bijou," and heaven knows how many more, wherein the cheerful multitudes of R.I. folk scream with laughter and weep over unreal dramas.

I no longer played the monotonous second fiddle in the orchestra of the music hall; we sat, a happy trio, the smiling occupants of orchestral stalls, where I saw the Indian squaw fade to a shadow and die rather than sell her honour; and the American missionary weep over the grave of the half-caste Zulu in Timbuctoo who had died sooner than he would drink rum! Here was no painting of true life, no dramatic, realistic scene showing the besotted derelict who died far away in the isolation of some alien land—the man from nowhere, who took the wrong turning twenty years before, being hurried into his roughly made coffin: then his two lonely comrades watching the sunrise gleam in his dead eyes, and the half-boyish smile on the silent lips, as they place the coffin lid on, and creep along at daybreak, carrying him under the mahogany-trees to the hole by the swamp. They say a prayer and murmur: "Pity, Bill, that we left the bottle of whisky by his bed. Didn't he rave about someone in the old country? Wonder what 'twas all about. The weather's hot. Buried him rather quick, eh? Here's the cross: 'Bill.' No name. 'Died of Fever, Remembered by Us.'"

Moonlight ferry trips, picnics, concerts and songs are as characteristic of Providence as of the South Sea islanders of Samoa and Tonga. One difference divides the Providence population from the islanders—the natives of Providence wear clothes; but the Yankee mechanics outdo the Savaii and Fiji islanders in tobacco-chewing, and can spit over their shoulders with even swifter certitude than my sailor comrades of San Francisco, whom I told you about in my first book of South Sea reminiscences. Boating is an essential feature in their amusements. Rhodes-on-the-Pawtucket is crammed with boats. On sunshiny days thousands of youths and girls paddle and sing away, and never reflect on the time when Red Indian canoes darted in the moonlight over those same waters.

My comrade was still with me, and we got several engagements to play at dances and concerts. My brother was in the ring, so to speak, and so we were received with an enthusiasm that we had greatly missed when we really wanted it. My friend eventually, however, went off to Alaska to some relations. He promised to write to me, but I never heard of him again.

My brother owned, and still owns, I hope, estates called Cranston Heights, an elevated, breezy place. On the hottest day a sleepy wind creeps about them. From that spot you can gaze down into the valleys and see a wall of cliffs about an eighth of a mile long, rising a hundred feet high. There on a large boulder, known as Middleton's Rock, my brother and I would sit reflectively smoking long Yankee corn-cob pipes, as we reclined, shaded by umbrellas of green-leafed trees from the hot sunlight. We sat there talking and dreaming of years ago when the Indians camped on Cranston Heights. I think my brother could outrival Fenimore Cooper and Cody in his knowledge of Indian history and the legends of the original tribes that owned America. Stone arrow-heads and Indian pottery to this day are often found there, and my brother showed me several relics which were dug out of his estate.

Rhode Island was of course originally an Indian settlement. Forests grew by the rushing rivers, and on the prairie landscapes stood native villages. The dominion was under a King Philip, and the island is sometimes called, for poetical purposes, "Land of King Philip." The forests have succumbed to the woodman's axe, though still patches of woods and prairie-land are left, and it was in that clump that I sat and played my violin and dreamed sometimes. Still the beautiful rivers run across the landscapes like veins of silver and gold fluid, glittering under the leafy clumps of beech, maple, hickory and many varieties of trees that resemble tropical types. The waters of those old rivers, like the coming and passing of singing humanity, have long since slipped into the distant seas, but still other waters flow on and are known by the ancient Indian names. The Seekonk river winds through Providence and throws its liquid mass into Narragansett Bay. From Cranston Heights you can see the exquisite scenery that is characteristic of the neighbourhood of Providence; across the valleys the hills fade before the eyes into dreamy distances as sunset floods the horizon. If you are poetical you can see the ghostly camp fires and dead Indian riders galloping and fading into the arched sunset of blood fire. The view reminded me of a South Sea modern shore village, for here and there were dotted bungalows, fenced by trees and green shrub and flowers. Things have altered a good deal since those days, for I have recently visited Providence.

Mr J———, whose palatial bungalow was among them, is one of Rhode Island's greatest business men, and his commercial success is deserved, through his unassuming philanthropy. He has given a great deal of land, parks and drives to Providence. I think it was in Meshanticut Park, one of his gifts to the city, that I met with an adventure. The weather was hot, and I spied a small lake by some trees. Immediately I undressed and, though my brother expostulated, I dived into the water: the park officials came and arrested me, but my brother explained and I got off with a caution. Years of wild life in the South Seas had taught me to bathe where and when I liked, and I had yet to learn that park lakes in Providence were not as lagoons on the isles of the wild South Seas, wherein the whole population bathe without even the modest fig leaf, gossip, mention the weather and go their ways.

Oaklawn is another pretty spot. I stayed there with some of my brother's friends, at Wilbur Avenue, I think. There is a little wooden bridge thereabouts, not far from an old stone mill. Near this spot in the old days a great Indian battle was fought, and there by that little bridge my brother would sit for hours, writing his articles for the provincial and New York papers.

It was at Oaklawn Bridge that I sat and told my brother of my various boyish experiences in the South Seas, of the island chiefs, and of my reminiscences of Robert Louis Stevenson, whom I had met at Apia and on ships at sea. My brother was deeply interested in all I told him. He was a great admirer of Stevenson's work and his perfect literary style. We talked of Stevenson's easy and careless manner that seemed such a contrast to his perfection and polish in writing. How he did not care a tinker's curse for the opinion of the conventional world, and loved to shock visitors to Samoa by appearing before them suddenly in old clothes, bare-headed and bootless. I saw him come aboard a ship dressed in that way; and I recalled how, on another occasion, I met him coming down the track inland from Saluafata, the native village. "Hello, youngster," he said; and, as I was going his way, off we tramped along the track together as he hummed beside me. Then, with the sunset, out came the native children rushing from the forest. Like tiny ghosts they glided, begging, in the shadows at our legs as we strode alone; and as Robert Louis Stevenson threw brass buttons to them, they raced after them, and then, half frightened that he might want to reclaim the prizes, they suddenly disappeared, racing back into the forest. The sunset died behind our backs and the stars crept over the Vaea Mountain top and the dark-branched coco-palms each side of the track; the shadows thickened as the stars brightened. So well do I remember that night that even now I seem to see my companion striding onward beside me, his loose neck-cloth fluttering in the wind that drifts in from the sea, stirring the coco-palms and pungent-smelling forest flowers as it passes. Still I see his ghost-like shadow, the clear eyes, the thin, æsthetic face; still he is humming a folk-song, while his right hand beats the moonlit bush with a stick—and yet he has lain there many years on the top of the Vaea Mountain—his rugged island tomb railed by the dim sky-lines of surrounding tropical seas, his vaulted roof the everlasting sky, studded with the brightest stars, as he lies with his stricken aspirations like some dead Christ of the lost children of the wild, solitary South.

A critic in *The Times*, reviewing my first book, *Sailor and Beachcomber*, after writing a column of critical appreciation, finished up by saying: "Mr Safroni-Middleton prides himself on having known Robert Louis Stevenson in the South Seas." My book has three hundred and four pages: on three of them I spoke of Stevenson; but I fail to see why I should pride myself on knowing him, except in this sense, that I am proud to have met him and to count him among the many men who followed after my own heart.

If he had not died before I returned, a little older, to Samoa, he would have welcomed me as I should have welcomed him; for he had several times expressed a wish that I should call on him and take my violin, but in the foolishness of a boy's thoughtlessness I did not go. Worldly greatness did not appeal to him, nor did my letters of introduction, for I had none, and he was, I am quite sure, aware of the fact.

Well, to return to my experiences in North America. After a time I left Providence, and then went down the Hudson river bound for New York.

There I stayed in a temperance hotel close to the Bowery, and I cannot forget the scene.

Along winding avenues that divide the towering wooden buildings rushed battalions of hurrying legs. The noise of car bells and gongs and the babble of shouting voices assailed my ears. All the races under the sun seemed to have emigrated to that spot to fight in scheming regiments for the almighty dollar. White men, Chinamen, black men, tawny men, yellow men, Armenians, Turks, Germans with thick necks—all were there. Over my head rushed express trains. No space seemed wasted. Indeed the Yankees in their commercial search for gold peg out claims in the sky, claim square miles of stars, as up go their buildings to the heavens. By the second-storey windows on elevated railway tracks crash along the trains. In those days they ran by steam, and the coal-dust showered down your neck and in your eyes as you moved along with the thick crowd below; a crowd so dense that you could shut your eyes, make no effort, and still be propelled along in the mighty rush, as you dreamed of other days of peace and solitude! I went across Brooklyn Bridge by night: swung on mighty steel cables, it dangles in space and has several divisions for vehicles and pedestrians. Below rushed the ferry-boats on the Hudson river, their port-holes ablaze with light, and the sound of music on deck fading as they passed underneath. Across the bridge hurried electric cars, racing along by the mechanical genius of man's brain, the light of the Universe—the stars switched on to wheels!

I only stayed one week in New York, for I met an old shipmate whom I had sailed with from Sydney. He was on a tramp steamer. One of the deck-hands had gone into hospital, so I yielded to my friend's persuasion, went on board, secured the job and signed on. For the rest, it is all like a dream now: I can hear the rattle of the rusty chain as they haul the anchor up, and the uncouth, shrill calls of the pulling crew rising above the clamour of the steam winches, just before the tramp steamer moves away from the wharf to put to sea. New York and its babble of voices with their nasal twang, its vast drama of scheming existence in a feverish hurry, fades away and becomes a memory of some monstrous "magic shadow show" lit by the sun far off somewhere across the lone sea miles astern.

The sea routine has commenced: deep down in the stokehold firemen with cadaverous faces turned to the furnace blaze are toiling away. They look like shadows in the flame-lit gloom, like dead men working out their penance in hell. Attired in pants and a sweater only, with their hairy chests steaming with running perspiration, they work furiously. Their conversation is made up chiefly of oaths and forcible criticism on the lack of generosity they found in Bill or Jim, who only stood them ten drinks ashore, after all they had treated them to on that first spree night of the last trip. They are not bad men, and as they spit out the coal-dust in a thick mass from their stained lips, and take a gulp of condensed water to quench their thirst, I feel deeply sorry for them, and realise that they are the unsung heroes of the sea. I look at the row of unshaved faces thrust forward to the roaring fires, and at their shrivelled hands and big arms moving the long steel stoking bars, and wonder at the marvellous strength and virtue of the hard-working ship's firemen.

On deck, like iced wine to my lips, I drink in the fresh sea breeze. It is dark. I cannot turn in, for I should not sleep, so I go into the fo'c'sle and watch the sailors playing cards, then return on deck and look over the ship's side. Under the pendulous, curved moon—for it seems to sway to the roll of the rigging—the mate's form moves to and fro as he tramps the bridge. The sailing ship that we sighted on the weather-side at sunset is now only a tiny travelling star low down on the ocean darkness far astern, where her mast head-light shines.

The weariness of the sea's monotony is on me; we have been to sea long enough to be half-way across the Atlantic. The weather is much colder. The moon is large and low, and looks like a ghostly arch to the south, for it seems half submerged far away on the edge of the ocean, that seems shivering for miles with silver mystery. Just over the side I watch the mirrored masts and rigging glide along with us as though a ghostly ship is following; and the hours fly and dawn breaks greyly, and once more the tramp steamer is surrounded by blue sky-lines, till sunset sinks to a wild blaze in the western arch of the sky. The sailors go on watch. The cook washes his pots and pans ere he cuts his corns and turns into his bunk.

The wind's voice murmurs mournfully in the rigging and round the bridge awnings; as the night grows older it swells to a tremendous voice that is really me! for it is the re-echo of my own hearing and dreaming consciousness. I fancy I hear the hounds of death racing across the wild sea moors as shadows dropping from the flying clouds go running over the moonlit sea, and now, as though a door in the sky is opened, the stars and moon are driven and shut away in the outer Universe. For a mighty sheet of storm-cloud slides across the heavens. The world is changed to an infinity of dark and wind, and the one dim figure of the look-out man on the fo'c'sle head. The thundering seas slowly rise with their white crests glowing in the ebon darkness as the brave old tramp steamer, like a frightened thing, stays her way a moment, and shivers as seas strike the weather bow. Then again she pitches onward, as wonderful little men, with bony, haggard faces with weary eyes in them, stare into the furnace fires of the steamer's bowels, and shovel and stoke to sustain an honest existence, and drink tank water. No wonder they drink beer when they get the chance. I am quite sure I should.

A week later we sighted the cliffs of England, and soon after the sea tramp touched the wharf at Liverpool with a jerk and a shiver, and went to sleep among a forest of masts and funnels till her next trip.

CHAPTER V

Home—On an Orient Liner—The Orchestra—A Sailing Ship—Paganini—Port Said—Honolulu

AGAIN I am home and meet familiar faces, and enjoy the sweet security of home life and respectability; but soon the flight of time brings its inevitable changes both to my feelings and to those around me. I am no longer the prodigal son and a romantic novelty to the many who welcomed me at my arrival in the monotonous suburb; but nevertheless we are all moody companions in the sad drama of respectability. I had made up my mind to go travelling no more, but my good resolutions have faded away, and my whole soul is centred on inventing the best excuse for my not being able to accept the good position in London that will make me, at last, the respected son of a respected father.

Well, I feel a bit ashamed of my incorrigible personality, and yet how much my soul is burdened with the thought that I must aspire to higher things, and go off to the city each day like Mr W.'s son does, to sit on a stool. I can never be the pride and joy of the family, and as I sit alone and dream I am miserable with dim forebodings. On the back of the chair is my very high white collar and the smart tweed suit, and by my washstand my beloved fiddle. Just over it, on a peg by my bed, is my big-rimmed Australian hat. Alas! that hat speaks of tropical sunshine and coco-palms. I can hear the arguing voices of bushmen in the grog shanty by "Bummer's Creek," and the trade wind in the shore banyans as the beachcomber laughs and nudges his pal in the ribs.

I cannot sleep, for the parrots are flying and muttering across the sky of my dreams; I hear the crack of the stock-whips on the slopes as the scampering, flying sheep go racing across my bedroom floor. I close my eyes, and the natives start singing in the Fijian village, and the drums are beating the sunset out ere I am wide awake, through the civilised jingle of the milkman's cans in the cold, windy street below.

The last dark wintry morning arrives. It has all been settled. I have signed on for a voyage as violinist and assistant purser on the Orient liner the *Britannia*. I am to catch the 4 A.M. train to London Bridge. How dark and cold it is as I get up and dress, then go up the next flight to kiss my three sisters a last good-bye. They lift their sleepy heads and put their arms around my neck. "Good-bye, Tiggy," they say once again, as I gently close their bedroom door and go downstairs. My father helps me on with my overcoat, and says very kind words. I try to answer, but my voice sounds husky and I keep placing the wrong arm in my overcoat sleeves. Now comes the greatest task of all, a task that will tax all my courage. I strive to hide my weakness and make a joke about the bad penny turning up again soon, and then neither of us speak, and once again I kiss her lips, the lips of the most beautiful woman this world ever gave me. I hurry down the streets. I am glad it's dark, for my eyes feel weak, and the windy light of the lamp-posts seem to swim about the street spaces. I am haunted by her face all down the Channel that night, for she caught my soul adrift among the stars ere I was born, and my heart still sings a sad song for the woman who was my mother.

There is a deal of sameness on a large liner's trip to the colonies. But for the complication of characters among the passengers and crew, and the ports that we put into on the voyage out, the passage would be extremely monotonous.

Forward, near the fo'c'sle, was the glory hole, between decks, wherein slept the crowd of stewards and cooks. They were a jolly lot of men, and when the steerage and fore-cabin passengers had finished their evening meal they would sit on their sea-chests yarning or playing cards far into the night. Sometimes they would sing songs, accompanied by the twang and tinkling of the assistant cook's banjo; and older men, who were tired out, thrust their fierce faces out of their bunks and swore at being kept awake, as once more the wild chorus of *I owe Ten Shillings to O'Grady* re-echoed through the "glory hole." Sleepless passengers up on deck clapped their hands with pleasure to hear the monotony broken, as the big pistons in the engine-rooms throbbed out their incessant pom-pe-te-pom, and the screws thrashed the racing liner across the world. In the morning at four-thirty the men would be dead to the world in their bunks as the second steward started shouting: "Now then, you sleepers! Now then, you sleepers, rise and shine!" or "Come out of it, you young b———!" and so on, as sleepy heads lifted up in the rows of bunks and then dropped helplessly again. Some were romantic boys who had read autobiographies, and some middle-aged men who had sickened of the workman's train and drifted to sea.

In the evenings I played the violin in the saloon and deck concerts aft, beyond the dividing rope which was the boundary line that told the fore-cabin passengers that they must not approach the élite in the first saloon.

Our orchestra consisted of three violins, 'cello, bass, and the usual brass and wind. I had an easy time, and often till midnight would stand on deck watching the stars and the world of waters below, and listening to the voices of passengers on deck outward bound for Australia, to find fame and fortune—or ill fame.

I became very friendly with a member of our ship's band, the solo cornet player. He was a quiet, elderly man, turning grey, and had once been a player in the orchestra of the Lyceum Theatre. A fine all-round musician he was too. He would sit on deck after dark, put a mute on his instrument, and extemporise melody and make it sound like a sweet-voiced girl singing softly to herself. He had the real temperament, and had received a first-class musical education.

Nothing reveals character, the intellectual calibre of the instrumental player, so much as the type of composition that makes up his private repertoire. For in that he only plays the compositions which appeal to him. Some are devoid of personality and only perform the stock pieces that are fashionable. Others revel in melody that tells of the light side of life, its gaiety, or the pathos of dramatic existence on the stage, the tragedian's mock grief before the footlights ere the curtain falls. Others find their musical heaven vaguely expressed by playing those pieces that seem to murmur, as a sea-shell murmurs of the ocean, that indefinable note of poetry, the voice of the unknown, the intense inner life of our existence. My friend was one of the latter kind. He gave me many useful hints which I profited by, (as I often did in my travels), and so received a free musical education, the only music lessons I ever really had.

But for the throb of the engines and thrashing screw, the vessel's motion, and the stewards' sea-legs aslant to the deck's list as they walk the saloons and cabin alley-ways, you could half think you were in some subterannean hotel. Travel on a liner, and the wild poetry of the sailing ships swerving to the swell of travelling seas, the climbing sailors aloft singing their chanteys among the storm-beaten sails, the flying clouds overhead that race the moon, all seem to be something that you dreamed of, or lived through ages ago.

Sea-boots and oilskins seem mythical things that faintly recall your yellow-backed old buccaneer novels, or the days when Drake sailed down the seas.

Officers on the P. & O. liners speak with university polish. "Ay, ay", "Hold hard!", "Look out, you son of a sea-cook!", "Holy Moses!", "Up she comes", "All together!", "Let go!", "Haul the mainsail up!". This is all changed now to "Make haste, Mr Pye-Smith" and "Yes, sir, I beg your pardon. What a draught!". Or a bell tinkles down in the engine-room, and the mammoth liner, like a mighty iron beast, slows obediently to half-speed, stops, or slashes her tail and goes full speed astern, without one song or oath.

The stormy night and head-wind, the huddled group of sailors in oilskins singing their wild chantey, *O, O, for Rio Grande*, on deck in the windy dark as they bend together and pull while the vast monotone of the ocean becomes the orchestral accompaniment to voices from strong, open, bearded mouths, and your world of stars suddenly veers as the dark canvas sails and yards swerve round; the chief mate shouting, "What the blazing hell—— Ay, there!" as on the wind comes faintly back, "Ay, ay, sir, all clear!": this smacks more of the sea. Why, on a sailing ship, the very sea-cook at the galley door, amidships, clutching his pans, gazing across the wild, lonely waters, where the leaping, white-bearded waves seem like old misers' hands plucking at the sunset's gold, is sheer downright poetry compared with the electric-lighted saloon crowded with munching, over-fed men and women with moving mouths and pince-nez on their respectable noses.

The sailing ship has its rough, uncomfortable side, for well I remember my last trip from 'Frisco round the Horn, when I stood on deck at night, with deadly cramp gripping my legs, my eyebrows frozen together, my nose pinched and blue with cold, the decks awash and our sea-chests afloat in the fo'c'sle and deck-house. I recollect the cook holding on to his pots and pans and swearing as only an old-time boatswain, and that cook, could swear as we begged for a pannikin of hot coffee: stuff that tasted like heaven-sent life-blood to our frozen lips as we two boys drank it. The weather-beaten boatswain in his oilskins and sea-boots went by us in the dark, as great seas came over, singing a song to himself as though he was soliloquising in some quiet bar off the Mile End Road instead of experiencing the wildest weather I have ever seen, or ever want to see.

How I admired those old seafarers! "Fetch that, matey," they'd say, and off I'd rush, eager to please and obey the orders of Horatio Nelson and Sir Francis Drake, for such men they seemed to me.

In the fo'c'sle at night they'd say: "Get that fiddle out and play to us." A thrill of boyish pride would go through me to notice their attention and respect as I played my best. Presently they would join in as I played the chanteys they had taught me, *Sailing down to Rio* or *Blow the Man Down*. Without removing their pipes or chewing quids, their cracked, hoarse-throated voices would join in.

Deep bass voices two or three had, and as they sat round me on their old sea-chests, and I scraped away to the tuneless, yelling, bearded mouths beneath the dim light of the fo'c'sle oil lamp, I drank in the last breath of the winds of sea romance. I see them now as I dream. There they sit on their sea-chests, oilskins and sea-boots on, with curios from other lands fastened over their bunks around them, as they open their big bearded mouths and sing. How ghost-like their eyes look by the light of the dim lamp, as the hazy tobacco smoke curls thickly to the low roof! Then their hollow voices fade and the visionary "Old Hands" vanish as the last breath of wind blows them like cobweb-fine things through the fo'c'sle door, along the moonlit deck, away seaward for ever as I dream.

How I recall these lonely nights and the sailors moving across the deck in the dark, or climbing aloft like shadows back to the sky. I used to stand alone and gaze over the ship's side and suddenly feel the intensity of living, as my thoughts half clung hopefully to the stars, like lost, migrating swallows that cling to the rigging of ships far out at sea; and the mighty, moving water all around me seemed to break with its monotone against eternity. I remember lying in my bunk, and by the oil lamp's light watching the ship's cockroaches go filing across the photographs of my parents and relatives which I had tacked on my bunk side to remind me of home, though I required no such reminder. Those silent faces intensified the difference between reality and my boyhood's dream; as a cold breath out of the grave of my beloved, who slept in the seas outside, blew through the door across my face as I dreamed of her—my beautiful dead romance!

Truly, sailing ships have their rough side as well as a wildly romantic one. Rolling down south, with gales behind bringing the seas up like majestic travelling hills as under the poop they go, and she rolls and swerves as the masts sweep across the sky, is the motion of sea poetry. If you are aloft you look down and could swear that she must turn turtle. Telling you this calls back my feelings when I first went aloft as a boy of fourteen years.

The ship was rolling heavily, and as I looked down on deck something seemed to have happened (I turned pale, I'm sure): she was turning right over. I clung on with might and main as the masts and yards went over; death seemed to stare me in the face: like a wild beast I hooked on with fingers, toes and teeth, prepared for the final plunge into the heaving ocean below, when lo! to the mysterious equal pull of gravity she slowly swerved and rose, the rigging jerked and rattled, the jib-boom lifted and the figure-head at the bows lifted her face from the weather-side and went right over to peep at the lee-side. Overjoyed, I looked over my shoulder astern and saw the chief mate yawning on the poop and the man at the wheel quite unconcerned, when I had instinctively thought they were clinging to anything movable, prepared to dive into the ocean when the ship turned clean over. That bronzed, broad-shouldered mate grinned when I stood on the poop. He asked me how I had felt. He was a good sort. He's dead now and under the sea, missing these many years; and the red-bearded Scotch skipper, who was like a father to me, is worse off, for the last I heard of him was that he was still alive and missing—mentally. "But this won't buy the baby a frock," as they say at sea when you go off dreaming and leave your work to yarn. So I must return to the P. & O. liner as she races across the Mediterranean, bound for Suez.

We had called in at Naples, where we had taken on board a batch of passengers. I remember one of them especially; he was a distinguished old Italian and his profile recalled to my mind the pictures I had seen of Dante. He wore a loose cloak and a cavalier hat, and carried a violin-case. His eyes were eagle-like, yet bilious-looking, for he was suffering from some kind of yellow jaundice and slow circulation. On the hottest nights his teeth chattered with the cold. When we were crossing the Red Sea and the passengers brought their beds on deck to sleep, hoping to get a whiff of air, he went into his cabin in the usual way, with his teeth chattering with the cold, crawled into his bunk and got into his bed-clothes—a large canvas sack heavily lined with wadding; bodily into this he would go and tie the tapes at the head of the sack tightly round his neck, so that no air could possibly get into the sack and give him a chill. The very sight of it all made me perspire and gasp in that stifling hot weather. I felt sorry for him, and I cannot imagine now that he could have lived very long after getting to Australia, where he was going for his health's sake. He was a splendid violin-player, but did not perform. I used to talk to him on deck, and discovered that he was a Genoese. I was greatly interested to hear that his father, who was also a musician, had known intimately the celebrated violin *maestro*, Paganini, and had had violin lessons from him. From broken English, and Italian gesticulations, I learnt that the great violinist had peculiar ways. He had stayed for a few days at my friend's childhood home and while there had upset the quiet routine of the family, for he was extremely superstitious and restless, and walked about the house all night. He declared that a ghostly woman stood with her face at his window whenever he played a certain melody that had come to him in his dreams. Beyond his family's enthusiastic reminiscences over Paganini's violin-playing, that is the only incident that vividly impressed me. My friend was a remarkable character and, though he was ill, extremely vivacious and always talking excitably. Sometimes he would sit on deck after dark, and plucking the strings of his violin, pizzicato, guitar style, would sing softly to himself in Italian with a clear, sweet, musical voice that was very effective.

I went with him ashore at Port Said. It was fearfully hot, but as my friend walked down the gangway with me he was well swathed in scarves, and wrapped up in shirts under his large fur-lined cloak. He seemed to have plenty of money and was anything but mean with it. It was a treat to get away from the hubbub of the natives coaling the steamer. I only have a dim, dream-like recollection of that particular visit ashore at Port Said. I remember the town with the white buildings and palm-trees dimly outlined under the stars, and the begging, dark-faced descendants of the Egyptian Pharaohs who rushed forth out of alley-ways and sought our patronage. Signor Niccolo was terribly thirsty, and the English restaurant was so crowded with passengers from the boats that we both went off and sought elsewhere for refreshments. We went up a dark alleyway, directed there by a swarthy man who evidently misunderstood our requirements. In the darkness it seemed like some subterranean passage to an Egyptian ghost-land as we walked along and heard the uncouth voices of the inhabitants issuing from the little barred windows that were let in in the high walls on each side. Shuffling by us went the sandalled feet of black men with white turbans on that looked like towels swathed about their heads. Presently we arrived at a tunnel-like entrance that led into a suspicious, dimly lit little restaurant. As we sat at one of the small tables and sniffed peculiar odours, that smelt like scented tea and aromatic herbs, four dusky beauties came through a little secret door and laughingly revealed their teeth, then asked in broken English what we would like to drink. Signor Niccolo called for wine and I had coffee. Off rushed the dark female attendants to execute our orders. "Funny plaze and funny girlees, eh?" said Signor Niccolo to me. "Seems so," I answered, for the waitresses were only dressed in little singlets, with a loose piece hanging to their knees and a scarf swathed about their bosoms for modesty's sake, which was the only modesty that we saw there, as they lifted their scanty robes to dust the furniture. We drank our refreshment and hurriedly escaped from the place.

I do not think there are any missionaries at Port Said; possibly the English and American officials look upon it as hopeless. Port Said was a veritable hell of iniquity in those days, and still is. Passengers often went ashore and lost the boat, or disappeared altogether. After we left a Yankee saloon passenger sat on the settee and told us of his experiences there. He had gone into an isolated restaurant at the north end of the town and called for a drink. In his button-hole he wore a large red camellia blossom which, though he did not know it, was a kind of Masonic sign. So directly he had ordered his whisky and sat down in the large arm-chair, the attendant, who was an old black Arab mute with a heavy grey beard, suddenly touched a spring in the wall, and lo! up went a partition on each side and he was shut in a little room, staring with surprise at the old mute, who, to his astonishment, now spoke in a musical voice. The old man's beard and eyebrows dropped off and with the old cloak fell rustling to the floor, and there, with shining dark eyes and pouting lips, a dusky harem beauty stood before him! Even the sedate P. & O. chief officer smiled behind his napkin as the Yankee told us that yarn, and we tried to keep straight faces over all the details which I have left out!

Three or four weeks later I arrived in Melbourne, where I stayed a week in Collins Street and at length succeeded in getting a berth on a boat that was bound for the Islands. Eventually I arrived at Honolulu, where I had some luck with my violin-playing which enabled me to take a cheap passage to Apia, where I had lived before.

CHAPTER VI

Changes in Samoa—Curios—A Moonlit Scene—Saints and Fakirs—Indians—Apia Town—Vailima—The Chief Mataaga—A Forest Ballroom—The Wandering Scribe—A Legend of Samoa—An old Shellback's Yarns—Tuputa and the Sinless Lands—A Tribal Waltz

IT was some time since I had left Samoa. Things there seemed to have considerably changed. Many of my friends, both natives and white men, had gone away to another island. I went up to Mulinuu village, expecting to see my friend Raeltoa, the Samoan, and to my great regret learnt that his wife had died of consumption and that he had gone away to the Line Islands, in the Equatorial Group. Robert Louis Stevenson had died some months before, and was at rest on the top of Vaea Mountain. Indeed with his death the old Samoa seemed to have passed away.

I felt rather depressed for a time, but I met an American tourist, staying at the German hotel in Apia, who was very eccentric, and he cheered me up considerably. He was a collector of native curios, and his whole life seemed to be centred on his strange hobby. He invited me into his apartments, and I could hardly move for the lumber and his large crates of native pottery, old breech-loading weapons, cutlasses, mummified human heads, dried native feet cut off at the ankles, war-clubs, human teeth and skeletons, native musical instruments and barbarian furniture. He talked of nothing else but his gruesome collection. He had a high, bald head and beak-like nose, whereon he was eternally fingering his pince-nez, which kept falling off whilst he enthusiastically held up relics for my inspection. His passion for getting curios seemed never satisfied. We dined at a native's house together; suddenly he lifted the cloth and saw that the table was a rough, native-made table of platted cane and bamboo. Immediately he bargained for it, and to the native's delight purchased it, and off we went with it. How he got them all away from the hotel I don't know, for he had a regular cargo of stuff, but eventually he got his curios on board a steamer and went off to San Francisco.

I stayed on in Apia for several weeks, joining a party of tourists, and with them I visited the various scenes and islands of the group. As I write, in a dream I see the slopes rising from the sea, lying silent in the moonlight. The curling smoke from the camp fires steals above the still coco-palms that shelter the huts of the native villages. The big, hive-shaped houses are musical with humming melody and the jabbering voices of rough-haired native girls and women. Some squat cross-legged by door-holes, whence emerge tiny, brown, naked children, to turn head over heels, or race like joyful puppies after each other round the dens. Big full-blooded Samoan chiefs smile and show their white teeth as they roll banana-leaf cigarettes between their dusky fingers. Across the flat lies Apia town with its one main street; beyond the inland plateaux rise, and far off you can see the moonlit waves breaking into patches like white moss on the level ocean plains.

By the copra and coco plantations are the emigrant settlements, where tired coolies, most of them Malay Indians, rest after their toil. Native women linger near them, for they are generous men those coolies, and give the velvet-skinned native girls sham jewellery. The Indian *sadhu* (saint) sits by the line of dens and stores under the palms; he looks like some carved holy image as he stares with bright, unblinking eyes. The natives' wooden idols have long since been smashed, or have rotted away, and that living idol of the East is one from many cargoes that have arrived to take the place of the old deaf South Sea idols. The new idols are real; they have live tongues and eyes that lure on true believers, converts to Allah, to do monstrous things. The deaf, dumb wooden gods of heathen times were sanctified compared with these new immigrant idols that breathe!

That old fakir, with outstretched withered arm that brings him reverence and cash, represents Hinduism, or Buddha. His thick beard is almost solid with filth, where-from at intervals, out to the hot sky, buzz big blow-flies. Just across the track is the bazaar, wooden cabins under the mangroves and coco-palms, where the Indians sell jewellery, the Koran, and richly coloured dress materials to the Samoan women. The Indians appear fine-looking men when dressed, with their dark, brilliant eyes and curly, close-cropped beards. They swear to all things by the holy prophet Mahomet, and wear a poetic smile that enlarges when you are not looking to a sardonic grin! Native women meet them at dark under the coco-palms, stroke their beards and gaze secretly up into their faces with passionate admiration.

That pretty Samoan girl, with staring, romantic eyes and rough, bronze-coloured hair, who only a week ago gave herself body and soul to some Indian, the scum of the East, sits alone under the dark mangroves by the lagoon and thinks and thinks of the day before her fall. A red, decorated loin-cloth reaches to her waist, the forest winds kiss the maiden curves of her brown, flower-like bosom. She is very young: her childhood's dolls are still unbroken, and are being loved and nursed by her little sisters who live on the neighbouring Savaii Isle. Her father was eaten by a shark last year, and her mother is married to a white man who is never sober.

Not far away sit a group of Indian women, dark and evil-looking, with round faces. Dressed in gorgeous garments of rich yellow and crimson, they are certainly attractive; earrings dangle from their ears and some of them have a silver hoop through the nose. They loll under the coco-palms, whisper viciousness, and mortally hate the handsome Samoan girls.

The mail steamer arrived in Apia harbour a few hours ago. Along the white, dusty, inland track goes the fair, handsome white woman, Maria Mandy. She is off to her bungalow up the hill, a secluded, romantic spot. Her round, pretty face is getting quite sunburnt and brown. By her side walks an aristocratic-looking tourist; he wears pince-nez, is deeply religious and in a great hurry! Maria is dressed up to "the nines," is scented and looks fine and sweet: the "light o' Love" of a score of German naval officers and men of respectable repute, she has grown wealthy and intends to go soon to Sydney. With her wit and courtly polish she will get on well in Australia, and will probably get into Government House society, be extremely virtuous and so shocked that she will suggest the removal from the select clique of such suspicious characters as old Colonel B——, who will foam at the mouth and wonder why he is snubbed. Mrs S. A. and Lady H. B. will go into hysterics, weep, grind their delicate white teeth, look at the ceiling of their bedroom and ask heaven who could possibly have guessed about those intrigues; and they will never dream of the knowing Apia harlot—handsome Maria Mandy.

That fat, thick-necked German official, who likes Samoa better than the Berlin suburbs, is out walking alone; he is just off to see Salvao Marva and gaze upon her through those big-rimmed, academic spectacles. He is nearly sixty, and pretty Marva is nearly fifteen years old! No one knows about it though. He is a good man at home, plays the Austrian zither perfectly, and sings in a deep religious bass voice folk-songs of the Fatherland. Romantic Marva loves those songs, and knows them all by heart; she has a voice like a wild bird, and you do not feel so hard upon the in-auspicious fall of German culture. He is due back in Berlin soon, for his time is up in six months, so he is quite safe, and poor Marva can place the parental responsibility for her baby on to the back of the beachcomber, Bill Grimes, who will say, "Well I'm blowed, if this ain't all right," then accept the position and make his home in the South Seas after all.

HONGIS TRACK, ROTORUA, N.Z.

Maria Mandy is not the only lady who will become respectable and make the devil rub his hands and chuckle with delight. On the beach stroll other white women, and droves of pretty half-caste girls who will eventually get jobs as "ladies' maids" to touring families that call at Apia on the homeward voyage to New York and London. They have fine times those girls with the German and English sailors, or with "perfect gentlemen," and sometimes a black-sheep missionary who has been dismissed from the L.M.S. Off they go on the spree and forget themselves and do things that make even the beachcomber Bill Grimes rub his eyes and stare; for, after all, he's not so bad; he *can* some day, in that "far-off event of perfect good," buy a new suit of clothes; but the beachcombers that loaf and eat the fruit of frailty in this Eden of the South Seas can never buy another soul.

Hark! the harbour is musical with voices, for this is fair Italy of the Southern Seas, where natives paddle their canoes and sing their weird melodies as naturally as men breathe. You can hear the splash of the paddles and oars as they cut the thickly star-mirrored water. The native boats are bringing sailors ashore from the ships that arrived at twilight. The moonlit shore and the palm-clad slopes look like fairyland to the silent ships lying out in the harbour. The men step ashore, pay one shilling, or one mark, each, then off go the canoes back to the ships for other crews, as the groups of sailors go up to Apia town. Before they get there dusky guides offer their services, and they see the sights—such sights too! No missionaries could ever reform such creatures as they see. One of them, she is one of many, wears almost nothing, the curved, thick lips in her wide mouth murmur forth alluring Samoan speech. Her girth is enormous, and her brown bosom heaves with simulated professional passion, like a wave on the treacherous deep dark ocean of sensuality—whereon so often travelling men are shipwrecked. Her eyes are large, the pupils widely encircled with white, and warm with the sunlight gleam of downright wickedness; she has been taught her art in the vast university of experience with white men in the foremost ranks of civilisation's pioneer tramp! Paid vice was never known in Samoa till the white men came; but now she lures to her velvety brown arms the unwary innocence of fragile sailormen and tourists who come from London on the civilised Thames; where the missionaries hail from, who in our land of purity, of course, cannot exert and bring into play their noble efforts, and so through innocence, O England, my England, your children fall before the lure of the wicked South!

Low-caste Samoan women are not all hideous; some have large, innocent eyes alive with wonder; half angel and half devil they look as they stand before the camera and, answering the stern voice of the operator, strive to look modest and sweet.

By the edge of the small lagoon, under those tall coco-nut-trees sit four little naked baby girls. It is dark, but their brown faces imaged in the water can be seen by the brilliant moonlight; they look like truant cherubims from Paradise out on the spree, as they sit side by side whispering musical Samoan baby words, and kissing the rag doll that was made in Germany. Their Samoan father is away in a far village on a visit to a wedding feast; if you listen you can hear the far-off sounds of tom-toms and cymbal-clanging coming across on the drifting forest wind that brings with it odours of wild, decaying flowers and fruit. Their mother is fast asleep by the door of their native home close by; she sleeps soundly, and the mongrel dog's snout is couched softly on her bare, warm, brown breast. It looks a mystical, beautiful world, like some spiritual land beyond the stars, as the bright eyes of those tiny faces peep through the wind-blown palm leaves; and I watch them in my dreams to-night, though long since those little girls are women and now meet the eyes of Indian, Chinese and European men.

Civilisation's iron foot is on the hills, and along the tracks that lead inland where mission schools and churches stand, to collect on weekdays and Sundays the high-class native folk who live in comfortable Polynesian homes. The night is hot, starry and almost windless, and handsome Samoan youths attired in the *lava-lava* (loin-cloth) patter swift-footed along the tracks under the coco-nut and tropical trees that shelter the primitive homes of the South Sea paradise. Samoan girls with wild, bright eyes, round, plump, brown faces, and curved figures as perfect as sculptural art, pass and repass up the forest tracks. They are singing Samoan songs that intensify the romantic, dream-like atmosphere of the tropical night—an atmosphere not even to be dispelled by the wailing cry of the native babies, who give short, wild, smothered screams as they lose and then suddenly recover the breasts of sleeping mothers in those thatched homes by the palms and banana groves. The vast night sky, agleam with stars, shines like a mighty mirror. You can see the red glow of the reflection from the volcanic crater miles away on Savaii's Isle.

If you go up the slope and stand on the plateau, away inland, when dawn is stealing in grey tints along the ocean horizon, awakening the birds on Vaea Mountain, and the native homes are astir, you can distinctly see afar something that looks like a cow-shed by coco-palms and thick jungle growth. It is Vailima, the home of Robert Louis Stevenson. One light gleams in the large shed-room, and the intellectual, sensitive face of the poet-author moves there in the gloom. He has come back from Apia town and is tired, yet secretly as pleased as the two old shellbacks who have carried his curios back, and who hitch up their trousers and cough respectfully as the world-famous author sneaks them in and gives each a bumping glass of the best brand. How quietly his keen eyes gaze upon them as they drink! On a shelf the large clock ticks warningly. He glances at it now and again as the belated sailors yarn on, grow more and more garrulous and continue their strange experiences, that cling to the wonderful, distilling brain of the listener as moonlight clings to deep, dark waters. At last, with intellectual delicacy, they are hurriedly slipped off; for soon the respectable folk, whom he gave the slip to early in the evening, will return, and he must not be seen in such company again. The old shellbacks grip the extended, thin, delicate hand, look into the keen eyes and wipe their mouths as they go down the narrow track. "He's a gentleman 'e is, d———d if 'e ain't," they say to each other, as the silent, lonely man they have just left sits and dreams on alone, and thinks and feels those things that no book ever did, or ever can, tell.

A few miles away lives the great high chief Mataafa; he knows Tusitala, the writer of tales. Mataafa is the old King of Samoa: his warriors have charged up those slopes and the sound of the guns from the enemy's warships echoed and re-echoed across the bay. It is all like some far-off dream to me that in my boyhood I should have met and fiddled to the Napoleon of the South Seas, for Mataafa was exiled, though there the similarity ends. I can still see the handsome, intelligent face and remember the quick, kind eyes of Samoa's dethroned king. I did not know, or at least realise, who Mataafa was, as he sat on a chest in the schooner's cabin in Apia harbour. I knew he was someone important by the skipper's behaviour and respectful attention. Only long after did I clearly realise that I was in at the death at one of the most tragic periods of Samoa's history. I helped row the exiled king ashore and went with him to Mulinuu village, where I stayed the night, and then rowed him back in the ship's boat again. Had I known the truth I would have clung to the old king with all the romantic vigour of my soul. The opportunity of my boyish dreams had presented itself, but I knew it not. How I would have striven to lean on that chieftain's right arm, helping in some tragical drama of war and intrigue that would have given me the fame that my boyish aspirations yearned for as I read the novels of Alexandre Dumas. Alas! I can only remember a sad, aged face in a South Sea forest homestead, in a schooner's dingy cabin, or earnestly talking under the forest trees by night to loyal chiefs ere he returned to the ship. I saw him three or four times ashore, and entertained him in the refuge where he lived with his faithful chiefs. Also I played the violin to him several times, while he smiled gravely and the garrulous skipper drank whisky and sang out of tune, or read out loudly snatches from *The Samoan Times*, which was a paper something after the style in size of *The Dead Bird*, published in Sydney, but suppressed and issued again as *The Bird of Freedom*.

Behind the stores in Apia's street is the primeval ballroom where I played the violin to the Samoan grandees, and to tripping, white-shoed German officials, while five half-caste girls in pink frocks, with crimson ribbons in their forests of hair, went through the Siva dances. Robert Louis Stevenson gazed on, or argued with the crusty German official, who was red in the face as Stevenson expressed his opinions on Samoan politics. Just below too, down the street, is the bar-room, where I played the violin with the manager's wife, who was a good pianist. I only performed there once: a trader was half-seas over and was arguing with a German official; suddenly he picked my violin up and hit the German over the head with it. There was a great scene and the trader was thrown out. Everyone laughed to see the look on my face as I scanned the fiddle to see if it had been damaged; even the manager and his wife put their fists in their mouths to hide a noisy smile. The German shouted: "Mein Gott! I vill see that this mans be arrested! Mein Gott! Mein Gott!"

It's a lively place, this Samoan isle. There sits an aged, tattooed native from Motootua village. He is a wandering scribe, a poet and author of the South Seas, and well beloved by all his critics, who mostly wear no clothes! He does not write on paper, but engraves on the brains of his audiences his memories, impromptu poems and improvisations; or he tells of Samoan history and poetic lore. He wears the primitive *ridi* to his bony knees and a large shawl of native tappu-cloth round his brown shoulders; tall and majestic-looking, with strong, imaginative face, when he stands quite still and lifts one arm to heaven he looks like an exiled scapegrace god.

With eyes shining brilliantly he tells you the tale of creation, how man- and woman-kind came on earth. Ages ago a giant turtle, like a fish that walked on a thousand legs, came up from the bottom of the ocean and saw the blue sky for the first time, and far away the coral reefs and forest-clad shores of Samoa. Full of excitement, it slashed its tail, swam to the isle and crept ashore. Once on dry land it could not move and get back to its native ocean again. The sun blazed on its tremendous back as it crouched and died, and underneath its vast shell a plot of tiny crimson and blue flowers trembled with fear in the sudden darkness that had fallen over them. When the giant turtle was dead its crumbling flesh fed the flowers with moisture, while they cried bitterly at being hidden from the beautiful golden sunlight. When only the shell was left, and the sun was shining beautifully, the flowers peeped out and saw the green hills and coco-palms, and found that they were able to move: out they all ran and tripped up the shore, a delighted flock of laughing faces, and climbed the coco-nut and palm trees—they were Samoan girls!

That same night a cloud was leisurely travelling across the clear skies with a cargo of male stars asleep on its breast; and as it passed right over the very spot where the new girls were climbing and clinging to the trees, the high chief of the stars, who was old and grey, looked over the side of the cloud and was astonished, for he saw the girls and at once called loudly to the youthful, sleeping stars, who rubbed their eyes and jumped up. They were beautiful youths with bright faces. "Look down there," said the old, grey star, and all the young stars looked and saw the Samoan maidens climbing about the tree-tops. "Oh, what shall we do to get down to them?" they all wailed, and the old, grey star said, "Ah, you were happy till I awoke you from sleep, but now your passions are awake and you cry aloud for sorrow." Then they all became impatient and fierce, and cried out: "Stop the cloud, stop the cloud"; and the old, grey-bearded star sighed and said: "So shall it be." The moon at once shone out in the sky and the old leader put his hand up to the orb and filled his arms with beautiful moonlight ere he struck the cloud with his magic breath and the thick, dark mist dissolving fell as sparkling rain softly to the isle far below. The bright moonlight clinging to the falling drops made ropes of moonbeams dangle to the forest tree-tops, on which the laughing stars slid as they went down, down—as beautiful youths, to fall into the outstretched arms of the surprised maidens. And that's how man and woman first came to the Samoan Isles!

Many more were the strange but really poetic tales told by him and by other wandering authors, but their memories and the children of their poetic imaginations are forgotten for ever. I do not think many of the old-time South Sea legends have ever been collected and translated, and so they only survive in the biographical writing of men who visited the islands and happened to have retentive memories for such things as poetic lore, and so preserved some of those old fragments of Samoan stories, as I have attempted to do from my recollection of many of them.

The lore of the South Seas has faded and has been replaced by tragic human drama and rumour. Subject matter for three-volume novels is plentiful in Samoa; indeed throughout the whole of the South Seas you could draw and never drain dry the living fountains of human drama.

Peaceful-looking homesteads, clean, religious and happy, abound, but some are tense with passion. By the mission room down at Mulinuu lives pretty Lavo; she is only sixteen and deeply religious. She loves the handsome white missionary with all her soul, but dares not speak out or confess. Eventually he goes away back to his own country, and a few days later they find poor Lavo's body in the lagoon. She looks beautiful even in death, as she still clutches the photograph of the homeward-bound missionary. Her native relatives wring their hands and wail; they lay her in the native cemetery just by the plateau, and sing sadly of her childhood till she is forgotten.

A white man was found with the side of his head blown off last night; he arrived at Apia a week ago, looking worried and haggard. All evidence of his identity had been destroyed by him, excepting a torn, half-obliterated letter which reads like this:

"MY OWN DEAR R——. Yes, I still love you, and will not believe you did that. I read the full account in this morning's *Chronicle*. My heart is heavy, dear; give yourself up and face it. Oh, my darling, don't leave the country. I love you, and will die, I am sure, if you go away. Meet me to-night at same place. I long to see your poor dear face. God watch over you. Yours ever,

E——."

The German High Commissioner kept the revolver that was found by the dead man's side, and his fat old wife took possession of the photograph that was found on him. She has tacked it up on her bedroom wall; it's such a nice, happy-looking, girlish face. They buried the suicide in the whites' cemetery, at the far end, among the "no-name graves."

On the slopes around Apia a few emigrants from far-off countries live in comfortable bungalows. They are happy with their wives and children. Their memory of the cities and turmoil of the old country is sweeter for the dreaming distance; they were a bit homesick at first, but now they have become contented and love the new peaceful surroundings, and look forward to the arrival of the mails. They still suffer, though, with the unrestful disease of the far-away suburban towns of advanced civilisation, and so cannot sleep for wondering who the strange couple are who rent the solitary bungalow on the edge of the forest up in the hills. It is quite evident that the new-comer is a gentleman, for he speaks well and has polished ways, but his wife talks like a servant-girl; she's pretty, though. They arrived suddenly in Apia, and three months after the baby was born. He seems very fond of the baby, and the mother too, but he often gets very despondent. He's a handsome man and does not look a bit practical; indeed he looks as though for the sake of affection and his word he would sacrifice all ambition and leave the world behind him. He seems to hate respectable people, and only goes down to the Apia bar-rooms to mix with old sailors and traders and the remnants of the beach; he stands treat and is a godsend to them, for he seems to have plenty of cash. One old shellback entertains him for hours with wonderful tales of other days, and his comrades sit by and silently smoke and drink as the bar becomes hazy with tobacco smoke. The lights grow dim as the old sailor's yarn rolls the world back, and in the now romantic atmosphere of the bar shades of old pioneers dance ghostly wise; old schooners and slave galleons are anchored in the harbour; you can hear the laughter and song of dead sailors and traders. They are dancing jigs, their sea-boots shuffle, under the coco-palms just outside the bar-room, the bright eyes of dark native girls shine as they whirl clinging to their arms: how they welcome the white men from the far-away Western world—the men whose ships long ago died down the seaward sunsets, and faded away beyond the sky-line into Time's silent sea ere our generation was born.

Out on the promontory sits the high chief Tuputo in his homestead. He has a noble, wrinkled, tattooed face, and, though he belongs to the old school, he wears glasses. The lizard slips across his moonlit floor, and through his door he can see the silvered waves and the wind-stirred coco-nut trees twinkling by the barrier reefs; the waves are breaking and wailing as they wailed and broke in his childhood. He has been a sailor in the South Seas; he remembers tribal wars in Fiji and Samoa and has refused many invitations to secret cannibalistic festivals. Now he sits reading the English newspapers, for long ago they taught him to read English, and he is a staunch Catholic. Often he reads and wonders over the terrible crimes that are reported in the police news of his late-dated London newspapers. He had once, long ago, thought that England and New York were sinless lands ethereal with Christian dreams, imparadised cities, their spires glittering in the sunlight of the Golden

Age. If not, why did missionaries leave them to come across the big seas to Samoa, and all the isles of the Southern Seas?

The great world war has not commenced yet, but even now his withered hands itch to clutch his disused war-club and sally forth to take revenge on those white men who laugh at his majestic bearing; those men who stole his isles and brought rum and vice to contaminate the virtue of his race. How spiteful will he feel when he wipes his spectacles, and, astonished, reads the truth! But then he will cool down, look at his innocent old war-club on his homestead wall and offer his humble services for the vast tribalistic war clash in the white man's lands, while Thakambau and Tano, the cannibal kings, and Ritova and King Naulivan, who never heard the word culture, sigh and turn in their graves to think that they are dead, while the very world is trembling with glorious, bloodthirsty battle. Ah, well, their children's children are coming to help us: may the old Thakambau spirit still be alive in their blood to help the advance of culture—the civilisation of sad humanity. Let us hope, too, that our semi-savage Allies will not eat the fallen foe! But I must proceed with my own wanderings, for I have a long way to travel yet.

Samoa still rises silently in moonlight out of the sea of my dreams. I can hear the barbarian orchestra clanging away down in the native village, as Samoan girls and youths, and two or three white men, waltz under the palms just below the plateau, where groves of orange-trees hang their golden fruit amongst dark leaves. As I play the violin the semi-savage people whirl to the wild rhythm of the forest ballroom music of a tribal waltz.

TRIBAL WALTZ.
(*Barbarian.*)

Composed by
A. S. M.

CHAPTER VII

Robert Louis Stevenson—Bohemian Incidents—I lead a Tribal Orchestra—The Big Drum—Robert Louis Stevenson at a Tribal Wedding—Robert Louis Stevenson in the Grog Shanty—Mr and Mrs Stevenson—The Last Man-eater of the Marquesan Group

I NOTICED that the brief incidents in my first book, *Sailor and Beachcomber*, concerning my personal recollections of Robert Louis Stevenson were received with an interest which I had not expected. Had I anticipated this, or had he struck me as an adventurous old shellback of crime and sea-lore, I should have dwelt more on the subject, but so much has been written about Stevenson's life in the South Seas, by men who have devoted volumes to their reminiscences of that novelist, that I deliberately left the matter alone.

As far as Stevenson the literary man is concerned I, of course, have nothing whatever to add, excepting, perhaps, that Stevenson's books dealing with the South Seas did not strike me as being as realistic and breezy as I had expected them to be, coming from such fresh experience and so able a pen. But having often seen him in Samoa and elsewhere, out of the limelight and under circumstances that have never, as far as I know, been written about before, I feel that I may as well tell at length the few incidents that I think may be of interest. I cannot do this better than by pursuing my own reminiscences, and so I will revert to my first visits to Samoa when I was a lad of about sixteen years of age.

Stevenson was at that time residing at Vailima, Upulo. I had met him several times in Apia and at sea, for at that time I was always cruising on the trading schooners and visited most of the chief islands in the North and South Pacific. I eventually got on a schooner that ran between Samoa and Suva (Fiji), and it was on these return trips to Apia, and during my sojourns there, that I saw Stevenson frequently, which was natural enough, since he lived there and hundreds of men became acquainted with him in that isolated paradise, where conventionality, as it is known in Western civilisation, was completely dropped, and all men became hail-fellow-well-met as soon as they sighted each other. Even missionaries practised this outward appearance of brotherhood.

I recall how I was sitting in a German store in April one afternoon when a Samoan, who knew me well, approached me and asked me if I would like to come that same evening to a grand tribal wedding festival that was to be held five miles off, round the coast. "And will you bring your violin?" he inquired. I accepted, and my companion, a young American sailor who had a banjo, agreed to go with me. I was well known among the chiefs and natives as an obliging violinist, for I seldom refused to perform at native ceremonies; the scenes that I witnessed, indeed the novelty and romance of it all, amply repaid me for all the trouble I was ever put to, though that is saying a good deal, for my troubles were sometimes serious ones.

That same afternoon my friend and I tuned our instruments up and made ourselves look as smart as possible, for the chief who was giving the ball was one of high standing, and a well-known follower of Mataafa, the ex-King of Samoa.

In high spirits we started off to tramp the five miles which had to be covered before we reached our destination. We had not walked more than three hundred yards from Apia's main street when suddenly Stevenson appeared with several of his acquaintances, coming across the slopes carrying fish which they had purchased from the natives down by the beach.

WHANGAREI FALLS, NORTH AUCKLAND, N.Z.

Stevenson turned and saw us, and noticing that we were carrying musical instruments, he came up and said in a jocular way: "Where are you hurrying off to? The Lyceum Orchestra?" Whereupon I told him our destination and he immediately became interested. "Are you in a hurry? I should like to come," he said quickly. I assured him that we were in no hurry, and told him we would wait; but as his friends were becoming impatient he said that he would come on later, and so off we went without him.

When we arrived at the coast village where the ball was to be given, my friend and I sat down under the palms exhausted, for the walk was a long one and the heat terrific. Just before us was the native village, groups of conical, shed-like houses, sheltered by coco-palms growing to the shore's edge.

As we sat wiping the perspiration from our brows, the village was all astir with excitement over the approaching festival. Native girls, dressed in picturesque style, passed by us along the track: they were jabbering excitedly to each other over the beauty of the bride who had been married that day, and who was to appear at the feast that evening to dance and reveal her manifold beauties to the village maids and youths ere she went off on the honeymoon to the bridegroom's home.

The shadows were falling over the palm-clad shores of the wild coast and village of Samoa as the sun dropped seaward. So my friend and I started off once more and arrived at Kalofa's distinguished residence. Kalofa was the bride's father, and a wealthy man for a native. We were greeted with loud cries in joyous Samoan phrases as we arrived, carrying the violin and banjo under our arms. As we entered the large primitive ballroom, a shed that held about two hundred people, an old Samoan at once started crashing away at a monster wooden drum, and another drum-player inside the shed did likewise. The noise was deafening, and the more so because the ballroom instrument was a large European drum that had been purchased from one of the American warships that had come into Apia harbour. This drum was lent out at a high charge on special occasions by the chiefs. I forget who was the original owner, but I know that he was quite a wealthy man through the money he received from his drum receipts, and I often regretted that I had not known the tastes of Samoans, or I should have arrived at Samoa with a cargo of old army drums and made a fortune.

Well, as we entered the ballroom Kalofa himself rushed forward and greeted us affectionately before all the chiefs as though he had known us for many years. I had only seen him once before, and my cheerful companion the banjoist had never seen him till that moment. Nevertheless we met him as though we were the oldest friends, and bowed respectfully as the whole audience arose and waved their dark hands as they cheered us. It was a wonderful sight that we saw round us, for right to the far end of the large, low room sat in half circles the élite of the native village, dressed in all the colours and grotesque garments imaginable. Handsome Samoan girls, half dressed and quarter dressed, were squatting amongst old tattooed chiefs who wore the ridi only, while lines of old women sat with the handsome youths, who glanced behind them at the girls who, I suppose, were being looked after by the chiefs. The code of morals in Samoa was becoming very strict, so many maids having been tempted by the amorous youths to do things which they ought not to do. In the centre of the throng was the barbaric orchestra. I have led and conducted many orchestras and bands during my time, but never such a deliberately planned inharmonious ear-torturing lot of musicians as I led that night. I think the instrumentation was chiefly strings and wind; the former consisted of wires strung across gourds and the latter of bamboo flutes, old coppers and the drum which I have previously mentioned.

I sat down in the middle of the orchestral players, squatting, with my comrade by my side, on a mat, and all the native musicians around me gazed with great curiosity as I started to tune the violin, and my comrade to pink-ee-tee-ponk on his banjo; indeed, so great was their curiosity that they arose from their mats and poked their faces against our instruments. Hitting my violin with the bow, so—tap-tap, I made a sign to them to take their seats, and then the overture commenced! My comrade and I tore away at the strings. I forget what we had proposed to play, but as soon as we started and the members of the orchestra heard the violin wailing, they went completely mad with delight, and then tried to outdo us; so placing their flutes to their dusky mouths they all started to blow terrifically, and the drums started off and the stringed gourds twanged! In a moment I realised that to keep up our musical reputation we must outdo the barbarian music, so I signed to my comrade, who looked at me as though he had gone mad, and then started to grind away at all my violin strings at once! I believe we both caught the primitive, barbarian fever, for though the row was terrible my memory of it all is one of some far-off event of supreme musical delight! Not Wagner's wildest dreams, no Futurist's idea of harmony could have outdone the reality of that tribal music. Then suddenly it all changed from thunder to weird sweetness, minor melodies of sad, forgotten loves and dreams, for on a little elevated bamboo platform the bride stood before us. She was a dusky, tender-limbed maiden of about sixteen years of age. Dressed in a blue frock that went no higher than her brown bosom, fastened on by a red sash, her thick hair bedecked with tropical blossoms, she looked like the beautiful dusky princess from a South Sea novel. Her husband, a fine-looking Samoan of about thirty, stood beside her as she gazed up into his admiring eyes and sang a tender song of love. It was a really beautiful melody and I at once caught the spirit of it, and as she sang on sweetly I extemporised a delicate accompaniment on my violin, interspersed with minor pizzicatos. As soon as she ceased her song a tiny child stepped forth, and kissing her feet handed her a large bouquet of richly coloured forest flowers; then the bridegroom stooped and kissed the child on the brow as all the audience solemnly murmured "O whey—O whey" three times. This child was a relative of the bride's, and not her own child; though, to tell the truth, this was often the case in tribal weddings at which I had officiated as violinist, where often the custom was that the bride's first-born came as chief witness to the altar, and sometimes was old enough to toddle all the way!

When she had sung one more island ditty to her delighted husband the Siva dance commenced. Through a little door behind the stage came about a dozen girls clad only in flowers and grass, and when they had squatted in a circle on the stage they started to beat their bare limbs with their hands as they chanted, and the orchestra went tootle-tootle on the bamboo flutes.

As the time passed the audience increased; chiefs, half-castes and many high-caste natives were there. Robert Louis Stevenson arrived, with his face wreathed with smiles, and stood just inside the door, watching and talking to the natives. The old ex-King Mataafa, who was at that time residing at Malie with his faithful followers, was also there and stood talking to our host, who was, I believe, related to Samoan royalty. Mataafa was a very intelligent-looking old man, well dressed and with a majestic walk. About that time there was a deal of trouble brewing between the subjects of Mataafa and those who stood by King Malietoa, and possibly the old king was travelling incognito, for he hardly revealed himself, but stopped in the shadows.

Stevenson went round behind the audience to him and was greeted very warmly; they evidently knew each other well.

As the festival proceeded, and the bowl of kava was handed round, the chiefs and women-folk became excited, while outside under the moonlit coco-palms the girls and youths started to dance and caper about. My friend and I took the first opportunity to get outside, for the heat was stifling inside "the hall."

When we arrived in the fresh air Stevenson was standing by the doorway smoking. "Hallo! there you are; I'm sorry, but I was too late to see the beginning," he said, and then added: "That bride was a beautiful girl, wasn't she?"

"Yes," I answered, as several native girls came up to us, and, laughing, seized us and invited us to dance. The girl who had gripped hold of Stevenson was a very wild but good-looking maid, and gazing up into his face she started to make eyes at him. Stevenson looked round laughingly and then accepted the invitation of the girl to dance with her, and so off they went! As far as I can remember the novelist was a good dancer and looked at his ease as he held the Samoan beauty in his arms and gently whirled with her under the coco-palms.

All the time that Stevenson and I were dancing the native orchestra was booming and shrieking away in the festival shed, and often we heard the old native drum-conductor cry out "O Le Sivo," and then came a terrible crash as he struck the old army drum with a war-club!

Stevenson seemed delighted with himself for a little while, and then we got too hot and, much to the disgust of the maids, stopped. They were cool enough in their scanty attire, but we were bathed in perspiration and fairly steamed in the moonlight as we suddenly stood still.

Now I am coming to the comical part of it all, for Stevenson's partner proceeded to make violent love to him, and the look on his face made it quite obvious that he was beginning to feel uncomfortable, for he eventually walked off and she at once followed him! He made several attempts to get rid of her by talking to a native who stood by, but still the girl persisted, till he suddenly walked up to me and said, "I say, for God's sake get her away somewhere; dance with her, do anything to attract her attention." I at once went to the rescue and asked her to dance. I was not much of a dancer, but as a lover I have always been passable! Stevenson seemed very grateful, but only expressed it by walking off in great haste as I clutched the girl tightly.

No sooner had Stevenson got out of sight than she started on me, threw her arms about my neck and began to say loving things about my beauty, I suppose, in her own language. Several natives were standing under the trees, shaking with laughter as they watched us: one of them touched his forehead significantly and then I realised that the girl was not quite right in the head! "I say, Hill," I said, as I quickly turned to my comrade, "she wants you to dance with her; do take her, old fellow." "Right you are," he answered, for he was an obliging fellow in that way, and then I also bolted and went off, toward the chief's Fale-Faipule (the head residence), to get my violin, which I had left in his care for safety. As I approached the bamboo door I saw Stevenson peeping through a chink! "Has she gone?" he said. "Yes, I've got rid of her; she is a bit wrong in the head," I answered. Then, as Stevenson came out into the open, ready to start away home, to our astonishment the girl we were talking about ran across the grass and embraced him once more! "Well I'm d———d!" he said, and at that moment two natives came across the track and collared her. I think they were her parents; anyway they took her off, and Stevenson hurried off also, for the hour was late and the code of morals strict in the Vailima domestic establishment.

My friend and I got back to Apia soon after. I slept soundly and dreamed of dusky brides and mad lovers. So ended that wedding as far as I was concerned.

A few days after the preceding events I saw Stevenson again. It was in the daytime, and I and my friend were busy packing up cases of tinned food, which had just arrived from Sydney on the s.s. *Lubeck*, which generally called at Apia every month. Adjoining the stateroom—where we were assisting in packing the cases—was a grog shanty's bar-room. The reputation that this shanty had was an evil one, for it was only visited by the beach fraternity who lived solely on rum, and by Samoan women who welcomed German sailors to their dusky arms after dark. In broad daylight it was a *bona-fide* beach hotel, frequented by traders who had no reputation to lose, yet who seemed the happiest of men as they told fearless tales to their rough comrades, squirted tobacco juice in endless streams through the open door and drank fiery rum.

Well, suddenly Stevenson walked into the bar, and placing a coin on the counter called for drinks. He seemed full of glee, and laughed heartily as his two companions told him something that was evidently humorous. These two men, whom Stevenson had most probably just met, and who interested him, were shellbacks of the roughest type. One was positively comical-looking with dissipation, and had a warty grog-nose; the other seldom spoke, but simply nodded his head, as an umpire of truth, when his companion told Stevenson the wonders of the South Seas. They were telling him about earlier black-birding days, when native men and girls were lured on to the schooners and carried off to slavery and worse. I cannot remember the things that they told him, but I distinctly remember Stevenson's deep interest as he stood by them, with his head nearly touching the low roof of the shanty, and called for more rum for his companions, though he did not drink himself.

The convivial old rogues were delighted with Stevenson's generosity, and seeing that he listened eagerly to their yarns the chief speaker became more garrulous and dramatic than ever as he lifted his hands up to the roof and said: "Sir, them things that I tells you is nothing to what I could tell you." Meanwhile the novelist listened and looked out of the grog shanty door, to see that no one was about who would carry the news to Vailima that Robert Louis Stevenson was full of glee, treating old rogues to rum, in a grog-house of mystery and lurking crime.

There was a native woman in the bar, whom the barkeeper called Frizzy. She had a large mop of frizzly hair and I suppose got her name from that. She was one of the abandoned class, had four half-caste children and was a half-widow, for the father of the children, a German official, had gone back to Berlin.

Whilst Stevenson was listening to his newly acquired friends this woman approached him with her ghastly smile, at the same time offering for sale her little plaited baskets of red coral. Stevenson shook his head, and as she was still persistent one of the old shellbacks pushed her away as though she was a mangy dog. Stevenson looked at him with disapproval, for, though he was naturally opposed to women of her class, he was a champion for the unfortunates who had been lured to their mode of life by white men. He then called the woman, who had walked away, and asking her the price of the coral bought two baskets, though I am sure he did not want them.

At that moment a white man came into the bar and gave a start at seeing Stevenson standing there. It was a "new chum" from Sydney, and the last man you would have expected to see in that place. Looking up at Stevenson, he said: "Well, who would have ever thought of seeing you here!" On which the other responded in a surprised voice: "Who on earth expected to see you here!" Then they both laughed, and Stevenson said something about being a writer of books and seeking inspiration from natural sources, and with intense amusement in his eyes he introduced the two grimy reprobates to his friend, who shook them heartily by the hand and asked them what they drank.

At this moment a Samoan youth rushed in at the bar door very excited, and before we could understand his gesticulations a native girl came in behind him, snatched a large mug from the counter and gave the youth a crack over the head! As she made another rush to repeat the attack Stevenson gripped her tightly, and she turned on him furiously, and then, as quickly, calmed down and relented. She seemed to regret bitterly her attack on her lover, for such he was, though he had been paying attention to another maid. The youth had a gash on his forehead, and though it was not a deep cut the large flow of blood made a serious-looking affair of it all. Out of the native's home, not far off, the children and women came rushing to see what the row was about, for, unfortunately, the jealous girl had screamed out when she struck him. A German patrol came running across, and had not Stevenson expostulated, and got on the right side of him, the girl would have been arrested. The whole affair would have been in *The Samoan Times*, Stevenson and his friend would have been brought forward as witnesses, and though Stevenson was perfectly innocent a lot of scandal would have been the result.

About eight miles from Apia, in one of the coast villages, lived a Marquesan who had married a Samoan woman, whom I knew, as she had resided in Satuafata village. One day, when I was walking along in Apia town, I was suddenly greeted by her cheery laugh, and she invited me out to their home, an invitation which I at once accepted, and so the next day I started off alone. The weather was beautiful and the sky cloudless as I passed under the coco-palms, and heard the green doves cooing in the branches around me, as the *katafa* (frigate-bird) sailed across the sky bound seaward. Through the trees I could see the Pacific, bright under the hot sun, and in Apia harbour the hanging canvas sails of a few anchored schooners. As I walked along I felt perfectly happy in the company of my own thoughts, which were only disturbed as I passed the native homesteads and returned the hand-waves and salutations of "Kaoha!" from the pretty native girls who stood at the doors. Samoan girls were, as I have told you, born flirts, and longed for the romantic white youth who would love them and make them "Te boomte Matan,"[1] as they had read maids were loved in the South Sea novels which they bought from the old store shops in Apia. Far away along the coast I saw droves of native children standing knee-deep in the shaded lagoon waters that joined the ocean just outside.

> 1. Wife of a white man.

I passed a beautiful spot where I had often stood at night, when the island was asleep and the moon hung over the water, and the view appeared like some mighty painting done in silver and mystic colours, framed by the starlit skies. The palms perfectly still, stretching to the slopes of the Vaea Mountains, stood all round, only a wave gently breaking over the far-off barrier reefs, or the wavering smoke from the moonlit village huts, destroyed the impression of something dream-like and unreal around me as the wind came and moaned in the palm-tops, humming beautifully, till it seemed the chiming of the starry worlds across the sky could be faintly heard.

About three miles from Apia I left the track to cut across a plantation towards the coast, when I was suddenly surprised to see two white people some distance off coming toward the village that I was making for. Ambushed in the thick scrub, I peered up the track to see what they might be, and was again surprised to see that it was Stevenson and his wife. Stevenson had a large bamboo rod in his hand, and was waving it about violently and seemed very excited. Indeed I thought they were quarrelling, but as they approached a group of village homesteads just near the track I saw that he was gesticulating, and pointing with pleasure at the surrounding scenery, which was extremely beautiful there. They did not notice me, and so I remained unobserved. Stevenson was dressed in white trousers and had an old cheesecutter cap on. As they approached the native homes a lot of children came rushing across the clearing to welcome them. Mrs Stevenson picked one of them up in her arms and kissed it, while her husband in fun ran after the rest with his bamboo stick, and they all scampered away in delight.

At the far end of the plantation, wherein grew coco-nuts, yams and pine-apples, was the home of my native friends. I crossed the space and passing between the lines of white native houses arrived at my destination. Mrs Laota and her husband gave me an enthusiastic welcome, with the usual hospitality of Samoans, and in a very short space of time I sat down before an appetising meal of poi-poi, taro, bread-fruit,[2] yams and boiled fowl. There were two families living in the homestead, and the native children climbed over me as I sat down to eat, and, though I am fond of children, at that moment they were a fearful pest. However, as in England, I had to put up with it and assume a happiness which I was far from feeling, while the delighted eyes of the parents gazed upon me and on their children; but they were semi-savages and, of course, it was all excusable.

> 2. Bread-fruit is baked in the red-hot ash, like baked potatoes. When it is cooked properly the outer rind cracks and falls off.

After I had finished my meal I stood at the door, smoking and talking to my host, who seemed a very intelligent native. He was a Marquesan, and his father, an old chief, was also in our company. It was just at this moment that Stevenson, whose wife was still visiting in the village, came strolling along; he had evidently been to the village before, because my host and his wife at once called him and he came across and greeted us all with a cheery laugh, accepting a slice of pine-apple from the children and sitting down on the bench with us.

Well, Koro, the old Marquesan chief, had lived in the stirring times when his tribe had suffered from the ravages of cannibalism, and he started off yarning almost directly Stevenson sat down. From his lips we were told many things that seemed almost unbelievable. Koro even darkly hinted that Samoans up till very recently had been addicted to the awful appetite, which was probable; but, being an intellectual race and superior in every way to the other races of the Pacific, Samoans had not allowed the stain of cannibalism to rest on the history of their people, letting the memory of it die out with the custom. Stevenson was alert with interest as the old chief told us of past cannibalistic orgies of his islands, and, as the old man yarned on in pidgin-English, kept saying "Well now, really me!" for very surprise at the things we heard. One tale he told us was so bloodthirsty and cruel, and the truth so evident from the manner in which it was told, that I must repeat it here.

It appeared that in the Marquesa Group, on Hiva-oa, at a period not distant from the time that I am telling you of, there was a ferocious cannibal who was the last survivor of a tribe which had ravaged the surrounding villages and preyed on the flesh of the people. In Koro's time this hated man-eater lurked in the forest, and the village was obliged to have sentinels on watch each night. For the terrible cannibal had a passion for the flesh of their children, and often by night the whole village was awakened by hearing the screams of one of their little ones, who had been seized whilst asleep, and was being carried off into the forest. The method of this monster was to crawl on his belly through the thickets and watch the village for hours, and once or twice a girl had been carried off in broad daylight to be strangled and eaten. Many of the things the old chief told us were too terrible to write down here; it is enough to say that he did not strangle his female victims at once, but kept them lashed in his hiding-place to be killed and eaten at leisure. The people knew this, because a native girl had managed to escape, after being a prisoner of the monster's for several days. It is impossible to describe here Koro's dramatic attitude, and his wonderful way of telling the story. The listening children in the hut crept closer to us for fright, and Stevenson laughed almost hysterically and said "Good Lord!" as the old fellow continued. "Well, Marser Stesson, one night Chief Swae, who had just got married, had a great dance, and we all be happy and dance; and that night when the moon was getting old we all did sleep and Swae's bride did sleep beside him, for the night was very hot and we did all sleep in the open under the *fifis* (palms). Suddenly we were all awake and jumping about in the village, for Swae was shouting out with a great voice: 'The man-eater has stolen my wife.' In one moment we had all seized our war-clubs, old cutlasses and muskets and rushed off into the forest, Swae the bridegroom leading the way. Presently we did hear a far-off scream coming from the direction of the sea. Swiftly we turned and went toward the shore, and it was then that we all looked through the mangroves and saw the great man-eater holding Swae's bride in his arms as though she was a caught bird. He was leaning against a tree and had stopped because she did cling to one of his legs; he was a mighty big fellow of great strength, and his face was very, very dark and wrinkled with wickedness. Swae ran with all his might round the shore and got behind the cannibal, and, creeping up behind him, with one sweep of his cutlass cut his head from his shoulders. It fell to the forest floor and the body still stood upright, while the cannibal's head lay on the ground with the mouth still half laughing at the thought of what he would do with Swae's wife! When we got up to the bride she lay as one dead, still clinging to the man-eater's leg. Then Swae called her softly by her name and she opened her eyes and sprang into his eager arms. We cooked the body of the cannibal and gave it to our grunting swine. No one of my tribe would eat the swine after that, so we sold them to the white sailors who came in on the big ships and they were much pleased that they were so cheap!" And saying this the old chief gave a chuckle in his wrinkled throat, being hardly able to disguise his inward delight. Stevenson, too, saw the grim humour of it and also smiled and said: "Well now!"

As Koro finished Mrs Stevenson arrived on the scene, carrying a large bunch of flowers, and when Stevenson told her that which we had been listening to she said: "Ugh, I am glad I wasn't here to listen; you love gruesome things, I know." Stevenson grinned like a schoolboy as he started mischievously to tell her some of the most gruesome details which we had just heard.

CHAPTER VIII

Robert Louis Stevenson and his Friends—Stevenson as a Roadmaker—Timbo—Stevenson on the Schooner—The Skipper—"Tusitala" and the Natives—Conventionality—A Visit to King Malietoa—Stevenson's Love of Adventure—Stevenson the Writer—Genius in the Southern Seas—Socialism

I SAW Stevenson several times after that at society balls and concerts in Apia, where sometimes he seemed full of merriment and indeed the life of the party, and again at other times strangely silent, revealing the man of moods. I have never heard that he was fond of being alone, but I can vouch for it that he was as often alone in his wanderings over the islands as he was with friends; indeed I think I saw him more often alone than otherwise. I met Mr Strong twice, I think, when he was with Stevenson. Mr Moore too, who wrote *With Stevenson in Samoa*, was a pleasant man, and Robert Louis Stevenson and he were as familiar as brothers.

Almost the last time I saw Stevenson was at the Tivoli in Apia; he was with Mr Moore and several other men whom I cannot recall. They were all taking refreshments and talking. Stevenson was flushed a bit, his eyes were very bright, and with his hat off, revealing a lofty, pale brow, he looked unlike the ordinary run of men. He was in an excellent mood, and Mr Moore and another member of the party were so intensely amused at what he was saying that they almost upset their glasses and spluttered as they laughed; which gave Stevenson very obviously great pleasure, for he was as fond of a joke as any of them.

On that special occasion I was in the company of the chief mate of a large schooner which was leaving Apia the next day for Honolulu. Stevenson, or one of the party, called us across and offered us drinks and cigars. Soon after my companion, who had to get on board his ship, left and I went with him; and as we got outside we still heard the jovial exclamations of Stevenson and his friends as they yarned on, their voices fading behind us as we walked away into the moonlight and shadows of the coco-palms many years ago.

Stevenson would often tackle rough work, such as tree-chopping and digging; and was often to be seen perspiring and covered with grime as he helped the natives to make tracks across the rough jungle and forest land that surrounded Vailima. Bare-footed, dressed in old clothes and a seaman's cast-off cap, he looked like some vagabond dust-man. His manner to the natives who worked for him was jovial enough; he would shout: "Go it, Sambo, that's right, te rom and te pakea[3] if you work hard"; and then with a twinkle in his eyes he'd stand and watch them lugging the wheelbarrows up the slope as they jabbered like school-children and worked their hardest. Several of

Stevenson's friends also worked with him: one of them would be cutting the trees down as the novelist smoked, and jocularly criticising him, telling him to "keep moving and not be such a loafer." Mrs Stevenson arrived on the scene of hard work once and chided him for exerting himself. "Don't do that, dear, or you will be ill again," she would say; and the novelist would look up and then work harder than ever.

    3. Meaning rum, refreshments and tobacco.

He was to be found in all the out-of-the-way places and would go miles alone, usually on foot; though he had an old horse or ass, I forget which, he seldom rode it.

One day I was walking along near the coast when a little native boy of about six years of age, came limping out of the jungle scrub just by the track. I picked the little fellow up and discovered he had trodden on some glass, and had a deep gash in his foot. As I was carrying him down to the shore to wash his wound, Stevenson and a boy came strolling by. Stevenson, who was always very kind to children, examined the wound, took out his pocket-handkerchief and bound the foot up, after we had well bathed it: his manner to the little outcast was one of extreme tenderness.

I was living with two kindly disposed old natives at that time, so I picked the child up and carried him home. We found out the next day that the poor little fellow's parents had been drowned by the upsetting of a canoe in a typhoon off Apia harbour. He was very thin and looked ill, so I gave my hosts some money and told them to feed him up, which they did. I became very fond of him; he had thick curls all over his head, and his cheery little brown face was lit up by a pair of beautiful brown eyes. He slept near me, and every morning he would jump off his bed-mat and caper about like a puppy and would insist in helping me put my boots on. He heard me play the violin and was deeply interested in it. I was always catching him looking at my violin, and each time he looked up at me artfully, as much as to say: "I must not touch your wonderful music. Oh no, I'm not that kind of Samoan baby!"

I only chided him once, when I caught the little dark tinker unscrewing all my violin pegs. He gave a terrified shriek as I ran after him, and was off like a frightened rabbit. When I at length caught him, and regained my property, he looked up at me with pleading eyes, gave a baby-like cry, and in musical, infantile Samoan phrases asked to be forgiven. So I at once placed him on my shoulder and gave him a ride to his heart's delight; and after that he stood guard over my violin, and came rushing up to me if even the dog went near it. I let him sleep with me sometimes, and he placed his arms about my neck as though I were some sweet-bosomed mother; and so in that way fell asleep the little brown savage in the arms of Western civilisation.

Of course this is not telling you much of Robert Louis Stevenson, but to me, and in my memory of it all, it's just as important, perhaps even more so. The old Samoan wife became very fond of Timbo, as I called him, and he became quite plump. So I secured a good home for him for life, or till he grew up, and therefore you will see that I have also done good mission work in the South Seas!

I heard when I came home afterwards that Stevenson had seen Timbo and given him some presents, including a box of tin German soldiers. Timbo gave me half of them. I was obliged to accept them to please him. If he's alive still he must be a fine young fellow, for he was affectionate and plucky even as a tiny child. I remember how I once took him for a canoe ride, and his delight as I rocked the small craft in the shallow water till he fell overside, for he could swim like a fish. Once I took him out in Apia harbour and we went aboard a schooner that had encountered a typhoon; she was being overhauled, for her deck was almost washed clean, the rigging was a mass of tangle and the galley had been washed away. The skipper was a pleasant enough man; he hailed from San Francisco and had a voice that could compete with the wildest gale's thunder, but nevertheless his heart was in the right place when whisky was scarce. I had met him ashore and, hearing that I came from Sydney, and had lived near his home in San Francisco, he got into conversation with me and hinted that there was a chance of a berth aboard for me, if I felt inclined to take it.

While I was on this schooner one afternoon suddenly Stevenson and his wife came on board; they had been brought out in one of the small native canoes that were always hovering by the beach, awaiting passengers wanting to visit the anchored crafts in the harbour. The novelist was in high spirits and helped Mrs Stevenson up the rope ladder in great mirth. Mrs Robert Louis Stevenson was an excellent sailor and made no fuss about the ascent, as she clambered up and leapt on the deck with a bounce!

The skipper knew them well and was very polite to them. A young American or Australian lady, I forget which, was also visiting on board, and the skipper introduced her to Mr and Mrs Stevenson. She devoted all her attention to the novelist, and as they were having lunch together in the schooner's cuddy Stevenson's misery, as she plied him with questions and reiterated her flattering approval of his books, was very evident. "Oh, I think your books most delightful; how do you think of such things? Was it really true about that rich uncle and the derelict piano? Have you read *Lady Audley's Secret?*" So she rattled on. Stevenson looked appealingly at his wife, in an attempt to get her to engage the girl's attention, but still she persisted in reiterating those things which she thought were music to the novelist's ears. Suddenly Stevenson looked up, and with his fine eyes alive with satire said something to the effect that "he did not write books for ladies to read," punctuating the remark with a look that made the garrulous visitor immediately retire into her shell.

The convivial equilibrium was not restored till the skipper sat down at the cuddy's harmonium and, with his feet pedalling away at full speed, started to sing with his thunderous voice:

"Fifteen men on a dead man's chest,

Yo! Ho! Ho! for a bottle of rum!"

The young lady who had so annoyed Stevenson joined in, and revealed the fact that her voice as a musical medium was a deal more pleasant than when it tried to flatter a writer of books. Stevenson seemed delighted to find such an opportunity insidiously to apologise for his previous irritability, and so at once started to applaud the lady's singing in an almost exaggerated fashion.

A bottle of whisky was opened, and the skipper drank half-a-tumblerful, just to sample it and see if he had really opened the special brand which he had been recommending to his visitors. Finding there was no mistake, with all the liberality of a sailor, he allotted to each a due portion; whereby the dimly lit cabin festival was immensely enhanced. Stevenson's mirth was frequently stimulated by the drunken mate, who repeatedly poked his head into the cuddy door and, with a half-apologetic leer at the ladies, looked at the skipper and said: "All's well, sir. I'm going ashore." The skipper, who was half-seas-over himself, looked at him contemptuously and said: "Clear out of it." "Ay, ay, sir," responded the mate, and in a few minutes he was back again, and out came the same information, "All's well, sir. I'm off ashore."

Suddenly the skipper arose and went on deck and a loud argument commenced, interspersed with those maritime epithets which enforce sea law and are not to be found in navigation books. After a brief interval of silence the skipper could be heard shouting out oaths as he shook his fist to the mate, who was being rowed away ashore by the natives who always haunted the gangways of anchored ships.

At sunset the party left the schooner, and the skipper went with them, and we heard their laughter fading away over the darkening waters as the singing natives paddled them away to Apia's island town.

That same night I also went ashore with the sailors. Timbo sat in the middle of the ship's boat; he had been entertained by the hands in the forecastle. As soon as I arrived on the beach I made my way to my friendly natives' home, for the hour was late and I wanted to get Timbo off to bed. I was deep in thought, and as he toddled beside me I held his hand. Suddenly I was startled by hearing the child make throaty gurgles as though he wanted to be sick, his little brown face wrinkling up as he made fearful grimaces. "What's the matter, Timbo?" I said, somewhat alarmed, and for answer he looked up at me helplessly and dropped several objects in the scrub. I picked them up and found that he had been sucking away at a large, rank meerschaum pipe, which I at once recognised as belonging to the boatswain of the schooner which we had just left. The boy had also stolen a purse with a few coppers in it and a small leather belt purse full of brass buttons. I felt pretty wild with the little fellow at first, because it meant that I had to go back to the schooner and return the things.

Taking Timbo up, I sat on a log and laid him across my knees, ready to give him a good spanking, for it was not his first misdemeanour; indeed, he had done many things which I have left untold. As I laid him face downwards, so that I might administer chastisement, he twisted his little curly head round and looked appealingly up at me with his big brown eyes: as if to say: "Oh, noble white man from the far-off moral integrity of Western civilisation, may I beg of you to overlook the sad indiscretion of a Samoan child?" That part whereon I was about to administer justice looked so small and helpless that I did that which I should have liked to have been done to me in my earlier years, for I relented and stood Timbo on his feet. Then I said: "Timbo, for that which you have done you will be arrested and taken to Mulinuu Jail, where the wicked chiefs are imprisoned." Hearing this, he clung to me and sobbed, and large tears rolled down his cheeks and splashed on to his small mahogany-coloured toes. So I said: "Timbo, I forgive you." For I knew, deep down in my heart, that, though I was white, I had in my childish days committed several little indiscretions very similar to Timbo's. He was only a tiny fellow, and I thought of English babies who at his age were still in arms and busy sucking dummies; and I knew that civilisation itself was a monstrous baby, devoid of wit, sucking away at the dry, windy dummy and soothing itself with the thought that it was swallowing kindly feeding milk. As I thought I looked at Timbo, and the expression of gratitude on his little half-wild face, as he stood on his head and waved his feet to the skies, seemed to applaud my mild philosophy.

In all that I recall of Robert Louis Stevenson—his manner to strangers, his ever-ready attention to those who would earnestly tell him something, his kindness to the natives and to all who were in a conventional sense beneath him—was revealed a large mind with a sympathetic, human outlook.

Often little actions, something done on the impulse of the moment, told of simplicity and tenderness and the greatness which reveals a spirit that sees the link of fellowship between men, no matter what their caste or position in human affairs.

At times he might have appeared theatrical to those around him; but it was the expression of an intellectual, dramatic instinct, not for the stage, but for the drama played by men of this world, as though he were ever gazing critically on mortals before the limelight of existence and saying, half to himself: "There you are! I told you so. What would you say to all that you've just heard if you read it in a book? You wouldn't believe it, I'll be bound."

His manner to Mrs Stevenson revealed an affectionate, confiding nature that loved attention. I should think it was the affection of a boy's heart, with the strong strain of a discerning man who knew the nature of women. He would always treat native women with the same deference that he showed to the women of his own race; a deference always delicately courteous, excepting on those occasions when women might court his criticism by criticising him, or by casting aside the delicate armour of their sex and assuming man's rôle.

His kindness and the trouble he took on behalf of the Samoans is well known, and the natives earnestly expressed their gratitude by listening to and following the advice of "Tusitala," as they called him, and when he died they loudly bewailed his death. The poet-author's coffin was borne on the strong shoulders of Samoan chiefs, and the sound of their wailing, as they carried the coffin onwards up the slopes, with slow footsteps, to the grave on Vaea's sea-girt height, was his funeral chant.

I saw Robert Louis Stevenson in many places and in many moods, and looking back, as I now can, the perspective clearly shows me that he was a religious man in the true sense of that term. In no wise bigoted, he often fell into the ranks of Christianity and beat time, with a smile on his lips, as though he wished to set an example to those around him, in his knowledge that the example was better than his own half-sad, hopeful smile. At times, too, he would fall out of the ranks and become a harum-scarum renegade, and at such moments he seemed to have no idea of the existence of the barrier-lines that men, before the public, draw between the jovial rogue and the respectable citizen. "Well, captain, how goes it? Got an eye-opener aboard?" he would say as he jumped aboard the schooner's deck; and then he would turn to the sailor who might be cleaning brass close by and offer him a cigarette, or walk into the forecastle and chum with the crew, or look over the ship's side and shy a copper to the swimming natives who haunted the bay, with the sea-birds, looking for a living. Such was Stevenson's manner in the isles of Samoa, where, notwithstanding the wildness and the proximity to primitive life, many of the emigrant citizens still did things, or did not do things, because of the standard set by a majority.

It does not matter where you go, or how remote from civilisation your dwelling-place may be, you are sure to have some living illustration before you to tell you that the chains of conventionality are forged from the natures of men. I believe that if we could come back to this world a myriad years hence, when the sun has cooled down to a ghostly moon, when the seas are frozen and swinging to the tideless desolation that precedes the final crashing of the planetary system, and the human race has dwindled to a camp of twelve shivering mortals wrapped in bearskins, we should find them sitting over the last log fire without wood, with gloomy faces, anxiously awaiting Monday—because it is Sunday!

Mrs Stevenson was as much a Bohemian as her husband. She accompanied him on his short visits to Apia town, and on those occasions she was generally to be seen hurriedly rushing back to get, or inquire for, that which had been left behind. The novelist walked ahead and, as he went on dreaming, forgot that his wife was out with him till the domestic voice came again. Mrs Stevenson was very pleasant to talk to; she invited me to Vailima, but I was not able to go. Indeed, I was only a lad and, not being a lady's man, would have run twenty miles to escape Vailima fashion.

I recall many men who were acquaintances of Robert Louis Stevenson, and whom I have never heard of since. I remember one old man in particular whom Stevenson was always glad to meet. Indeed, the novelist's face lit up directly he saw him. His name was Callard, and he was a bit of a scallawag, was a character and had plenty of spare cash. He was never silent, but talked all day long and nearly all night, and always had some new trouble to relate. I slept in his room one night with two other men and he kept on and on about some friend who had swindled him out of five dollars in San Francisco, for that was his native place. "Yes, he did me, by heaven he did"; and saying this he would start reckoning up on a bit of paper, and sit on the side of the bed swearing till my friend and I said: "If you won't worry any more about it we'll give you the five dollars." About a week after he took a passage on the 'Frisco mail-boat. I really believe that he hurried home and spent five hundred dollars to ease his mind about that five dollars, and would have spent a thousand dollars sooner than be done. I am rather like that myself, but I do not let such losses prey on my mind, for if I did, and tried to get even with the culprit, I should be incessantly travelling off somewhere or other.

Well, Stevenson often met Callard, and the old chap treated him as though he was a boy, told the novelist jokes, spun yarns and repeatedly nudged him in the ribs; and the two would finally end up by retiring to the bar and standing each other treat.

Callard's great ambition at that time was to see King Malietoa Laupepa at Mulinuu. I went off with him, and with the assistance of some Malietoans got him an introduction at the royal court. Callard behaved with great propriety, indeed, bowed to almost all the native servants of the court retinue!

I played the violin to the King, who was a most agreeable gentleman, and carried himself with a deal more importance than Mataafa did. Callard spoke day and night of the King's handshake, and chuckled in his very sleep at the thought of what his friends in America would think when they heard of Callard and the King of Samoa together. He went especially to Vailima to tell Stevenson about King Malietoa, and kept the novelist amused the whole evening.

Callard's eyebrows were about half-an-inch long and they stuck straight out, and as he spoke his eyelids kept closing as though he was in deep thought; and what with that and his high, bald head, he was a cheerful-looking man. He always drank whisky, and Stevenson tucked him up to sleep on his couch at Vailima when he was too full of it to walk back to his lodgings! I am quite sure if Stevenson had lived the world would have heard of Callard.

WANGANUI RIVER, N.Z.

Stevenson had a sneaking regard for vagabonds, and his eyes twinkled with delight in their company. He was very credulous and believed a deal that he heard. I think he would have gone off exploring for some new country, or a treasure island, in five minutes, if he had been encouraged by some of the fearless adventurers whom he mixed with through his love of vagabondage and adventure. The questions he used to ask men of the seafaring class revealed how implicitly he believed that which they were telling him, yet at other times he seemed alert with suspicion and in a mood to disbelieve actual facts.

Though I heard Stevenson make several attempts to play the violin, and also heard him pedalling at the harmonium, I cannot recall that he accomplished anything that struck me as showing musical talent—that is, talent revealing a quick ear to distinguish the scales and intervals of mechanical music. Indeed the pedals made more noise and sounded more rhythmical than the time he played; and he looked like some careworn priest toiling away on the treadmill of penance to save his soul. But still I can say that Stevenson had a gift that was something much greater than an ear for light melody. He was a great tone poet! His mind was a shell that caught echoes from the vastness of creation, and the murmurs of humanity in all its joy, passion and sorrow. Otherwise he could never have even noticed, let alone described as he did, for not in all literature will you find another who describes *sound* so perfectly at one stroke as Stevenson did. You can *hear* Nature's moods, in all her wild grandeur of seas and the winds in the mountain forests, as you read his books. The seas beating over the barrier reefs, the vast silence of the tropical night, the starlit coco-palms and the coughing derelict beachcomber sleeping beneath them, become realities that haunt your mind, because they are made and played by a great musician who was an artist in Nature's great orchestra.

I think if Stevenson had been able to cast aside all thought of the critical inspection of lovers of polite literature, and the mechanical niceties of phrase and thought, and had written his reminiscences down in a book, the characters therein would have walked, talked and laughed with cinema realism. Down in the magical world of words, before the mind's eye and ear, we should have seen the vast tropical Pacific, and the stars over it reflected in the lagoons of the far-scattered isles clad with coco-palms as if painted by the magical silver oils of moonlight. We should have heard the cry of the traders and seen the beachcombers' ragged clothes fluttering by tossing waters, and paddled canoes filled with the swarthy faces of wild men, on the waves that were breaking over the shores of his wonderful pages.

But, unfortunately, it was not to be, because of the great truth that we cannot do differently from that which we do. We are born in the chains of grim conventionality that become inevitably a part of us. Indeed he who professes to be utterly free from it, and to have no regard for it in his work, has his published book as strong evidence against his sincerity.

I've met far greater geniuses than Robert Louis Stevenson in the Southern Seas—geniuses so intense with pathos, wit, insight and heroic courage that though they had never even read a book, or learnt to write, their minds were gold mines of truth and experience and all that men have ever attempted to tell in polite phrase. Could they, by some magical means, have turned a handle and so written down in a book their reminiscences, and their thoughts on human affairs, modern literature would not have to bewail the loss of its Golden Age, but would be absorbed with delight, filled with ecstatic charm over the pathos and the wonderful touches of truth, in what would be the great classic, the new Odyssey of modern times.

But to return to Stevenson. I once heard him arguing violently on board a ship, when he was at dinner in the saloon. At the time I was busily cleaning the brass door handle. It grieves me to have to confess to this humble occupation while I was seeking fame and fortune in far countries, but it was the execution of this little detail of one of my many professions that gave me the opportunity of hearing the celebrated author's opinion on Socialism.

One of the diners, who sat opposite Robert Louis Stevenson, was a big red-faced man, weighing about sixteen stone, a quantity of heavy jewellery which adorned his clothing being included. He breathed violently as he ate and kept insisting on the wonderful virtues of Socialism. Stevenson combated with him in fine style, winning every point. All I can remember of the conversation was that the author said: "Socialism is based on ideas of equality and the freedom of the individual; yet its principal aim in practice would be to destroy individuality and freedom, and the equality would be a system producing nothing else but a nation of slaves."

I think Stevenson was right, for I have noticed that socialists are not continually busy in giving away anything. Indeed, socialists have so developed the instinct of commercial grab that they can always perceive, "by the cut of your jib" (a socialistic phrase), how much you are worth and whether you would part with it without the use of muscular force. I am not well read in the ethics of Socialism, because I cannot waste my time. If a burglar broke into my house, and I caught him stealing my goods as his fair share, I should not want to read his private correspondence and hear his views on human affairs, or wish to know if he had a clean shirt on ere I threw him out of the window or fetched the police. Socialists do not like sharing their property with others any more than I do.

I have striven to tell in the brief foregoing details my impressions and experiences of Robert Louis Stevenson. I hope they may be interesting. In the books that deal with his life in the South Seas it is little short of marvellous how tamely his life there is painted, especially when one thinks that his island home was overrun by semi-civilised natives and a white population of the most mixed and adventurous people the world could well place together; and certainly Stevenson was not the kind of man to travel to the South Seas and seek no other excitement beyond an afternoon walk or a fashionable dance in an Apia ballroom.

It was somewhere about the period which I am dealing with that a discussion was going on concerning Father Damien, the celebrated Catholic priest who had sacrificed his life for the sake of the lepers at the dread lazaretto on the Isle of Molokai. In my first book of reminiscences in the South Seas I touched briefly on the few incidents which I heard from a native friend of mine, Raeltoa the Samoan. And before I proceed with my later reminiscences of Samoa and elsewhere I will tell you all I heard about Father Damien whilst I was in Honolulu.

CHAPTER IX

Honolulu—King Lunalilo—Chinese Leprosy—Kooma's Reminiscences of Father Damien—Molokai—The Leper-Hunters—Father Damien at Molokai—Robert Stevenson's Open Letter to Dr C. M. Hyde

AFTER Samoa I think the Sandwich Isles are the most attractive islands in the Pacific. They are mountainous and the summits of Hawaii—pronounced Ha-wy-ee—rise to fourteen or fifteen thousand feet. All the islands of the group are volcanic, and rich both in live and extinct craters. I should not be surprised if some day the bowels of the Sandwich Group suddenly exploded and blew the isles to smithereens!

When, from the sea, you sight the coast, its promontories covered with coco-palms and gorgeous tropical trees, waving over slopes that lead down to lazy, shore-curling waves, you think of the Biblical Garden of Paradise. Native hut homes, conical-shaped, with tiny verandahs, peep out of the bamboo and clumps of bananas beneath mighty bread-fruit trees.

I stayed several weeks in the Sandwich Group. The natives are mirthful and well dressed, far in advance of the Marquesan and Solomon islanders. They are all Christians, but decidedly immoral according to European codes. Honolulu is a well-shaded city, with the spires of advanced civilisation rising. Missionaries are there in plenty, and possibly they feel thankful that barbarian ideas of virtue have given them a profession on islands of tropical beauty, whereon they can live in extreme comfort while they work among, and are kind to, the natives.

While there I saw the palace of the Hawaiian queen, who I think was the widow of King Kale-Conalain. She was as polished as a Parisian prima donna. I also saw the new king, Lunalilo, a fine-looking Hawaiian, six feet high, full-lipped and very majestic-looking. He was dressed in a frock-coat and fashionable felt hat. As he appeared before the people and stood on the palace steps, the crowds waved and cheered as the British do to their King and Queen.

The Hawaiian climate is healthy; but Chinese leprosy attacks the natives and the white population, which consists of French, English, Kanakas negroes, Chinamen and ex-convicts. Swarms of mosquitoes find the Sandwich Isles a happy hunting ground for their race, and are one of its drawbacks.

I toured on the island steamer *Kilanea* to all the various isles, and then stopped near Honolulu with Kooma, who was a Hawaiian. He was an old man, yet straight figured, well tattooed and with intelligent eyes. His high brow denoted intellectual qualities which were usually conspicuous through their absence from the heads of his race. Hawaiians are like all the South Sea

Islanders, and have a deeply rooted hatred for work. As they have embraced Christianity, heathen songs have ceased, and now, like caged birds on the polished perches of civilisation, they sit and quote, parrot-like, all that the missionaries teach them.

Kooma at that time had no calling. He was aged, and had reared up a large family, and his athletic sons, who worked on shipping wharves at Honolulu, repaid Kooma for his past kindness. He had several married daughters also. I was not very well off at the time and gladly accepted the old Hawaiian's offer to let me occupy rooms in his home at a charge that nicely suited the state of my exchequer.

Kooma had known Father Damien[4] intimately, that heroic leper priest who had devoted his life to combating heathenism and nursing the lepers on the Isle of Molokai, and had, a year or so before, died of the dreaded disease. So I was fortunately able to hear, directly from him, details of deep interest to me concerning the life and character of the celebrated priest, who had emigrated from Louvain as a missionary to Honolulu, and after a strenuous life of self-sacrifice lay in his grave near his stricken children on the lonely lazaretto isle, Molokai.

> 4. Joseph Damien de Veuster was born at Tremeloo, a small peasant village near Louvain, in 1840; and in peaceful scenes that are now ravaged by the relentless tramp of materialistic battalions he, as a boy, dreamed and fed his imagination and intense genius for helping humanity. He died on 15th April 1889.

It appeared that my friend had known Damien many years before he went to Molokai; had officiated as his servant, and helped the missionary build some of the extemporised churches and homes at Kohala and elsewhere.

Sitting by his side, by the window of his humble homestead, while native children romped under the palms out in the hot sunlight, I talked to Kooma of many things, and hearing that he had known Father Damien I at once plied him with questions. "Was Damien a kind and good man, Kooma?" I asked, and then, with much pride that he was able to give me information concerning such a popular white man, he blew whiffs of tobacco through his thin, wrinkled lips and answered: "I have cut wood and dug hundreds of post-holes for the great white priest, and he no pay me."

"Did not pay you?" I said, astonished.

"No," he answered. "I knew that he was poor and had no money, and so I work for no wages." After many questions and replies which dealt chiefly with the Hawaiian's own character and importance, I gathered that Kooma had collected firewood for the lonely priest, and had done many services for him, both as a friend and a servant, out of a good heart, for it appeared that

Damien was not by any means an austere man or master, but one who worked with those around him in a spirit of good comradeship.

If anyone imposed upon the natives and Damien heard of it, he would hotly resent the imposition, and with flashing eyes shout and fight for their rights as though they were his own children.

Years before Damien went to Molokai a handsome Hawaiian girl, who lived at Kahalo, loved a Society Island youth who had, with his parents, emigrated to the Sandwich Islands. The father of the maid disliked the youth, who was an idle, good-for-nothing fellow, and so would not encourage the lad's attentions to his daughter. For some time the lovers met in secret, for love laughs at locksmiths in Hawaii as well as elsewhere. One night, as Damien sat by his fireside in his lonely hut having his humble meal, the love-sick maid appeared at his door. Crossing her hands on her breast, she bowed, half frightened, and after much hesitation pleaded to the Catholic Father on the youth's behalf, begging him to help her, for she was in great distress; and knowing that Damien was a great missionary and priest of the white God, she suddenly fell on her knees and confessed all. She was in trouble through the lad, and, telling Damien this, she laid her head on his knee and cried bitterly; for the kindness of his eyes soothed her and made her feel like a little child. Gently bidding her to rise, the Father told her to cease from troubling, and said: "Go, my child, home; tell thy father all; also that thou hast told this thing to me, and I will come and see him."

The priest did all that he promised; and the next evening the sinful youth who had brought sorrow to Ramao, for that was her name, appeared before the hut door wherein lived Father Damien and, shamefaced, hung his head for a long while. Kooma, who sat telling me all this, added: "And the great white Father put the spirit of Christ in Juno's (the lad's) heart; for he became good, and worked hard, and was forgiven for that which he did, and they were happy and had many children; and I learnt to love Juno in his manhood, for he was a good father and kind to the maid who was my daughter!" And, saying all this, he pushed the window higher up and pointed to a tall maid who, in her ridi robe, came singing down the track by the jungle ferns. On her bare shoulders she humped baskets of live fish which had been just caught below in the sea. "She," Kooma said, "is my granddaughter, and was the unborn child of the fallen maid whom Father Damien was kind to"; and there she stood in the doorway and gazed on us both with laughing, sparkling eyes, bare from the waist upwards, excepting for a thread of beads hanging at her breast and a Catholic cross, with a tiny figure of the Virgin Mary, swinging below. I looked at her with deep interest, and thought of the kindness of the missionary priest, dead in his grave at Molokai.

Kooma showed me a Bible which had been given him by Father Damien. It was well thumb-marked, torn, and pencilled by the priest at those pages where he had made my friend memorise different passages. On the front leaf was Damien's signature. On my handing the sacred gift back to the Hawaiian he carefully placed it at the bottom of his chest; and I knew that it would be no use my attempting to get it from him, however much I might want the book. Many interesting things did I learn from my stay at this native's house, for night after night I would get him in a reminiscent mood. It appeared that as time wore on the young priest, who was a handsome, healthy-looking man, became somewhat subdued and saddened, and aged considerably in the space of three or four years. At times he was morose and unapproachable, though afterwards he would gaze with kindly eyes on those whom he might have spoken to in anger.

"Did he ever go away?" I asked Kooma, and he answered: "Sometimes he would go for one or two days, and often at night-time go off wandering alone in the forestlands about his house; and night after night at sunset he would sit with his chin on his hands and gaze toward the seaward sunset, with eyes that saw far away." And then Kooma added: "And I would say, 'Master, shall I get thee more firewood?' and he would not answer, but would steadily gaze on, and I could see the tears in his eyes, and I knew that he sorrowed over that which I knew not of." So earnest was Kooma's manner that, as he told me these things, I saw the past, the lonely hut home and the exiled priest gazing into the sunset, sick at heart as he dreamed of his childhood's home across the world. I wondered somewhat, and thought over the stories Raeltoa of Samoa had told me, which I have written about in my earlier book of reminiscences. For Raeltoa the Samoan had also known Father Damien, as, of course, hundreds of natives did, and had told me, unasked, of his kindness and heart-felt sorrow for those who hid from the leper captors as they searched for the stricken people.

For leprosy had wiped out thousands of the natives of the Sandwich Islands and elsewhere. When once the victims revealed the purplish-yellow patch on their bodies they were doomed, for no cure was, or is, known for the scourge of leprosy.

In Kooma's house dwelt a chief who lived in Oahu. He had elephantiasis, which had swelled his legs to three times their normal size. He used to sit under the pandanus-trees reading his Bible as I talked with Kooma, and I was extremely pleased to hear, on inquiring, that his complaint was not contagious; for when he squatted with his knees up in front of him, so swollen were his limbs that his body and head were hidden from view.

But to go back to Kooma's reminiscences. "What happened before Father Damien went away to the Leper Isle of Molokai?" I asked, and Kooma answered: "He became most sad, and then wished many of my people who had the leper patch good-bye, and promised to go one day and see them, and made them happier with smiles and promises; and often he would go a long way off to comfort those whose relatives had been taken to the dreaded lazaretto."

"Did you see Father Damien after he had gone to the lazaretto?" I asked. "Yes," he replied; "and he looked most sad and very, very much older: and I asked him of my sister, whom he had seen at Molokai, for she was stricken with the plague, and he said, 'Kooma, your sister is happy; the spirit is well, though the flesh, which is nothing, is ill.'"

Then Kooma told me much of the doings of the Flemish priest: how he had toiled incessantly for the welfare of his native children, ministering to their souls; and how his influence had soothed their hearts, hearts that still half nursed the old traditions; for the Hawaiians were originally a wild race, and still their songs told of heathen mythology, of mighty warriors, of love and ravishment, and of cannibalistic times, so Damien's task of reforming them was no easy one.

For many years the dreadful scourge had crept, with its fatal grip, over the whole of the Sandwich Group, and as time went on it became so prevalent that the Hawaiian Government decided that the best step to take to stay the horror of fetid rot which was annihilating the race was to isolate all those afflicted with the disease and send them to Molokai.

Molokai was a lonely, half-barren isle surrounded by rough, beaten shores of crag and fortress reef that for ever withstood the charges of the seas as eternally they clashed, broke and moaned through the caves of the death-stricken isle, echoing and mingling with the moan of memories and deathly cries that faded on the dying lips of the plague-stricken men, women and children who rotted till they became lipless skeletons, still alive in their tomb—the grey, gloomy lazaretto of the Leper Isle. Terrible was the grief of the natives as those employed to separate the lepers sought out all those who were spotted with the livid leper patch. Father Damien's heart was sick within him as he heard the lamentations of forced farewells, as, standing by their captors, helpless men and women, gazing over their shoulders, looked into the eyes of those they loved and went away for ever!

Father Damien, who had devotedly administered comfort to the stricken ones who were scattered over the isle, saw and felt deeply the grief of those around him; but he was powerless to help the unhappy people; he knew the enforced separation was decreed by the authorities, and was for the best.

It was well known that many of the unfortunate victims were hidden away in the forest-lands, or in caves by the shores: maidens secreting their lovers, and lovers hiding the pleading maids, husbands their wives, and wives their children. Often in the night, as the dread inquisition discovered some trembling, hidden victim, a scream would break the silence of the jungle as the victim was muffled, gagged and taken away; for the leper-hunters were not the tenderest and most poetical of men. Money was their reward for all the lepers they captured, and the men hired for the job were chosen for their evil reputations and the expression of brutality on their dark faces. Father Damien's heart was indeed wretched over the fate of his children.

As Kooma the Hawaiian sat telling me all this, and the shadows fell and the island nightingale sang up in the pandanus-trees, I watched his earnest face and listened attentively, for I knew that I was hearing the truth of much that was hidden from the world. I learnt that the sad priest would sit at night for hours under the coco-palms, deep in thought, and have no sleep, so troubled was he over the fate of the flock that he loved; and many times did he help the afflicted ones, and long and deeply did he hesitate ere he told the authorities that which he had to tell, and which his tender heart stayed him from telling. As Kooma told me this I saw that his memories of the priest were sincere and loving enough. Then he called out "Pooline! Pooline!" and a native girl came and poked her head in at the doorway; it was his granddaughter, whom Father Damien had christened. They had called her after Damien's sister Pauline (which they pronounced Pooline); for the priest often spoke of his sister in Flanders, and told Kooma that some day she would come out to him to share his work and help him in it, and several times he wrote home and asked her to think the matter over.

Few were surprised when at length Father Damien volunteered to go to Molokai and administer faith and comfort to his lost children in exile. He taught them to be patient as he walked amongst them and crept by the lazaretto huts of death, knitting their shrouds and gazing with kind eyes on their faces till they ceased to see and feel, and he buried them. Lonely indeed those nights must have been as, alone with grief and silence, his bent form hammered and hammered, beating out the muffled notes that drove in coffin nails: for he made the last beds of his dead children, digging their graves and burying with his own hands many scores of the stricken dead, until he at last succumbed to the scourge himself. He lies buried with those he died for, and has, let us hope, found a reward for his self-sacrifice in heaven.

From Kooma I heard much of Damien's true character, his love of justice and his impulsiveness in hastening to help the weak, regardless of all consequences. Once, while Father Damien was eating his supper, a Hawaiian appeared at the door and said, "Master, trouble has befallen me and my home"; and then told the priest of a tragedy that had occurred. A native girl through jealousy had stabbed another who had sought her lover, and was either hiding in the forest or shore caves or had killed herself. All night the native and Father Damien searched, and at length the girl was found almost lifeless, covered in blood, on the shore reefs seaward from Kilanea, her body lying half on the sands and half in the waves. She had slashed herself and had nearly bled to death. Damien carried the girl for miles in his arms, bandaged her and saved her life; also the life of the girl she had stabbed so viciously in her jealousy. When they were both well again he brought them together, made them embrace each other and swear to forget all, with the result that they became greater friends through being erstwhile enemies. Each secured a lover to her liking, and ever blessed the great Father who had befriended them instead of handing them over to the authorities at Honolulu—authorities whom Damien hated, for they moved on material lines and looked upon cruel force as the best means of discouraging crime, and on kindness as insanity more dangerous than the crime it forgave.

In a corner of Father Damien's lonely little homestead he kept the cherished letters that arrived from his homeland across the sea. Night after night he would take those letters out and read them through again, and then tenderly place them in a small pot and hide them beneath his trestle bed. They were letters from his sister Pauline and other relatives in Flanders.

One night he sought them and they were missing. Great was Father Damien's grief, and even rage flushed his face as he demanded of Kooma if he knew of their whereabouts. For hours he searched, "and never was the Master in so great a temper; he look much fierce and his eyes fire and then cry," said Kooma, as I listened. "What did he do then?" I asked. "Did he find the letters?" "Yes," said Kooma, "he did find letters: a dog that Father Damien had been kind to had smelt and pawed them up and run off with the pot, which we found in the scrub. The great Father was then good to us and did ask me to forgive him for that which he said; which I did do; and the dog too he forgave; and Father Damien once more smiled, stroked the shaggy thief, and it sat up, looked at the Father's eyes, wagged its tail and was happy."

I often heard a lot of discussion about Father Damien's life and work, sometimes between rough island traders, and sometimes between men of the conventional middle class. A few of the former had met Father Damien, or knew those who were acquainted with him, but most of them expressed opinions from hearsay and the low or high order of their own instincts. Robert Louis Stevenson's celebrated open letter to Dr Hyde had much to do with the popular nature of the controversy and the growing enthusiasm for the self-sacrifice of the dead priest.

For those who may not know the exact facts I relate them here.

After Father Damien's death Robert Louis Stevenson, whilst cruising in the South Seas, happened to read a paper that contained a letter written by Dr

Hyde, of Honolulu, to the Rev. Mr Gage, of Sydney, who in turn sent it to *The Sydney Presbyterian* for publication. Here is the letter:

To The Rev. H. B. GAGE.

HONOLULU, *2nd August 1889.*

DEAR BROTHER,—In answer to your inquiries about Father Damien, I can only reply that we who knew the man are surprised at the extravagant newspaper laudations, as if he was a most saintly philanthropist. The simple truth is, he was a coarse, dirty man, headstrong and bigoted. He was not sent to Molokai, but went there without orders; did not stay at the leper settlement before he became one himself, but circulated freely over the whole island (less than half the island is devoted to lepers), and he came often to Honolulu. He had no hand in the reforms and improvements inaugurated, which were the work of our Board of Health, as occasion required and means were provided. The leprosy of which he died should be attributed to his vices and carelessness.

Others having done much for the lepers, our own ministers, the Government physicians and so forth, but never with the Catholic idea of meriting eternal life. Yours, etc.,

C. M. HYDE.

(Published in *The Sydney Presbyterian*, 26th October 1889.)

When Robert Louis Stevenson read the above letter, and the comments upon it, he was deeply incensed, and wrote a defence of the priest about which the world knows.

Mr Melville, whom I met at Apia, told me an interesting story about Robert Louis Stevenson and his championship of Father Damien. While Mr Melville was a passenger on a ship, the *Lubeck*, I think, he sat near Stevenson, who was dining in the saloon. The conversation touched on Father Damien and Dr Hyde's letter, and when a passenger revealed by his remarks that he was half willing to believe Hyde, Stevenson almost shouted and insulted him. The passenger, irritated, persevered with his opinions and said something further, whereupon Stevenson said: "Some of you men still make one think of the danger of Christ's mission and His risks on earth," or something to that effect. On this the passenger answered: "Mr Stevenson, you forget yourself," and Stevenson immediately replied: "I would to God that some of you fellows would forget yourselves and remember the virtues of others."

When Mr Melville told me this I smiled, for from my own personal recollections of Robert Louis Stevenson I knew that he did not need a battalion of supporters to help him maintain his own opinion when he felt that he upheld a noble purpose: for Stevenson was a fearless, though gentle soul, even apart from his literary life and work. Indeed Damien found in him a kindred and worthy champion. Not always are men able so well to express outwardly that which they beautifully write and feel.

As I have said, much rumour and discussion followed both Dr Hyde's letter and Stevenson's powerful retaliation, and it was not uncommon for Catholic and Protestant divines engaged in arguments on the matter to come even to blows. Now all men admit that Dr Hyde's letter of denunciation was indirectly one incentive that drew the attention and praise of the world at large to the heroism of the martyr priest, and was responsible for Robert Louis Stevenson's reply and vindication of him. Personally I do not think Dr Hyde was as deliberately hypocritical as Rumour has painted him. Of course this does not imply that Robert Louis Stevenson's counter-denunciation of Hyde's epistle was unjust or too fierce; he wrote as the first champion voice, and wrote from the white-hot intensity of indignation over what he felt was a deadly wrong done to the memory of a great man. This can, too, in the consciousness of man's fallibility, be applied to motive on the other side, for Dr Hyde, of Honolulu, also wrote to his friend, the Rev. Mr Gage, from a firm belief in his heart that rumour was truth and Father Damien's memory was not deserving of "extravagant laudation." Many others of his own denomination had devoted their lives to the lepers, both on the islands and at the lazaretto at Molokai, and so Dr Hyde's great sin was in believing that which he was told and remembering the self-sacrifice of his own brethren who had also toiled on behalf of the lepers.

The voice of Rumour has many forked tongues of envy and the carelessness of thoughtless scandal. Our religion is founded on the sorrow and disastrous result of its tongue, for did not Christ suffer crucifixion through this weakness in mankind? Through doubt and envy to this day some nations believe one side, and others the other; and are there not millions now who do not believe in that which our religion is founded on? Was Dr Hyde so wicked? I for one do not think so. Do we know what he thought after he had written that mighty atom of a letter? What were his reflections, misgivings and regrets over his first belief and hasty conclusions, and over that celebrated blazing challenge of Stevenson's to the world, revealing in words of fire the complete vindication of Damien's life, work and Christ-like heroic virtue? We can imagine what he felt like, for we all make mistakes, but not with such drastic results.

The stern note of intense application to a set purpose reveals in Stevenson's letter the fact that he felt that Damien needed an immediate champion. Stevenson was at heart a Christian man, in the full, true sense of the word, and I have not the slightest doubt that after his open letter had fulfilled the purpose which he intended it to fulfil, and the first heat of his just indignation had cooled down, he himself would have withdrawn it from publication, if he could have done so, and let the whole matter slumber; for he of all men would not have wished vindictive roots to spread and twine about the hearts of men who thus would strangely nourish the very thoughts that their creed specially preaches against.

Stevenson well knew man's weakness, and the bigotry of men who differ on religious subjects and are opposed to each other by the difference of creed. Certainly the imputations of undeserved praise which were suddenly hurled at the self-exiled priest's reputation only served one end: to bring out, if possible in brighter relief, the splendid heroism of Father Damien's life, both before and after his going back to Molokai. Even had it been bitterly proved that the Flemish missionary was not a spiritual saint, but fallible flesh and blood flowing through earthly channels, which resisted, but did not always overthrow, temptation, still he would stand before us a beautiful man (and he was a man); and to do all that he did, and still have the weaknesses of mankind, makes the martyr stand out greater to our eyes than if he did his wonderful life's work through some effortless, inborn virtue of heavenly inheritance.

The sad peasant priest of Louvain has been dead these many years; he lived and died without ambition, and only in heaven may know the earthly fame he achieved. Well may we believe how beautifully he would smile, forgive and touch with his lips the brows of his erring detractors, with the same spirit that made him live and die for his fellow-men with the certainty of one final reward—a stricken leper's grave in far away Kalawao, on Molokai Isle.

Out of grey crags by warder-seas they creep

With wailing voices as the stars steal by;

Dead men—fast rotting on dark shores of sleep,

Their earthly eyes still shape the shadowed sky!

Poor skeletons, they moan, laugh, grin and weep;

In loathsome amorous arms some still lie.

Entombed, they curse the sun—Time's cruel dial

Above that vault—the South Sea Leper Isle.

Hark to the midnight scream! Then silence after

Of desolation voiced by waves that leap

By sepulchres—damp huts of sheltered rafter,

Where dreaming dead men shout thro' shroudless sleep!

As windy trees wail dreams of long-dead laughter;
As o'er each wattle hut the night winds sweep,
And dying eyes watch ships out o'er the night,
Pass shores of death with port-holes gleaming bright!

'Twas on that Charnel-isle, with watching eyes
He toiled for dead men who still heard the waves
Beat shoreward: saw the South Sea white moonrise
Bathe their-to-be forgotten flowerless graves!
Exiled pale hero-priest! Full oft their cries
Smote his sad listening ears; like unto caves
That voice the mournful tone of ocean's roll,
Infinity entombed sang in his soul.

Lonely as God, he sat: enthroned o'er pain
Brave music made of desolation's sorrow,
Christ-like gazed on the deathless, crying slain!
His eyes breathed light—foretelling some bright morrow
Till from their tombs they rose—the dead again!
Dark skeletons of woe, they rose to borrow
Life from Molokai's hero:—men denied
That leper-priest—like Christ—when Damien died.

CHAPTER X

An Inland March—The Great Chief—A Siva Dance—A Sailor's Party—Nina's Samoan Fairy Tale—Death—The Golden Horn—Idols—A Marquesan Village—We ship as Stowaways

I EASILY recall to mind my farewell days in Samoa, and the native trader with whom I lodged. His homestead was a comfortable bungalow, sheltered by coco-palms, and not far from Saluafata village. I had not much money at that time, and my friendly native only charged me just what I could afford to give him, which was, unfortunately, very little. He had three daughters and two grown-up sons who were just about my age; they spoke good English, were good companions, and we had merry times together. I gave the eldest daughter music lessons during my short stay. Her father purchased a cheap German violin down in the stores at Apia, and the Samoan's daughter made rapid progress. I taught her to play by ear. Her relatives came in from the districts to hear her play her first Samoan hymn. I have never been so complimented for my teaching ability in my life as I was over that dusky girl's progress. I felt well repaid by their gratitude. They fed me up, for I had been ill for a fortnight with a severe cold and was getting thin. I went off almost every evening with the sons fishing, and lived in real native style. I enjoyed the various native dishes, for Mrs Pompo, my host's wife, was a clever cook, and served up the cooked fish with stewed yams and many more island delicacies. Poi-poi was a favourite dish: a mixture of taro, bread-fruit, yams and wild bananas.

My host had several wealthy relatives living inland, and at last the sons, young Pompy and Tango, succeeded in persuading me to go off to the inland villages with my violin to visit them. I well remember the long, hot march they gave me, as I tramped between them for miles and miles along tracks just by the coast, and then inland across paths by the coco-palms. Some of the journey was over rough jungle country beautiful with tropical trees and flowers. Merrily my comrades sang as I plucked the fiddle strings, banjo fashion, marching along far away, with the civilised cities thousands of miles behind.

We slept out the first night, as indeed I often did in my travels. Pompy and Tango lay asleep on each side of me as, sleepless, I looked round my bedroom floor and saw my palm-trees standing windless and still and my bright stars over me flashing in the midnight skies.

Next day we passed across thick island jungle and then suddenly emerged on to a large clearing, where by a river stood several isolated huts. Through the doors came rushing brown-faced native girls, with delight and wonder shining in their dark eyes at hearing the music of the fiddle! Like little dark devils bare-footed children came running behind us, and then, just as we were passing close by the half-open hut door, out came the picturesque bigger girls for the second time, for they had seen my white face and had rushed indoors with haste, all screaming out, "Papalangi!" They had forgotten their fig-leaf, so to speak. At the very most, natives, boys and girls who lived inland, wore little dress beyond the primitive ridi, and if they wore more than usual it was some remnant of European clothes, given them in exchange for curios, or as wages by artful traders.

On the green, scrubby slope, under a palm-tree by her hut door, stood a full-figured, dark Samoan mother, showing her white teeth as she smiled. She looked like some grotesque statue as she stood there quite still beneath the blue tropical sky, for she wore a delicate undergarment as a robe, which just covered half of her bronzed figure—a present, possibly, from some trader's wife.

As the native girls came down and walked by me, gazing sideways with great curiosity, the tall grass brushed their bare knees and their eyes shone as they revealed their pearly rows of teeth and laughed, calling out to each other, "Arika pakea!"[5] Samoan girls are great flirts, yet I felt that I trod some enchanted land where vice was unknown. The faint inland wind stirred their loose, bronze-coloured hair, wherein they had stuck white and crimson hibiscus blossoms or grass. Several little mites, with tiny wild faces, came close up to us and stood with boastful bravery a moment in front of me, their little demon-like eyes anxiously striving to examine my violin, and when I suddenly struck all the strings together—r-h-r-r-r-r-r r-r-n-k—off they rushed back to the hut doors and gave a frightened scream. Out poked the frizzy heads of all the mothers to see what the hullabaloo was about. When they saw me they waved their dark hands and shouted, "Kaoha!" or "How do you do?" as I tramped by between my two comrades.

    5. White man.

About a mile farther on we came across another small group of huts, not far from a grove of orange-trees, where we picked the golden fruit out of the deep grass; it tasted like pine-apples and oranges mixed. Only two old native women were in sight. They were very busy, it was their washing day, and one of them stooped over an old salt pork ship's barrel, washing the village clothes: on a line hard by, stretched between two coco-nut trees, hung a row of newly washed ridis, steaming in the hot sun. As we approached, Pompy and Tango intimated that it was the abode of one of their great relatives. On the ground beneath a clump of bamboos, stretched out flat, was an old Samoan chief. "O Le Tula!" Pompy shouted, and the old fellow slowly lifted his wrinkled face and welcomed us. My comrades, his grandsons, jabbered away to him in native lingo, and introduced me with pride, telling me that I was gazing on one of the past great chiefs who had been King Malietoa's special favourite. He had a classical profile that was slightly spoilt, for one of his ears was missing; it had been blown off by a gun-shot in a tribal battle some years before. As I gazed upon him with reverence his eyes looked straight in front of him and he pulled himself up majestically. His large frame was well tattooed. Suddenly he signed to me and said something over and over again in broken English. When I at last understood I forced a smile to my lips and handed him my last shilling. I could not very well refuse, as I had walked many miles to see him. He grabbed the coin, and his face went into a mass of wrinkles as he grunted out "Mitar." On a slope about five hundred yards off was a tin-roofed mission room, and a missionary's homestead close by. There was only a half-caste assistant there; "the Boss" had gone off to Apia. The half-caste seemed a decent fellow, and gave us a cup of German tea; for Malietoa's old chief had bolted off to the nearest rum shop, miles away probably, directly he had got possession of my shilling, to get *te rom*.[6]

6. Gin or rum.

That night I witnessed a native dance, resembling in character the dances which I have already described in my first book of reminiscences. But this dance slightly differed from the dance scenes of my previous experience. It was more rhythmical and, instead of being grotesque, was a weirdly beautiful sight; for as the large, low moon, half submerged by the distant hill, sent a flood of light through the coco-palms and banyan-trees, it lit up the moving, dark faces on the forest stage floor, which was a cleared patch. A picturesque Samoan girl stood swathed in a girdle of festival flowers and sang, while the squatting Siva dancers rocked their bodies to and fro and clapped their hands. I stood close by and played on my violin a minor melody; and its silvery wails were accompanied by the full orchestral moan of the whole forest of giant moonlit trees as the wind blew fitfully through them. Then came the wild chorus, as the circle of girls rose and, like a crowd of wood nymphs made of moonshine, embraced each other and then divided, whirling and waving their arms fantastically in the glimpsing moonlight that poured through the palms. As for me, I stood in the middle of the dancers playing my violin and firing away double forte, and presto velocity, to keep in with the barbarian tempo. About a mile off was the spot to which I had been dragged by a tribe of natives, who had forced me to play at a cannibalistic feast during my previous sojourn in Samoa.

After the forest ball had closed, and the performers were dispersing and going off to their homes, a well-dressed native, who had known me when I was in Samoa before, recognised me, and I was extremely pleased to see him. He was a trader and an intimate friend of Hornecastle's—my convivial old friend of earlier days. I learnt from him that Hornecastle had gone away to the Gilbert Group, or to the Solomon Isles, I forget which. The trader invited us to his house, where we spent the night. We had no sooner got under the shelter of his welcome roof than clouds slid over the sky and a terrific storm came on. It lasted well into the night and nearly blew me off my sleeping-mat, for the Samoan's house was open all round. To ease my restlessness I rose and looked out on to the sleeping village. The rain had ceased and the moon, low on the ranges of Vaea Mountain, looked like a globe lamp wedged between the sky and the earth. Space was quite clear for miles, but far away was a travelling wreck of foaming cloud that looked like a serried line of mighty breakers silently charging across a shore of starlit blue. I well recall this particular night, for I was greatly impressed by a sad sight. Under some coco-palms just below I saw a light glimmering in one of the natives' shed-like huts, and I heard native voices. Going down the slope, I spoke to a Samoan who was standing by the door, and from him I understood that a native youth was dying. He had been ailing for some time and had been suddenly taken worse. The relatives had fetched the priest, who was kneeling by the bed-mat giving the last benediction. I saw the outline of the sick boy's face and the half-conscious smile of faith on his quivering lips ere he died. I will draw a veil over the rest, which would make very uncheerful reading.

The following day, on our way back, we met a crowd of English sailors going inland. They had several natives with them who had been drinking rather heavily down in Apia. As we approached, the sailors, spying me and my violin, shouted out: "Hallo! matey, where did you get that hat? Any girls round these parts?", and then all started to do a double shuffle. Not far off was a small village, and when I offered to go there with them Pompy and Tango jumped about and laughed with delight; and the eldest seaman of the crowd, the boatswain, I think, smacked me genially on the back with such force that I looked up at him a bit wildly at first; but I quickly recovered as he gleefully gave me another nudge in the ribs, saying, as he winked with good fellowship: "Don't kill me, youngster."

As they approached the village, loudly singing the latest London hit, and emerged from the thickets of bamboo, a covey of native boys and girls came running down the slope, from a group of native huts, to welcome the jolly white men: two of the wild crew were blowing their hardest, mouth organs at their lips, and the eldest, who had goatee whiskers, and wore a Tam o' Shanter kind of seaman's cap, sang lustily, with wide opened mouth, just behind them; at intervals he stumbled slightly through being half-seas-over.

Sunset was fading on the horizon out seaward and touching the coco-palms and the distant mountain range with golden light as the shadows fell over the island. From the hut doors the naked children peeped and clapped their hands with delight. The primitive town fairly buzzed with excitement when, under the palms, Samoan maids whirled around, clasped in the arms of the joyful sailors, who made the wild island country echo to their singing voices.

A crowd of stalwart Samoan men left their work on the banana plantation close by and came to watch the sailors ashore. Dressed in their ridis only they stood, with their white teeth shining and their eyes sparkling merrily to see the novel sight. The pretty Samoan girls screamed with laughter, and their long brown legs went up and swung across the grass and fern-carpeted floor of the primitive ballroom, as they twirled round and round in the sailors' arms, and looked over their brown shoulders at a corpulent, fat native woman, who hailed from the Solomon Isles. For she imitated the drunken boatswain's high kicks and fell down, purposely, on her heavy bareness, to the shrieking delight of the whole onlooking village, as I played the fiddle. "Birds of a feather flock together" is a true saying; and I must confess I enjoyed myself seeing my countrymen so happy.

At the far end of the village was a native store, run by a half-caste who sold kava and terrible stuff called the "finest whisky." When the first dance was over, with their bashful partners on their arms, dark eyes looking up admiringly into blue ones, they all went across the slope to get refreshments. The sailors had money and treated the natives, who were all on their own, for the missionaries were away on the coast somewhere, attending a festival. So the mission rooms were deserted, and the lotu songs unsung that night, and the sailors were welcomed by them all as missionaries had never been. Pompy, Tango and I followed the crew about and they treated us to lime-juice drinks; we refused the whisky. When they were all primed up again with native spirit, and the stars flashed over the windless palms, they had another dance, and six native women, who did not care a "tinker's cuss" for anyone on earth when the missionaries were away, stood opposite the sailormen all in a row, mimicking them in a jig, the hibiscus blossoms stuck in their thick hair tossing about.

The missionaries somehow got to hear of it all and there was an awful row. Some of the women were taken before the *fakali*, or native judge, and fined a dollar, one month's wages, and they sat with shamed faces for hours in the mission room, counting their beads (about the only dress they had worn that night), doing penance, while the real culprits went on to their ship out in the bay.

When we got back, in the early hours of the morning, old Pompo jumped off his sleeping-mat and started bellowing at his two sons for overstaying their leave. I took all the blame, and explained that the old grandfather, the late high chief Tuloa, had been so pleased to see us that we had been compelled, through sheer courtesy, after his enthusiastic welcome, to accept his invitation to stay on. Hearing this, the old chap toned down, and we went to bed and slept soundly.

I went on the tramp steamer S—— next day and applied for a berth. The chief mate promised me a job; so I went back to my friend the Samoan's home and stayed there till the matter was settled.

Nina, the youngest daughter of my host, who was about twelve years of age, was an extremely pretty girl, and very romantic. A day or two before I left Samoa I came across her sitting by the shore holding a sea-shell to her ear, listening attentively to its murmur and singing to herself.

"Why do you listen to the shell's voice, Nina?" I asked.

"They are singing to me," she said, as she looked up into my face with earnest, wondering eyes.

"Who is singing to you, Nina?" I responded, rather surprised at her remark and the assurance in her manner that someone was singing to her in the shell. Then I heard from her lips an example of the poetical *Arabian Nights* of the South Seas. Crossing her legs, she arranged her pretty yellow frock, then put her finger up as though to tell me a great secret, and as I sat by her on the rock she told me the following story:—"There still lives an old heathen god deep down under the sea. His home is a large cavern, so big that its roof is the floor of all the ocean. In this big cavern is a beautiful country, lit up by the light of all the sunsets that have ever sunk down into the great waters out in the west. For it is in the west, deep down in the sea, where the old grey-bearded god's door is. Every night, just as the days are going to bed, the lonely god stands by his door, with his big watching eyes gazing up through the waters, as the sun sinks slowly down into the sea. For he knows it is on the sunset fires that he will catch the shadows of dead Samoan sailors who have been drowned by the upsetting of their canoes when the great storms blow. For when they die their shadows swim away to the sun directly it commences to sink, and then, clinging to the golden light, they go down, down, and are caught by the big god as he stands by his door under the sea, pulling the sunset in as a fisherman does his nets."

"And what does the god do with them, Nina?" I said, as she sat hesitating and looking up at me with her pretty brown eyes.

"Well," she continued, as she put her finger to her lips and dabbled her little brown feet in the waves that crept up the shore in foamy curls, "for thousands and thousands of years he has been watching and catching the dead sailors, and all those who are drowned in the storms; and as he stalks along through his wonderful countries, his endless forests under the sea, moving through the light of yesterday's sunsets, all the shadows of the dead sailors follow behind him, singing, and begging him to catch also the dead girls and women who have been drowned. But in a deep voice that echoes, and is the thunder you hear when the storms blow, he says: '*Mia fantoes*' (my children), 'you must only love me and not love mere women.' But still the shadows follow him, imploring and singing, 'Oh, bring us the beautiful dead girls and women'; and their voices, for ever echoing through the cavern roof, come up to the top of the ocean shores and caves, and you can hear them, though they are far away, faintly calling, calling to the big god under the sea. So all the girls and women come down to the shore and, if they have no one to love them, they put the shells to their ears and listen to the calling voices of the dead sailormen."

"Do you believe that, Nina?" I said, as I looked at her.

Then she nodded her pretty head with absolute conviction; and I too listened to the shell's murmur and pretended to be astonished and convinced. "Nina, and what becomes of the dead girls who are drowned?"

For answer she looked up at me sorrowfully for a while, then said: "The big sea-god is jealous of women, so he takes them out of his nets of sunset and throws them back into the waters, just as a fisherman does with the fish that are of no use to him."

"And what becomes of them then, Nina?"

"They turn to *ruios*" (sea-swallows), "and you can see them very early after dawn flying away into the fire of the rising sun, whence all that is beautiful comes"; and saying that she looked up at me with her pretty eyes staring thoughtfully.

"Who told you all those beautiful things, Nina?" I said.

A RIVER WHARF, WEST AFRICA

Then she looked up and told me that when she went to see her grandfather, who was that old chief, "O Le Tula," he told her many wonderful things about the sea-gods, and the old heathen gods who once lived in the clouds and the forest of Samoa. So I tell you that which Nina told me, though I could never infuse into her beautiful, simple story the earnestness of her pretty eyes, the note of certitude in her innocent voice, or the poetry of her childish imagination.

I liked that little Samoan maid. "Good-bye, Nina," I said, after bidding the others farewell.

"You go away on *te kaibuke*[7] and never come again?"

[7]. A ship.

"I may come back some day," I answered. I saw the tears in her eyes as I left her. She's a woman now. I wonder if she remembers me.

Before I proceed I must relate an adventure I had while passing along a forest track after playing at a native dance. It was a beautiful evening; the coco-palms, mangroves and dark orange and lime trees were bathed in the sunset's light, and the soft wind from seaward drifted sweet scents to my nostrils. I was hurrying towards Apia town before dark came on. Suddenly I heard a scream! The knight-errant fever of other days leapt like lightning to my eyes: a woman was in distress. I stood still and cursed inwardly, for I had only my violin as a weapon. I threw my shoulders back, looked swiftly at the skies, then rushed up to the slope's top. A white man stood under an orange-tree; in front of him was a beautiful Samoan girl. He seemed to be a large-framed, well-knit man, and I felt a tiny thrill of hesitation; but in the forest shadows just behind me my old heroes, with dauntless eyes, seemed to be shouting: "Forward to the rescue of distressed loveliness—onward!"

The white man had once more gripped the native girl and was shaking her. Her eyes looked around appealingly. The supreme moment to do or die thrilled me. I dropped my violin-case and, longing for a comrade, with a bound I was on him! For a moment we wrestled silently. "Ach Gott!" and "D—n!" the villainous seducer muttered as I gripped him by the throat! Crash! On my head came a blow—the Samoan girl had struck me on the back of the head with my violin-case! I heard the fiddle within hum trr-err-rh, as the four strings vibrated to the blow. They were jealous, quarrelling lovers, and the girl, seeing that I was getting the better of the German, had suddenly relented. I had a thundering headache all night and have never rescued a woman since.

I saw an old Mataafan chief die of old age in Saluafata village. I shall never forget the sight, or my feelings at the time. He lifted his aged, shrivelled face from the sleeping-mat, whereon he died, and begged the heavens to save him. Around him wailed his children and grandchildren; he was well loved, for all seemed earnest in their grief. I saw his eyelids close; I heard him murmur in Samoan a prayer to the gods of old, for the child's belief revives at death. His dying frame tried to sit up; the tattoo engraving on his breast, of warriors and weapons, went out of shape as his skin wrinkled in agony, and then his eyelids closed for ever. His death forced me to wonder on the mysterious cruelty of the Universe. Theologies give death a divine intention, but that sight affected a sense in my innermost soul, and death did not appear to me as a boon.

Soon after I joined the ship in Apia harbour. We stayed in port a few days, and then I shipped on the *Golden Horn*, bound for the Marquesas Islands. I had been there a year or two before and had a fancy that I should like to see the old spots once more. The schooner's crew were mostly Samoans, the cook being a German. The skipper, Alfred Richardson, an Englishman, was not more than thirty years of age. I slept in the cuddy. The "Old Man" took a fancy to me, or at least to my violin-playing, so he, the English mate and I had a fine time together.

The weather was squally for a week and kept the crew busy, and then a calm fell and we hardly moved. The boat was a splendid sailer and ran like a hound with the yards almost squared. I remember the beautiful, calm nights as the sails half filled and flopped and the rigging rattled. The ocean about us was drenched with mirrored stars; so calm and bright was the water that we could look over the side and see the shadow of our ship and all the silent heavens over it, and the mirrored, beautiful *katafa* (frigate-bird) sail across the sky on silent wings.

The Samoan sailors squatted on deck and sang weird ditties; I played the violin, and even the skipper joined in in good fellowship. Sometimes we fished and caught bonito, a beautifully coloured fish. Soon the wind sprang up again, and we made rapid headway across the wonderful world of waters. One moonlight night I was standing on the starboard side thinking, and gazing at the sky-lines, ghostly bright in the moonlight for miles around us, when the great ocean silence was broken by a complaining monotone, such as you hear when you place a sea-shell to your ear. I instinctively gazed over the side and saw far off, opposite the weather-side of the moonlit sky-line, curling and tossing breakers, where liquid masses soared and dissolved on the coral reefs of an enchanted isle; for enchanted it looked to me as the tiny wind drifted us onward. Slowly the inland palm-clad mountain ranges rose, and the groves of coco-palms and dark-leafed tropical trees, and out of the creeks and bay came native canoes filled with paddling, singing savages! Presently we saw their dusky faces as they raced across the moonlit water, bringing their bargains of fruit, pine-apples, wild bananas and corals; and alas, two or three of them, who had no wares to sell, were accompanied by their immoral wives!

Up the side they came, clambering like savage mermen out of the ocean depths. Their frizzly, wet heads came above the rails and, puff! they leapt on deck and pattered about on naked feet. They were pleasant, bright-eyed, shaggy fellows and the world's greatest talkers: they jabbered and jabbered till sunrise burst over the ocean, and before us, over the bows, half-a-mile away, lay Hiva-oa.

I asked the skipper to give me a long leave of absence ashore. "Very well, Middleton, we are not going for a fortnight. You can go off; and mind you behave yourself and bring that fiddle back."

"All right, sir, and thank you," I said gratefully, for he really did treat me as though I were a passenger. I had played cards with him and taught him melodies by ear on the fiddle.

"Come on, Sam Slick," I said to my comrade, who was an American fellow and came from 'Frisco. I was reading *Sam Slick the Clock-maker*, and so gave him that name, for he was a kind of Slick. He was about twenty-six years old, but as boyish as I was; a merry-looking fellow, with a little straw-coloured moustache, grey, kind eyes, thin lips, good-natured and determined, and his long legs balanced on enormous feet. We went off, and I had not gone far before I met a Frenchman who had known me on my previous visit. I understood from him that a lot of the people I had been friendly with before were still living there.

Slick, who had not been to the Marquesas before, was enraptured with the sights we saw. I made him go up to Turoa village and see the natives *en déshabillé*. He made a splendid pioneer forest breaker, as his boots crashed down and levelled the jungle scrub, and I followed cautiously in the track he left behind him. The heat was terrific when we arrived, at last emerging from the thick tropical scrub and dust into the native town's open space.

There was a store erected by the village, a new wooden, one-roomed shed. We fairly steamed as we loosened our shirts and stood drinking native toddy, and the little wind blew through the pandanus and dark spreading palm leaves on to our bare breasts. Out from their beehive-shaped huts came the Marquesan girls, dressed in their undraped beauty. Their fine dark eyes shone and their somewhat sensual lips, laughing, revealed their pearl-like teeth. The Marquesan girls are slightly darker skinned than the Samoans, and do their hair very attractively, almost with a Parisian effect. Some of the youths also bunch their hair up, and it is impossible at times to tell the difference between the youths and the maids till they stand in the grass smiling before one, and one sees the straight limbs of the males and the feminine curves of the dusky, smiling Eves. Sam Slick's eyes twinkled with curiosity and very evident pleasure as they spoke to him in pidgin-English and by signs. One pretty girl, about fourteen years old, held her own baby up for our inspection. Slick held it in his hands. It was not much larger than a green coco-nut. Its skin was a pretty red-tinted brown colour. I held it on one hand and, to please the admiring mother, kissed its tiny bald head. Then all the little native children, who had crept up to us and were watching our white faces with childish interest, rushed back under the forest palms, screaming with delight. Off they went to tell the whole village population that the big white man had kissed Temarioa's *fantoe* (child) on the head. I gave the girls a coin each, and they clapped their hands and said: "Yuranah!"[8]

8. Thank you.

Man's imagination could never picture a paradise to outrival the beauty of that Marquesan village. But on we tramped, and as we turned up the winding tracks we sighted the sea, and the waves breaking in the hot sunlight over the reefs by the palm-clad shores, and far away we saw the masts of our schooner, the *Golden Horn*. We got hold of a half-caste, who took us off to the various tribal districts and then left us. In the solitude of the bush-land, sheltered by an enormous tree, we saw a large wooden god. As we approached, and our feet snapped the twigs, a frightened Marquesan girl, who was kneeling before the hideous, one-eyed, grimy wooden god, rose and fled like a frightened rabbit. We saw her hair flying in the wind over her bare shoulders as she faded away in the forest glooms, just looking over her shoulder once with awestruck eyes as she ran, and then disappeared!

Slick and I were quite impressed by the sight of the running wild girl, and then we stood and looked up at the heathen idol. It was about eight feet high, broad shouldered, and the acme of ugliness. It was considerably decayed, for one eye was gone, and swarms of large white-bodied ants filed in and out of the curved wooden lips. "Fancy praying to that thing," said Slick. "Yes, seems strange," I responded. My comrade caught hold of a large bough, and standing a little way off swung it back; and then crash! he smashed the old heathen deity's head in! Then we stood and gazed upon it, and across the forest silence came a low wail of anguish, as once more we saw the heathen girl run across a cleared patch, running so fast that we could only just see the twinkle of her bare legs as she fled in terrible fright at seeing us crash her god's skull in, and yet both stand unharmed!

Slick wasn't anything of a poet, or even of a reflective temperament, but the silence of that spot, the broken god and the poor, terror-stricken girl made him say: "Well now, did you ever, mate!"; while I too looked round half frightened and said, "No, I never; but I'm off." When I explained to him that the girl would rush and tell some more of her tribe, who were Christianised but worshipped idols on the sly, and that they would come into the forest and get their own back, probably by strangling us and serving us up at the next cannibalistic feast, he too agreed. Just as we turned away, and I had carefully placed the god's eye in my pocket as a valuable curio, we heard a noise and looked over our shoulders. About twenty stalwart Marquesan savages were leaping towards us, not half-a-mile away! I am tall, and to this day I thank God that my legs are long. I know not what my primitive ancestors were, or what deeds they were capable of, or what barbarian strain they have infused into my blood, but I always feel thankful that they gave me the capacity for fast running! I never knew that Sam Slick could show such swift movement either, as simultaneously we made an unprintable remark and like two race-horses, chin by chin and neck by neck, we bolted off. I had been to the Marquesas before, and I knew that the inland tribes still nursed old cannibalistic appetites, and an intense hatred for those who hurt their gods, and that knowledge electrified my feet. Only the mechanical pumping of our breath could be heard as we raced across the slopes. Presently I saw that I was gaining in the flight; my nose was moving through space just about one inch beyond Slick's nose! The savages were shouting behind us! I distinctly heard the wild, savage wails, and looking back I saw their dark faces coming through the forest of palms. Slick's face had gone white; mine, I think, had turned ashen-grey! The sound of running in the forest just behind us grew louder. If we did not reach the village before they overtook us we should have to fight for our lives. I had by then gained the courage of resignation, and turning slightly I gazed back through the great beads of perspiration dripping from my eyebrows. I told Slick to "P-p-pp-ick—up—sti-ick—as—you—r-run." Each word came out in jerks, for at that time we were almost tumbling down a steep slope. As we rushed up the next incline I spied some stout branches, and together we stooped and gripped one each. "I'm done, Slick," I muttered. "So am I," he breathed out, as we stood on the top of the slope and entrenched ourselves behind a lot of bush, prepared to sell our lives dearly. We both felt nearly dead as we leaned against each other and prepared to give battle to the semi-savage men who were rushing down the opposite slope.

Then the strangest thing happened, but one which I believe happens to most men. When we found that we *had* to fight a splendid delirium thrilled us. We piled the dead logs up, gripped our weapons and waited with a grim feeling of exultation at our hearts: we would go down to the festive board game!

Slick stood by my side, a real brick. "Let 'em come, the brutes," he said. Up came a stalwart fellow and almost leapt over our branch parapet. I lifted my club and down it came, crash! on Slick's head! I shall never forget that terrible miss of mine, or poor old Slick's cry as I fell, and the savage buried his teeth in my leg, while with both my hands clutching his hair I called loudly to Slick to help me. Down came my chum's club on to the foe's shoulder, and in a moment we had him up bodily and between us swung him and hurled him over the dead wood; and down the slope he went rolling!

All this had only taken a minute to happen, and the remaining members of the horde were all standing at the bottom of the slope to see the result of their leader's attack. When we returned their chief to them half dead they stood perfectly still, hesitating, and looking up to us tried to call a truce.

"Got any tobacco plug with you, Slick?" I said quickly. To my delight my comrade pulled out two plugs of ship's tobacco. I broke it into four pieces and holding it up in my hand I said, "Tobac! tobac!" and made friendly signs. In a moment the grim, savage faces of the foe were lit up with smiles. All the dusky lips grinned and, incredible as it may seem, they came rushing up the slope with outstretched hands. I at once made signs to them not to come too near, and then called the best-natured-looking one; and, as he came close up to me, I stretched forth my hand and said: "I give you te pakea."[9] Then I put a bit of tobacco plug in his dark fingers and signed to him that if they all went away I would give him a lot more. Upon which he went back; and presently all his companions went away up the slope opposite us, and standing at the top of the hill watched the truce-bearer return to us for the promised tobacco.

9. Tobacco.

"Don't you give it him till they go another mile off," said Slick; and after parleying again we got them out of sight, and then, to make doubly sure, gave them only half of the remaining tobacco. As soon as the truce-bearer went off with it to his companions we took to our heels and did not stop running till we arrived at the village where we had left the half-caste guide. Outside the guide's homestead we lay and rested for two or three hours before we recovered from our exertion in the sun, and the fright. We told the guide about the idol, and he said that if we told the authorities they would go and arrest the Marquesans. Then he asked us if we would be witnesses and not say that he had anything to do with giving them away. I at once declined, and so did Slick: we did not want the whole tribe to swear a vendetta and seek our lives.

We made ourselves comfortable and happy in the village. Many of the old chiefs lolled about by the huts, pretty little homes made of twisted bamboo, elevated on crossed palm stems. Scarred with old wounds which they had received in tribalistic battles, they looked grim, wonderful warriors. Some were tattooed extensively and had large hairy warts on their cheeks and ears. They loved to talk of the good old days ere the bloated whites came across the seas and the Marquesan Rome fell. Sly old native women, hideous and wonderful looking, peeped at us, then sighed, and went on chewing their tobacco or betel-nut. Pretty girls, with hats made of palm leaves and clad in a *mumu*[10] trimmed with flowers, passed along the tracks that lead from village to village.

10. A tappu-cloth chemise that reached to the knees.

As we went on after resting we heard the confusion of noises in the native huts. In some the occupants were singing happily and in others shouting with hot rage in family squabbles. Often a youth or a girl suddenly rushed forth from the den door, flying for dear life, as the old chief's gnarled, tattooed face peered forth, ablaze with anger that his own children should dare argue with him and say the heathen gods were only wood and stone! Sometimes babies disappeared in a mysterious way, and the native mothers wandered about the villages beating their hands together and wailing most mournfully. Terrible rumours floated about in those days, for some of the old chiefs had a taste for "sucking long pig": no man who had any respect for his soul would swear by it that the grizzly old chiefs, and old concubines, did not sit by the festive fires far away inland and gnaw the bones of those very missing children!

Slick and I bathed in a lagoon and felt greatly refreshed. I rubbed the bruise that my club had given him with palm-oil, and though he moaned a bit the lump soon went down. Next day we went to our schooner and slept on board. The skipper was away for a week, so we once more went off wandering, and when we returned to go aboard, to our surprise the *Golden Horn* had gone! She had been originally chartered to take a cargo of tinned meats and foodstuffs to Papeete and many of the isles and groups scattered about, and had suddenly received orders to sail. The skipper had sent off to try and find us, and then left word that he would probably be back in three weeks. Three days later, being stranded, we went aboard a trading steamer and asked for a job. She was bound for the Carolines, and then across to Samoa and Tonga. They did not want any hands, so at dusk, just before she sailed, Slick and I went down in the hold and stowed away. They put the hatch on about ten minutes after we had got below and we were then imprisoned in darkness. We lay side by side against some barrels and bunches of green bananas and unripe oranges, which are always plucked green for cargo purposes. We had a terrible time together. The days and nights became a blank. We lived on the bananas and green orange juice. At last in our desperation we climbed up over the barrels and thumped the decks, but no one heard us. As we lay down, trying to sleep, large hairy ship rats jumped at us and squeaked. I struck at them with my violin-case and smashed it, and as I lay half asleep I felt their soft snouts poke and sniff in my ears. Slick swore that they were flying rats, because they seemed everywhere and flapped about. We found out after that large island cockroaches were flying about us and the rats were leaping at them!

Slick became as downhearted as I did, though he was a good fellow and brave too. "I'd sooner have stopped in Hiva-oa for years than go through this, mate," he said. One night, when the steamer was rolling and pitching, I sat on the barrel by Slick's side and played the violin furiously. "Perhaps they will hear that," I said. "Go on, scrape the d——d thing," said my comrade, and I tore away at full speed. "It's no good, Slick. It's blowing hard. Can't you feel her rolling? We must wait till it's calm."

Next day, or night, it was silent, and we only heard the screw-shaft revolving, so I got the violin out and started scraping again. I must have torn away for two hours. Suddenly a stream of light flooded over us! The man-hatch had been lifted off! And the crew of astonished sailors, and the skipper, mate and chief engineer, were looking down!

"God d—n it! I wonder what next is going to happen on this old packet!" shouted the astonished skipper. "Come up, you men." Slick went up the iron ladder first and I followed after, while the chief mate looked grimly down at the bare banana stems and at heaps of green orange peel. They had heard the violin through the storm, during the first night's orchestral appeal for help, and had come to the conclusion that a ghost was aboard. For, as the mate told me afterwards, it was only a wail that sounded faint and far off above the storm. The skipper forgave us and we were treated well—considering our sins. I was placed in the stokehold and Slick was put to coal-trimming. When we arrived at Upolu (Samoa) Slick made up his mind to stay and go off with her to Honolulu. I left. Nina, Pompo and all my old native friends were delighted to see me again, and took me straight off on a fishing excursion round the coast.

I never saw Slick again; but if ever he chances to gaze upon these reminiscences he will see I have remembered him, and still feel that I could not have found a better comrade the world over for the escapades that we went through together.

CHAPTER XI

At Sea—A Fo'c'sle Argument—A Native's Confession—Sydney Harbour

THERE was a steamer in Apia harbour and I was lucky enough to get a berth aboard her. I think I had only been in Apia two days when she got steam up to leave for Fiji and New South Wales. I berthed forward in the forecastle. She was a tramp steamer and carried sail to help the decrepit engines and take the vessel to port when they broke down. Just before we left we took on a cargo of natives bound for somewhere! They were a mixed lot, most of them Samoans or Malay-Polynesians, and among them some Solomon Islanders who had arrived in Apia a week before, waiting to be transhipped. They were berthed forward between decks. Most of them were dressed in dead men's clothes, collected in the South Sea Island morgues, after the first occupants had no further use for them: dead sailors, beachcombers, coolies, suicides; indeed all the derelict corpses of life's drama who lay in their final resting-place in the unvisited cemeteries of the Pacific Islands.

These natives were a cheerful, indifferent lot of people—at least when they got over the first pang of parting from their relatives. But that grief was soon over, for they each believed that they were leaving their native isle to return some day with fortunes from the promised El Dorado: hope is as intense in natives of the South Seas as it is in white people. Next day they started to sing cheerfully, and came up on deck in shoals to cadge from the galley, and get the cook to bake their bread-fruit[11] and yams. Some had their wives with them, big fat women with glittering eyes. They were supposed to keep down below after dark, but they came up on deck and went pattering by us as we stood by the fore-peak hatchway smoking with the sailors. About three days after we left Apia, bound for Suva (Fiji), a hurricane came on, and the boat rolled and pitched till we thought she would turn a somersault, or turn turtle. The natives between decks were shut down; we heard their yells as the mass of clinging arms and bodies were hurled about as the boat rolled and shipped seas over the bows.

> 11. The name bread-fruit is more poetical than the flavour of the fruit, which tasted to the writer like sweet turnips.

At midday next morning the wind suddenly ceased and the sun burst out. Only those who had experienced the howling chaos of mountainous seas, blackness and wind would have believed what the weather had really been a few hours before.

The boatswain and the carpenter were interesting characters, both typical shellbacks of the island trading type. The boatswain looked like a priest: his face was weather-beaten and his nose twisted; he had no hair on his face, head or neck, and wore a cap to hide his polished skull. His chum the carpenter fairly wallowed in hair, had bristly eyebrows, a bristly beard, head and neck, and a vast moustache; you could only see his fierce, twinkling eyes as he sat arguing in the forecastle with the boatswain. Those two never agreed on any subject, but were inseparable companions. The boatswain, I believe, loved to be contradicted by his shipmate, and if no sudden response was made to any assertion he might make, he at once looked round fiercely and said that silence was equivalent to disbelief, and they might as well call him a liar and be done with it.

I recall how he sat by his bunk on his sea-chest and said: "Remember 'im? I should think I does. Very old man. He had been a skipper on the trader between the Samoan and Marquesas Group; a nice old fellow; he was blind, quite blind in both eyes." At this the argument commenced immediately, as the carpenter looked up and said: "Of course he was blind in both eyes; he wouldn't be blind if he could still see with one eye, would he?" Then, as he hammered at the hinge of the sea-chest he was mending, the boatswain shouted: "Stow yer gab, yer clever son of a nigger, d——n yer. Isn't a man blind if he's blind in his eye?"

"Course 'e ain't, he's only lost one hye!"

"Yer d——d swab! To h—— with yer! If 'e's lost his eye, ain't 'e blind in it?"

At this the carpenter's unshaved face fairly steamed with heat as he appealed to the sailor standing by: "A man ain't blind if he's lost 'is one eye, is 'e?"

"Well," slowly answered the sailor solemnly, "if he couldn't see out of the eye that was blind, I should say that he was blind in it."

At this the boatswain spat on the deck, the carpenter thrust his bearded chin forward, and they started to bet heavily on the matter; and the Norwegian cook, who had come in to see what the shouting was about, wiped his mouth with his dirty sack apron and said:

"Mein tear frients, vich eye was the mans vlind in?"

"Yer son of a German sea-cook, I said the man was stone blind in both eyes, so, d——n yer, he hadn't any eyes at all!" roared the infuriated boatswain.

"Vell, now," said the sea-cook, as he stroked his short Vandyke beard and looked astonished, "he vash not vlind then; he haf no eyes to be vlind in at all; for how cans a man be vlind in zee eyes if he haf no eyes?"

The boatswain turned purple, spluttered out "Yer God-d——d cheeky," then suddenly lost his temper, made a run and pushed the cook, who nearly fell to the deck.

"I vill show you vat a vlind eye is," shouted the enraged Norwegian sea-cook.

"Bear witness," shouted the boatswain, looking at the sailors and members of the black squad, who were all standing around to see fair play. "The cook has insulted me by saying that a blind man has no eyes." Then the Norwegian made a rush at the old boatswain. It gave the whole crew a lot of trouble to separate them. Then the boatswain cooled down and said it was his own fault for not simply saying the man was blind, and saying nothing whatever about his eyes if he hadn't got any. Then they all had a drop of rum together, and were good friends till the next argument cropped up and they took sides once more.

At other times they would sit yarning, and as I listened, sitting on my sea-chest, I heard many terrible and indescribable things: true enough too, I have not the slightest doubt, but only fit to be told here after considerable prunings from the facts. There was an old Solomon Island native just by us, down in the fore-peak. He was a kind of overseer, and had to look after the natives in the hold, and separate the various tribal characters if they fought, which they often did. Now this overseer was a garrulous chap, and though he was hideous enough it was interesting to hear what he said. He was over fifty years of age, and we gathered from what he let out that he had eaten "long pig" in his youth. One calm, hot night, when the engines were clanking steadily away, while the skipper walked the poop and the steward slept, we were all sitting in the forecastle; some of the sailors were in their bunks, and a few others smoking and playing cards beneath the dim oil lamp. The garrulous native overseer was talking away for all he was worth, when suddenly the boatswain leaned over his bunk and said: "Shut up, yer son of a cannibal."

"Me no heathen, I good Christian man. Once long ago I eat 'long pig'; but since then I have saved white sailor from being eaten, and been friend to white girl."

"Eh?" said the boatswain, as he pricked his ears up; the carpenter said, "Gor blimey, you've eaten———"; quickly a sailor nudged him, so that we might hear all about it, and one of the crew who had been playing cards shuffled the pack and said quietly: "Tell us all about it." The grim-looking, half-naked savage nodded his head and started off.

"Many years ago now a terrible hurricane was blowing off the Solomon Isle of Bourka, when the islanders suddenly sighted a full-rigged sailing ship in distress. Sunset blazed behind her, and they could see the torn sails and the decks taking the seas over, as she helplessly drifted before the gale that was bringing her shoreward. That night, when the stars were flashing through rifts in the clouds, which had broken up and left pools of blue in the sky, they saw the great ship within a mile of the shore, with walls of living waters breaking over her. One or two sailors were just discernible, clinging to the spars aloft; and then suddenly a mountain of water rose and the masts disappeared.

"In the early morning the natives gathered the bodies of the dead sailors together, put them in old salt-beef ship's barrels and hid them on the sands just under the water near the shore. For the bloodthirsty tribe who found them were cannibals. Four of the crew were still alive—the boatswain, the chief mate, the cook and the ship's doctor; and a girl, who was the skipper's daughter." The boatswain dropped his pipe on the floor, the sailors all looked round and left their cards, and one or two went phew! then listened, and the half-savage native continued to this effect:

"They took the four living men up the shore and put them in a cave, and hid them so that a rival tribe they had lately been fighting with should not get hold of them before they could eat them. The chief of the tribe claimed the pretty white girl; she was not more than seventeen years old. They took her up to the stronghold, made a big festival fire and had a feast from one of the dead sailors who had been washed ashore.

"While the whole tribe sat squatting in a circle, watching and waiting while the flames of the fire flickered and hissed, the white girl, tied to a coco-palm by the hands, looked round at them all with staring, frightened eyes. Then the hideous cannibal chief caught hold of her and told her that if she would be his wife he would save the four white men who were alive in the cave. For a while they could not stop her screaming, and then she looked up at the chief and said: 'Bring me the white men first'; and he shook his head and said, 'No.' Later, when they were eating, and dancing wildly round the terrible fire, another chief, of a tribe inland, came suddenly out of the forest close by and joined in the feast. When he saw the white girl staring, tied to a palm just behind them, he looked at her longingly, and offered to buy her from the first chief.

"I was a young man then, about twenty years old, and I had been a servant off and on to the white missionaries who lived twenty miles away round the coast. I made up my mind to steal away at daybreak and tell them about the white girl and the four sailors in the cave. For that old chief who had come and tried to buy the white girl was a bloodthirsty cannibal, and he only wanted to buy the girl so that he could eat her. It was well known by all the tribe that he loved the flesh of women, and would risk his life to eat a white girl's breasts.

"In the shadows by the trees she still sat, with her wildly staring eyes, appealing to the glittering eyes of the chief and to dumb heaven. Most of the tribe squatted or lay at full length round the dying fire, their hideous appetites satisfied and their bellies distended. I saw the two powerful chiefs stand arguing; and then the chief who longed for the white girl turned away from the other and looked with fierce, hungry eyes at the shivering girl a moment, ere his dark, naked limbs strode away into the forest. My heart leapt with joy as I saw his big form go. I felt that I could now easily save the white girl; for I knew that white men were brave and would come directly I arrived before them and told them all that had happened. Walking as near as I dared to the white girl, I spoke to her in English. I said four words only: 'I see white men.' I could not see her glance, as I dared not look her way; for the chief sat close by, rubbing his chin and grunting sleepily. I sat myself down by a tree and slept, thinking to go off and get help before the day broke. Suddenly I was awakened by a great noise of shouting and running. I jumped to my feet. The tribal chief was lifting his war-club and dashing it to the ground to ease his terrible rage; and then crash! he smashed the sentinel's skull; it cracked like an egg-shell. The man had slept instead of watching; the white girl had gone! At first I was delighted, for I thought she had escaped; but instead of that she had been carried off by the great girl-eating chief!"

Directly he said that all the forecastle swallowed their tobacco smoke and said, "Well, I'm——"; the boatswain muttered, "Holy heaven!"; and then one of the sailors said, "How did you know the stinking swine of a chief had her?"

We all somehow listened hopefully; for the overseer looked so earnest, and we did not want to think we were hearing the truth. A yarn was all right, but this made the hands restive and the eyes blaze. However, he continued:

"Some of the tribe, who were camping by a lagoon not far inland, were suddenly awakened by an agonised scream. Looking through the jungle, they saw several canoes being rapidly paddled across the moonlit waters, and in the foremost canoe they recognised the feared, bloodthirsty cannibal chief, Torao. He was a giant of a fellow, nearly seven feet in height and of tremendous girth, and so there was no mistaking him. He was paddling with one arm, and held the white girl under the other as you would hold a strangled rabbit."

"Lummy!" said one sailor; as one or two others wiped their perspiring faces with their red handkerchiefs, listening as they held on to the stanchion in the middle of the forecastle, while the tramp steamer rolled and pitched along across the Pacific, heaving at intervals to the heavy cross-swell.

"Vell, vell now," muttered the Norwegian cook, as he sat on the side of his bunk taking his trousers off. The Solomon Islander continued:

"I was young then and could run with the swiftness of a horse, and, knowing that there was no time to lose, I never stopped once as I ran across country and round the coast for miles. At length, about midday, I arrived at Tooka village, which is on the coast, rushed up the shore and thumped at the door of the first white man's bungalow that I saw. They all came rushing from their houses when they heard what I had to say. Directly they heard all they rushed back to their homes and got their guns and revolvers, and in no time were all astride on horseback galloping across the country.

"At sunset we arrived at the village where the caves were. I was brave, for I knew the white men would protect me, so I led the way at once to the caves; but we were too late; they were deserted; the sailors had been taken away. At once the leader of the white men, who was a big man with a heavy grey moustache, shouted to me that I should take them to the spot where they had eaten the sailor. Quickly I ran on in front, and they all came behind, their faces stern and white-looking. When we reached the place they said nothing, but all quietly tightened the reins of the horses and then, dismounting, crept together to the edge of the forest. The white man who led them made a terrible oath when they all peeped through the bamboos; for the savages had just clubbed two of the sailors and a great fire was blazing in the middle of the cleared patch by the huts; and not far off from the dead bodies stood the chief mate, bound hand and foot, waiting to be clubbed too. The white men hesitated one moment, then rushed across the cleared patch, firing their revolvers. Several of the natives fell dead as the tribe scampered off into the forest. They only saved the chief mate out of the four men who had survived that shipwreck. They burnt the village to the ground and buried the bodies of the boatswain and the cook. Not far from where the fire had been they found some shrivelled clothes and a small peaked cap; in the pockets were some little medicine phials, and, close by, the ship's doctor's feet—still in his boots! I told them about the ship's salt-beef barrels hidden under the shore sand. They dug them all up and took the bodies miles away and buried them. The skipper's daughter was never heard of any more. About two years after that high chief Torao, who stole the white girl, became a Christian, and taught the native children lotu songs in the mission rooms. I went and lived with the white men at Tooka; they gave me good clothes, and I was their servant, and found them good and kind masters."

"Clear out of this fo'c'sle, yer God-d——d son of a cannibal!" shouted the boatswain directly the overseer had finished; and though he had befriended our countrymen we too felt a bit disgusted, and knew how the boatswain felt as we looked up at the thick-lipped Solomon Islander's face.

The foregoing is as much as I can tell you of the main facts of the native's story. I have left out all the gruesome embellishments and the heart-rending cruelty of the native's description of the white girl's grief in the hands of the cannibal monsters. Let us hope it was not true; but I must admit many things made my heart thump as I listened to all that seemed too true. The boatswain and his shipmate never argued over that tale. The Norwegian cook at last pulled his trousers right off and said, "Vell now, it's too terrible to tink of," and swung his legs round into his bunk. I turned in also, just opposite him, and said: "Let's keep the lamp on; I don't feel sleepy to-night."

Next day we dropped anchor in Suva harbour and stayed there two days. I had previously been to the Fiji Group and stayed there for a considerable time, having various experiences with the natives and traders, experiences which will appear in the second half of these reminiscences.

The crew went ashore and had a fly round, walked the parade and visited all the drinking establishments. The boatswain and his mate came back arm in arm, arguing at the top of their voices; they had been drinking rather heavily. When they got on board the boatswain sighted the natives poking their heads out of the fore-peak hatchway, and, thinking of the tale the overseer had told us, he shouted at them, "Get down below, yer d——d cannibals," and then made a rush for them. We were obliged to hold on to him to keep him from going down between decks. At last we got him into his bunk; but none of us had any sleep, for he shouted about cannibals all night and swore that we had got thousands of them on board.

Next day, just before we left Suva, a passenger came on board. He was an old gentleman with bristly eyebrows, who wore a monocle. He carried two large portmanteaux and came puffing up the gangway, and directly he got on deck he started shouting: "Stew-ard! Stew-ard!" Spying the boatswain by the main hatch, he mistook him for the steward, and, looking through his eyeglass, said: "Where's the saloon?" At the same time he handed him the largest of the portmanteaux. With disgust wrinkling his florid nut-cracker face, the boatswain pointed forward. Off went the old man, muttering something under his breath about the discourteous behaviour of sailors. "Down there," shouted the boatswain, as the passenger got up against the fore-peak and called once more: "Steward!" Then down the fore-peak he went. In a few seconds we heard a wild yell, and up came the old fellow, hatless, with his face pallid with fright. He had landed in the middle of the huddled natives below.

"Help, help!" he shouted. I told him it was all right, put his hat on for him and went down quickly and fetched up his portmanteau, which he had dropped in his fright. He was "all of a-tremble"; his hand shook visibly as he clutched his property. The German steward came hurrying forward and, when he sighted the old gentleman's massive gold chain and jewelled fingers, almost fell forward on his face, bowing and scraping in his apologies.

When the old fellow recovered he swore he'd sue the boatswain, in Sydney, for damages.

We had a fairly fine passage across to New South Wales and in a week sighted Sydney Heads.

We dropped anchor out in the stream, and the old passenger went off in a tender. He had got over his adventure, and shook his umbrella good-naturedly at the boatswain, who grinned at him over the fo'c'sle head.

I was pleased to see the lovely shores of Sydney harbour again. That same night I stood on deck and saw the beautiful sea-board city rising grandly, with her spires and walls, as moonlight crept over the horizon.

Sydney by night is a sight that makes you easily understand the Cornstalks' pride in their beloved city. Next day we berthed by Circular Quay. It was fearfully hot, real dog-day weather. Hospitality abounds in Sydney, and one never need feel lonely, for on stepping on to the wharf I was once more enthusiastically welcomed by an immense crowd of mosquitoes! We can joke after, but I did not see life then as I do now.

How I recall it all, my beautiful youth—aye, as a woman's heart secretly remembers her first love, and gazing back feels the old passion, sees the rosy horizon of dreams, the absolute certitude of old vows, spoken by that voice that expressed all the happy Universe! Yes, so do I remember the sleepless, hungry nights under the stars that shone over the trees, nights radiant with dreams!

CHAPTER XII

Circular Quay—Figure-heads—A Derelict's Night—The World's Worst Men—Off to New Zealand—A Violin Prodigy—In the New Zealand Bush—My Maori Girl—A Pied Piper—A Recipe for the Happy Vagabond—The Philosophical Sun-downer

I HAD lived in Sydney five or six years before, when I had run away from a ship in Brisbane and had come across to Sydney full of dreams and hope. I was then only fourteen years of age. How vividly I recall those days and nights.

Once more I stand on old Circular Quay and seem again to breathe through my dreams the turbulent poetry of emigrant sin and sorrow; for ah! how many cargoes of human lives have been brought across the world and then dumped down on the quay. I dream on, and see the silent wool clipper-ships lying alongside the wharfs, the tall masts and long yards at rest beneath the sky. The fine carved figure-heads look alive, their grand, allegorical faces gazing, their outstretched arms pointing, towards Sydney's silent streets. They seem to express dimly to me some substance of great poetic thought, as though I stood on the mysterious shores of the heaven whence those spiritual minds that conceived them drew their inspiration, when with creating brain and moving fingers they carved such sad, wonderful faces; faces destined to be exiled for years on voyages across wild oceans.

I am a boy again, and am thrilled with such a feeling as a poet has when he treads visionary worlds and forgets his sad reality. How happy I feel as I move along in the white moonlight from wharf to wharf, gazing on each wooden ship and wondering on their past voyages, what seas they crossed ere I was born, and what the seaports looked like when they came sailing down, with weather-beaten sailors staring from the fo'c'sle head.

How distinctly I remember it all! I cannot move from one ship's side: the figure-head is that of some beautiful goddess with a crown of bronzed hair, wherein a dove flutters. Her face represents, exactly, my romantic ideal of all the tender beauty of woman as I dreamed of it in my early boyhood. It is a beautiful face. I gaze from the wharf at it with fascinated eyes: all is silent except for the plomp of the waters against the ship's side as the tide ebbs. Still I gaze at her praying hands, as with wide-opened eyelids she stares across the moonlit quay at the sleeping city.

I went back to my room and dreamed of that perfect face. So strangely was I impressed by its beauty that I felt a longing to find some living type resembling it. The next day I walked up the Sydney streets and earnestly scanned the faces of the Colonial girls. None of them seemed to me as beautiful as the thought of the artist who had fashioned the perfect outlines of my figure-head. The next night I went down to the quay and gazed once more at her, and then again the following night; but when I arrived on the wharf to my great sorrow I found her gone. She had left her beauty in my soul, and though she was only an insensate figure-head, the memory of her features and expression stirred and fired some devotional dream within me, and gave me a poetic reverence for womanhood, a gift from out the great strangeness of things, that I have ever cherished. Often in seaports, on my travels from land to land, my comrades wondered why I stood a moment and gazed at the silent sailing ships by the wharf. But, though I searched, I never saw that figure-head again. I suppose they have broken those old wooden ships up now and burnt them on the hearth fires of the cities, and by them other boys have probably dreamed of strange lands, and lovers gazed in the curling flames with shining eyes. Ah! little did they dream what their log of firewood had meant to me; and while they kissed with clinging lips the substance of my boyhood dreams, those features that lived spiritually in my imagination fell to ash as the flames faded in the homestead hearth fire.

The poetry of Sydney harbour, with its sights and turmoil of sound, lives in my memory as though to-day is far-off yesterday. I even remember, and feel again, my strange romantic loneliness as I watch the silent ships lying out in the bay. Night, like life, is on the deep, tide-moving waters; in the dark depths the fixed mirrored stars shine steadfastly like Eternity, while over them the waters ebb seaward or flow towards the shore. The outline of North Shore, like another continent, rises across the wide harbour, and exactly opposite are the spires of the grand, silent, sea-board city. Some drunken sailor's song floats across the bay from the wind-jammer that is lying at anchor out in the stream. Several lights are twinkling across by Miller's Point. The Orient liner, the giant aristocrat of the quay, is agleam with shining port-holes; her funnels belch forth smoke that ascends to the silence. We creep by—three homeless men and a boy—looking for a place to sleep! Our shadows suddenly hurry on with us, as in the moon's gleam we spy the quartermaster on watch at the gangway. No hope there for us, we think, so we go round to the anchored ferry-boats and leave the great liner behind. She's off for England to-morrow, dear old England! O magical word to how many exiles in the sleeping city, and especially to us, with our stomachs rumbling with emptiness. The big Manly Beach ferry-boat is moored by the wharf; our frightened eyes look carefully around, then down on board we go to seek the cushioned settees of the saloon. We slept there last night. Again we creep into the saloon, four of us: Roberts, the ship's stoker, villainous-looking, old, with unshaved face; Ross, the son of the Right Honourable, and the third man, who is a late schoolmaster from a school of great distinction. He is a pessimistic-looking chap, perhaps because he lent Ross his last ten shillings on the promise of five hundred per cent. interest when Ross got an expected cheque from England. "Ah, woeful when!" The night is getting old and cold; how comfortably the warmth of the dim saloon strikes us as we four derelicts creep across. The moonlight is streaming through the port-holes. Ross smothers a note of irresistible exultation, for he has spotted a large bunch of bananas on the saloon table! Such sudden unexpected affluence is too much for me, and even as I wonder why the saloon smells so strongly of fresh tobacco smoke, I sit down plomp! on the stomach of the ferry-boat's night watchman, who is asleep on the settee!

KAWIERI, N.Z.

A terrible yell of pain escapes the official's lips; like four shadows in one headlong leap we cross the saloon and rush up the gangway. How we scampered across the quay space and then rescued poor old Roberts, the stoker, as he puffed behind and stumbled on the kerb-side and fell with a crash! Under the trees in the domain he sat swearing terrifically, but calmed down as we held his blood-splashed face up and examined it by moonlight. The schoolmaster lent his handkerchief of other days to stanch the blood-flow. Ross promised another fifteen shillings when the cheque came. Then, under the big-leafed tree, with our heads pillowed on our coats or caps, we lay with our faces side by side to sleep. I can still see the many huddled derelicts under the gum-trees of Sydney's Hyde Park, disreputable old men, and young men, good and bad. I watch by my chums on our big bedroom floor and hear the far cry of the wild animals in the Botanical Gardens Zoo, and smell the dew-damp leaves and domain grass, as dawn steals over the windless trees away back beyond the horizon of more years than I like to count.

Some inexplicable kind of sadness comes over me as I look back to the lost splendour of my derelict days. How wealthy I was with all my youthful unfulfilled promises, and what security I found in the hopeful, manly eyes of men who went down to the sea in ships. How I stuck to them as they yarned together, or sang till the shore cave echoed. The shanty was a paradise, filled with men of mighty deeds, as I gazed with the eyes of boyish inexperience at the stalwart, unshaved men from 'Frisco and London, and listened to the stories of sad self-sacrifice, or great deeds on land and sea, performed in the valiant imagination of those wonderful brains of the world's worst men.

I often wonder what I have missed through the inherited taint of vagabondage that is in my blood. Should I have been happier and gained some wealth had I gone ashore in some far country, scorning vagabonds and marching down the track on honest feet, like some Dick Whittington, looking for the lights of some distant city, with my violin slung beside me? I doubt it. If one is really honest, one is sure, some day, to trust the wrong man through not being dishonest oneself. But to go back to my reminiscences at the moment when I arrived in Sydney from Samoa.

I did not stay in Sydney very long. I had three or four pounds in my pocket and did not want to get stranded, so once more I looked around and was lucky enough to secure a berth on a steamer that was going to New Zealand for a cargo of meat, and from there to London. I got a job down in the engine-room as a kind of snowman to look after the refrigerators. The chief engineer was a terrible pig; he was a Dutchman, and gave me no peace, but made me paint the lower-deck iron roof. We eventually had a fight, and I received a black eye which took a considerable time to cure itself. I made up my mind to leave at the first opportunity.

I smelt the freshness of the sea-water and tar when we dropped anchor in Oriental Bay. After the first old loafer who is always waiting in every Colonial seaport to say "This is God's own country" had said it, I looked about. Oh! the splendour of those days, the glorious homelessness and the thrilling uncertainty of everything! I stood on the wharf with my violin in my hand, and, though I was almost penniless, I felt like a monarch gazing on his multitude of toiling subjects. Ships of many nationalities lay alongside discharging their cargoes, and the crews mingled with the crowds of embarking or disembarking passengers, arriving from, or bound for, Australia, China, Japan, India; in fact everywhere wealth and poverty massed together. I saw white faces, black faces, yellowish faces, mahogany faces;

glittering eyes, blue eyes, black eyes, bilious eyes; Dantesque profiles, turbaned heads, thick, black lips, expressing carelessness and humour, and thin, cynical lips; also self-exiled, broken-down, sardonic-looking poets, authors and musicians from the British Isles. It seemed that the drama of life was being enacted on that wharf, with its hubbub of uncouth voices: Hindu men, and women with rings in their ears, multitudes from the Far East, South and West. A kind of miniature parade of existence, ere Time's hand swept the whole lot like pawns off the board, it seemed to me as I watched them embark on the ships to go seaward.

I eventually secured a position as violinist in the orchestra of the opera house in Wellington, and I had comfortable diggings with an English family. I think I should have settled down there, but, just as I got to like my landlady and her family, the old father made up his mind to go back to England again. This unsettled me, and I started off on my wanderings again. I got to know a man who hired concert halls. I played at many of his shows, performing Paganini's *Carnaval de Venise*, also De Bériot's and Spohr's concertos. I was received very well indeed, and I should have stopped on at the game, but I was very unfortunate. I could not live on the applause which I received through being billed as "The Sailor Violinist." I wore a cheesecutter cap, at the request of my employer, who indeed tried to go on the same lines as in London, where foreign prodigies of twenty, with baby collars on, appear! I barely got any wages; my employer secured the profits.

I never knew a man who could promise so much and give so little as that particular employer of mine did. And what he *did* give he gave with such an air of munificence, as though he was conferring a favour on me that I had never expected, or earned, that for the moment I was completely disarmed and my protest died on my lips.

So one day I started off with my violin "up country." The turmoil of the crowded city streets, and my commercial inability, had sickened me of trying to do well. When I got on the lonely roads the old knight-errant fever gripped me. As I stood on the bush track I saw the primeval forest trees all brightening in the sunlight, while singing winds, bending their tops, blew through them, and wings glittered where, overhead, flocks of cockatoos sped across the sky.

At midday, tired out, I came across a small bush town. It was by a river where, on the banks, Maoris camped. I stopped there only for a day and night, and I lodged with two old men who lived in a small wooden house by a paddock. They were grizzled, retired shellbacks, not from the sea, but from the trackless bush-lands. I unfortunately paid them for my lodging in advance, and they at once bought some rum and sat at their little wooden bench table yarning away till their mumbling voices seemed deep down in their dirty beards.

As the rum fumes got more and more to their brains they ceased telling me their experiences, grew argumentative, and, with fierce eyes, glared at each other till they fell asleep at two o'clock in the morning. The next day I heard from the farmer who lived in a shack just across the flat that they were always drunk, and that the whole bush town thought I was some relative of theirs who had come from abroad to see them, otherwise they could not think anyone would lodge with them. Once more I tramped off, and after doing about ten miles I "put up" at a homestead in which an Irishman and his wife lived. I was getting short of cash and was half inclined to sleep out; but though it was very hot by day, a cold wind had blown for several nights. I have quite forgotten the name of that little bush village, but I easily recall the picturesque Maoris who lived by a creek in their *pah* (stronghold), a beautiful spot, sheltered by karri trees.

I played the violin to them; and two old Maori chiefs, aged and wrinkled, squatted, with delight beaming in their deep eyes, listening to me. They were tattooed with dark blue curves from their lips to their eyebrows, and some of the girls were also decorated with tattoo. The Maori women were very cheerful, and brought me food, fresh water, fish and vegetables. An extremely beautiful Maori girl, dressed in picturesque Maori style, sat on the grass beside me and sang as I played the violin. The surroundings were wildly romantic, and I must confess that I almost fell in love with her. I kept thinking of her eyes as I lay sleeplessly on the extemporised bed that the Irishman's wife had made up for me in a shed adjoining their homestead. I went across to that pah several times; indeed I stopped at the Irishman's all the next day and night. When I went my Maori girl bade me good-bye, and then, with some little Maori children, she came to see me off, and crept by my side along the track till the pah was almost out of sight. Her eyes gazed earnestly into mine as she looked up to me; the wind fluttered her blue frock; in her wealth of hair were stuck crimson and white flowers. I seemed to live once again in the romance of my faded dreams of boyhood. How beautiful she looked as sunset deepened the mystery of her eyes. Gallantly I kissed her and then, on the top of the hill, waved my hand back to her, and she faded away, and mad Don Quixote, carrying his violin, faded away also.

Before it was quite dark I sat down on the bush grass and played the song she had sung to me on my violin. I half wished I was a Maori and lived in the old days. I am sure I should have gone with a tribe of warriors and attacked that pah and ridden off into the forest with that pretty Maori girl!

I slept out that night. I did not fall asleep till midnight, but I made a small fire in my forest bedroom and managed to keep warm; for I opened my violin-case out and with some bush grass made a good shelter, though the slight trade wind on the weather-side blew cold. In the morning I got up without bother as I had slept "all standing," had a wash in the stream just down by the gullies, and then tramped across the hills to where the smoke arose from a group of homesteads. I counted my money; I hadn't much, I know; but people in the New Zealand bush proved as generous to me as I had found them in the Australian bush a year or so before.

As I emerged from under the gum-trees I saw that the village was a decent-sized place of some fifty houses. A main road separated wooden shop buildings, and just behind were the small homes of the population. I had slept late, and the sun was blazing over the forest trees and shining on the tin roofs of the township.

As I went across the paddocks the cows lifted their heads, stared at me, slashed their tails and moved off. I heard the voices of romping children running about in the scrub of their fenceless gardens. Summing up my courage, I took up a position in the centre of the silent main street. Only one or two shops had their shutters down as I stood erect and started to play the violin! I was a good player, and before the first strain of the sentimental operatic selection wailed to a close the doors of all the shops and houses around me suddenly opened, and out came rushing the children, rosy girls and boys, and women and men, who gazed at me in astonishment.

I felt like some Pied Piper of Hamelin; but the Mayor did not turn blue "to pay a sum to a wandering fellow with a gipsy coat of red and yellow" as I fiddled away. The bushmen and the whole population grinned, as though with one mouth of delight, and sunburnt little children rushed up to me with shillings and half-crowns as I moved along and they scampered behind me.

I was well dressed; my grey suit was still new looking and my collar passably clean. I appeared outwardly to have a social standing that outrivalled that of my delighted audience. The vagrancy in my blood made me perfectly happy; and when the old storekeeper tapped me on the shoulder and invited me in, I accepted with alacrity and without a blush the breakfast he gave me. The little children's bonny brown faces looked in at the open door as I ate like a horse; then they all screamed with delight as I tossed the cat to the wooden ceiling and caught it with one hand. By midday I practically owned the township; for I played in the houses and the children invited me to stop. When I went away and passed up the track the whole population came to the end of the main street to see me go! They all waved their hands as I faded along the bush path.

One never forgets those few hours in life when one has been really happy, and so I have never forgotten that bush township.

WHAKAREWAREWA, ROTORUA, N.Z.

To the thousands of literary and commercial vagabonds living under the guise of respectability I give a recipe—how to be happy in vagabondage. First, you must have a firm belief in God and be able to keep the belief to yourself. This belief will help you when each great scheme unexpectedly fails; for if you be a true vagabond your schemes will only benefit others. Ere you go to sleep on the grass look upon the forest about you as your bedroom; examine the moon as though it were your lamp, trim it so that the shadows fall glimmering through the trees on to your face, and keep saying to yourself: "I am better off than anyone else; the world is certainly mine." In time you will believe this, and people will see the belief in your eyes and respect you. Be kind to little children you meet on the tramp, and write on your brain the wisdom they speak, for they are the cheeriest of vagabonds! Avoid luggage, and throw away your conscience with all your unpaid bills. When you have cast your socks into the bush, place palm or banana leaves in your boots as substitutes: they are cool. I've walked for miles quite happily in banana-leaf socks. If you can possibly play a musical instrument, well, take it with you; at the worst you can pawn it. Never worry; and when you have no money keep saying to yourself: "There was no money in the world for millions of years before money was invented." Have plenty of tobacco with you; and when you sit under the trees by your camp fire recall pleasant memories only; then the birds will serenade you cheerfully; and if you have a good comrade by your side you will be as two kings, your sentinels the stars, your domain extending to the sky-lines around you. Remember that when beggars die, before they put them to bed they wash their feet and place half-crowns on their eyelids so as to keep them closed in deep sleep. If they do that for the dead, what will they do for the living?

As I tramped along the sun blazed down, and I left the track for the shade of some majestic trees. Across the gullies I saw a camp fire burning and a man cooking food on it. I had run across a New Zealand sundowner!

"Hallo, matey, how goes it?" he said as I approached.

"All right," I answered cheerfully, as he looked at my violin and then up at me and said: "Want some tucker?" I accepted a lump of damper and, as his old dog greeted me affectionately and licked my hand, I sat down beside him. We tramped along together all that day and slept in a gully off the track. He was an experienced bushman, and made up two splendid soft mattresses of leaves and moss, and with the dog's soft muzzle crouched to the ground, its sentinel eyes agleam between us, we slept, and I dreamed of the Maori girl.

My companion did not seem extremely gifted, but he was a philosophical and kind companion and never argued, only listened. He had little thought of the morrow; dead yesterday was the land of his dreams, for he was generally retrospective in his conversation. Nevertheless he was agreeable, and though I understood little of what he said, the note of the mumble in his beard sounded pleasant. I gathered that he had been tramping for several years, and was off to see some friends who lived up country on a farm of their own. We had a sad misfortune together: about an hour after we had left a cattle yard that was just off the track, we were tramping along, and the old fellow was mumbling, when suddenly his dog ran in front of us and started to whimper and yelp, and then fell down. It had evidently eaten something that was poisonous. Before sunset it died in great agony. My friend, indeed both of us, were very much upset. The poor dog had travelled with him for some years. Before it got dark we went into the forest under the gum-trees, and I dug a hole at the foot of a large blue gum, then covered our silent sentinel over, as possums leapt overhead in the trees. I did everything, for my companion was too upset. I also cut its name, "Bill," on the tree trunk. He lent me his knife, and when he spoke his voice sounded husky. "I'm a bit of a fool," he mumbled. "No, you're not; I understand," I said. Next day I gave him a large tobacco plug and some money; but still he walked along by my side, looking in front and never even speaking, as the flocks of parakeets shrieked across the sky.

We came to a river with rushing falls, and a lagoon beside it caused by the overflow when torrential rain fell in the mountains, which rose miles away, brightening behind us in the sunset. I bathed my feet in the cool water. The bushman looked on, and when I asked him to bathe also he mumbled out that he had bathed like that once before and was afraid. That same evening we came across a deserted Maori stronghold. The *whares* (huts) were in ruins and overgrown. Where the garden had once been, among the tall grass and crowds of everlasting flowers, blossoms like vividly coloured crimson and yellow parchment, still grew rock melons, tomatoes and other fruit and vegetables, which the Maoris had cultivated. The silent old bushman, to my astonishment, joined me in my reflections as I stood and gazed on the relic of the once prosperous pah. "I guess we'll camp here to-night, for it's not too warm these times," he said; and so we went into the one hut that had withstood the rotting encroaching of time and still had a roof on. The floor was carpeted with weeds and flowers; even the hollow that had served for a fireplace had burst into bloom; and as my quiet old comrade, bending by the door, gathered dead scrub and gum wood to make a fire to boil the billy-can water, the wind moaned fitfully through the forest boughs overhead: I fancied I heard the dead Maoris' voices calling and echoing in the forest depths, and the laughter of girls who were long-ago dead.[12]

> 12. I was told by my comrade that it was the ruins of a pah stronghold that had been attacked by an enemy tribe, all of the defenders having been killed.

As the shadows closed, and sunset left a gleam out westward, we sat together. In the corner of the whare the sundowner had made our beds, so placed by the bushman's instinct that they were completely sheltered from the draughty weather-side. My comrade, who was so methodical in his habits, and had the night before pulled his boots off and "turned in" punctually at sunset, seemed wakeful and started talking to me. I understood all he said, for I had got used to his pronunciation, odd though it sounded, owing to his having lost all his teeth. I had been playing the violin to him, and as he sat intently listening, with his bearded chin on his hands, I played on, very pleased to find that he appreciated music. First I had played a commonplace jig, thinking that it would appeal to his uncultivated mind more than direct melody. But when I played a melody from some operatic selection he at once lifted his half-closed eyelids and said approvingly: "That's right." I inwardly said to myself: "He's an ignorant, low old fellow, but there's something in him; he's got feeling anyway," and I thought of his manner when I buried his dog. I had been reading a little book—I forget the name of it—but it quoted the philosophers a good deal, and dealt in such subjects as the human mind and the Universe as it appeared to the senses. As I looked up at the stars I pondered, and, half in earnest and half with an idea of showing the old bushman how clever I was, I said, "All those stars out there are other worlds"; and then I used such phrases as "infinite extension"—a lot of high-toned phrases that I did not understand myself. He listened silently, and that was sufficient. I felt that, though he had no imagination, he would look upon me with wonder in his eyes and think "how clever this youth is." So I rattled on with enthusiasm about the vastness of things and how, but for man's consciousness, there would be no big or little, sight, sound or time, and how the immensity of space was a mighty ocean of nothingness, a fungoid growth, wherein like jelly-fish universes floated in the eternal waters of darkness, and as they twirled and flashed, their sparkles were the stars!

Still he listened; and with pride I again delightedly attacked his profound inferiority, striving to explain that all material and immaterial things were chimeras of the mind's madness, that crept on shadowy feet through a vast Nothing, which was the Universe! I told him that he was not then listening to me by the camp fire, but was as the image of myself, an image that I saw at that moment in his wide-open eyes, as he suddenly looked up at me and said: "That'll do; if there's nothing, then your opinions, and those of all the philosophers, are nothing!" My hearing seemed to have gone wrong. He mumbled off a Latin phrase! I knew it was Latin, but that's about all I did know. His grey, deep-set eyes looked steadfastly at me. The lightning rapidity of intuition telegraphed to my brain a startling message, which in human speech would go this way: "Tick! tick! your old bushman, whom you think you are teaching, knows more than you think he does!" Two feelings struggled within me; one mockingly laughed at my discomfiture at being such a fool, and the other smiled with pleasure to find my old man was not one. I quickly recovered, and in my heart thanked the "fungoid universe" that it was dark, so that the old man could not see my blush as I dropped my pipe and groped for it in the shadows. And then I received another shock; for he quietly picked my violin up and very quietly started to play! His fingers were stiff, and the bow once slid over the bridge, but it was very evident that somewhere, back in the past, my mumbling old bushman had been a decent violin-player. Removing the fiddle from the depths of his dirty beard, he said quietly: "That's a French-made fiddle; not a bad tone either; you can tell that by the curve of the back and the shape. *Savez?*" Then he held it up in the moonlight and, moving his wrinkled finger along the fine curves of my violin, laid it down beside me. "You've been a good violin-player in your time," I replied.

OLD MAORI, SAID TO BE 105 YEARS OLD

"Yes," he said, and not a word more did I get out of him, except, as he knocked the ash from his corn-cob pipe, "It's getting late, chappie"; then with a sigh he lay down in the corner on his bed and almost immediately went off to sleep. He snored vigorously as I lay beside him, quite sleepless. I looked at the outline of his sleeping face, which I could just distinguish by the stream of moonlight that came through the broken wall opposite us. Whether it was because of my just acquired knowledge that he was not an uneducated derelict I don't know, but I fancied the outline of his face looked decidedly refined, notwithstanding the grey, unkempt beard and sweaty grime.

Next morning we rose early, and the bushman cooked the breakfast on a fire which he built by the deserted whare's doorless passage; and as he poured hot tea into a mug from his big billy can, and handed it to me, he placed in it the last remaining bit of sugar, going without sugar himself.

I noticed this; but when I remonstrated he simply said: "Never you mind, chappie; you're not as hardened as I am." I tried to learn something of his history, but to all my interrogations he was either silent or evasive. One thing I did learn, and that was that he was by birth an Englishman. That same day, after crossing some very rough but wildly beautiful country, we arrived at a homestead where there were several outhouses being built. It turned out to be my comrade's destination. The owners gave him a great welcome, took us both inside and in no time had a table laid ready and a good feed of meat and pumpkin for us. They also were emigrant English folk. As we sat at that grand table d'hôte a venerable old blind man, who had been a sailor, sat at the shanty door, secured from the blazing sun by the shade of the thickly clustered grape vines, and sang: "Oh, ho! Rio! We're bound for Rio Grande."

He had retired, in England, from the sea many years before, and was the father of our host, who had sent home for him and paid his passage out to New Zealand. He was a jolly old fellow and, though over eighty years of age, danced a hornpipe and sang, in spite of being quite blind. How his white whiskers and red beak nose tossed as I played the fiddle and he shuffled his feet and sang, and the boys from the next homestead, a mile over the slopes, watched with delighted eyes.

"Avast there! Turn to!" he would say, as he asked for a bit more of anything at the table to eat; and he loved to say that his rheumatism had given him a twinge on his weather-side, or on his starboard-side or his stern, as he moved his sightless eyes about and swayed, as though he walked a rolling deck, across the shanty floor.

The last I saw of my travelling comrade the bushman was when he was sawing poles in two and carefully measuring them with his little rule. Several new outhouses were being built, and his friends gave him a job for a few days. When the job was finished I have no doubt he went off once more on the track, with his home on his back. I never heard why he lived that life, or who he had been away back in the "has been" past, but I took good care after my experience with him not to try and talk philosophy or teach shabby-looking old men.

Very soon after I bade the New Zealand "bush-faller" good-bye I went off visiting various townships with my violin and became a wandering troubadour. I grew so well off that I was able to go on, devoid of all worries, and see a great deal of New Zealand's romantic scenery.

CHAPTER XIII

Matene-Te-Nga—A "Bush-faller's" Camp—A Maori Village—The Canoe Dance—Song of the Night—Mochau's Tale—An Open-air Concert—Violin Solos—The Brown-eyed Girl—Boyhood—Onward to the Past!

I VISITED many places during my wanderings in New Zealand, among them the beautiful Bay of Akaroa, and many other romantic scenes. The New Zealand bush is wild and grand enough, and the Maoris deeply interested me. I visited one aged Maori warrior, called Matene-Te-Nga. Samoan tattooing was nothing compared to the engraving on his big frame. He spoke English perfectly, but said little. He had kind, deep-set eyes and a wrinkled face that was also deeply carved; indeed he looked like a stalwart bit of brownish Greek sculptural work, covered with hieroglyphics, when he moved with majestic precision. Curves of artistic tattooing joined his stern, straight nose to his chin and upward to his eyebrows. He was the one surviving warrior of a time when New Zealand was a real Maori land, when the beautiful legendary lore of to-day was poetical reality to the land's original race. Matene had fought with the tribes while fleets of canoes were ambushed in the gulf.

At Rotorua too I interviewed Maoris in their native pah. They wore but few clothes. The girls and women had good-looking, stoical faces.

The Maoris strongly resemble the islanders of the Samoan and Tongan Groups; indeed so pronounced is the likeness that one cannot help thinking that the two races are allied by blood ties, and probably drifted from New Zealand to the Pacific Isles, or vice versa, ages ago. For several weeks I went off on my wanderings, accompanied by my beloved comrade—my violin. I had still a pound or so in my possession, which I intended to keep for the rainy day that would be sure to darken the blue sky of glorious vagabondage. So, while the skies were bright, I made my bed in the bush, and by the light of the moon read Byron's *Poems*. I had bought a paper-covered edition of them in Wellington and carried them in my violin-case. Oh! the romantic splendour of those days and nights, when I drank in the Byronic atmosphere. The glorious illusion of youth, the rosy glamour that is not what it seems and seems what it's not, hung about me, as I sat under the giant karri-trees by the track, or approached the Maori stronghold with Don Juan sparkling in my eyes.

On the west coast ranges, North Island, I came across a "bush-faller's" camp. I walked across the slope and introduced myself to the solitary occupant, an old Irishman. He turned out to be an interesting and congenial member of the wandering species. His camp was pitched by a creek that led to a lake, the banks of which were surrounded by beautiful ferns, eucalyptus and trees covered with fiery blossoms musical with the moan of bees. As we sat together and sunset touched the lake waters with fire, and primeval silence brooded over the forest, broken only by the weird note of birds, I could easily have imagined that I and my comrade occupied a new continent alone. Parakeets went shrieking across the forest and over the lake; we only saw their shadows in the still water and heard the tuneless beaks scream as they passed overhead and left a deeper silence behind. I stopped with the "bush-faller" one night. "Good-bye, mate," he said, as he looked up to me with his grateful, round blue eyes and placed my gift in his pocket. He had told me where there was a Maori pah several miles away, and had come stumbling with me through the undergrowth for a long way, to direct me to the track that led to the main road.

That same evening I came across several old whares by a sheet of water, at the foot of a tremendous range of hills that rolled to the southward. It was extremely hot weather, and, as I followed the track round by the water's edge, I saw the little Maori children paddling by the lake shores as the native women were fishing. On the other side of the lake were several wooden homesteads where some whites lived.

I walked into the Maori village and the children stared stolidly at me as they stood by the shed doors. Presently I came across an old Maori chief sitting under a mangrove. He looked very aged, possibly more so through his face being carved with dark blue tattoo. He spoke English well, and as I approached he welcomed me and said: "Play me your music." I at once sat down by him and began to talk. As we were speaking a crowd of Maori girls came round us, and some men, who wanted to hear me play the violin. The old chief took me into his dwelling. It was strikingly clean. I saw his wife squatting in the corner, reading a book printed in the Maori language. She was a very ugly old woman and when she smiled revealed bare gums that seemed to reach to her ears. Her hideousness intensified the youthful beauty of the Maori girls, who came rushing into the pah while I was speaking to the old man. They were beautiful girls, with the usual fine eyes, and a marvellous wealth of hair that glistened over their bare shoulders and fell to their bosoms. The sight of them reminded me of my pretty Maori girl, who had long haunted my dreams.

I stayed near that settlement for several days and attended the rehearsal of a canoe dance. The weird beauty of that scene in many ways recalled memories of the fantastic sights I had seen in the South Sea Islands. One night, when the moon was shining over the lake and forest, the Maori girls came forth from the pah, attired in scanty robes of woven grass and flowers reaching to their knees. Across the forest patch in front of the pah they ran with bare feet, waving their arms and singing a chant in their native language. Then lying down in a row, prone, in the deep grass, they moved their bodies and arms as though to imitate canoe-paddling, all the time chanting a Maori melody. It was an unforgettable sight, the moonlight glimpsing over their bodies as the night wind lifted their luxuriant hair. They looked like mermaids paddling in seaweed at the bottom of an ocean of moonlight. All the while the Maori men gazed with admiring eyes.

I heard many Maori songs. They struck me as being full of a wild, poetic atmosphere that suggested tribal battles and the legendary sadness of far-off deeds of passion and love.

I give here a few bars of melody which may faintly express my memory of their music:

I recall the solemn grandeur of the New Zealand bush, the cry of the melancholy curlew in the forest as I tramped along the wild tracks to Rotorua. I had my violin with me, and in the strange perspective of memory I still hear and see the romping, sunburnt bush children rushing out by the bush homesteads to welcome the troubadour who had suddenly appeared. Once or twice I got pretty hard up and had to resort to my violin's appealing voice for help.

Not far from a little bush township, by a range of hills that rolled to the westward, I came across another pah, where my fiddle and I were welcomed by the old Maori chiefs, whose blinking eyes lit up their tattooed faces. I remember I was warmly received by that primitive community. It seemed hard to believe that they were descendants of bloodthirsty cannibals as I sat among them and accompanied their songs, songs that breathed tenderness and poetry. The character of their music strikingly resembled Samoan melodies I had heard sung by the Siva chorus girls in the South Sea villages. The following suggests the atmosphere of Samoan or Maori music:—

I will tell you a native fairy tale, as nearly as I can remember just as the pretty mouth of Mochau, the Maori girl, told it to me. One evening she was singing sweetly while I strummed a tinkling accompaniment on my violin. The shadows were falling over the forest karri-trees and across the slanting roofs of the whares, and the sunset fire blazed the lake waters until they seemed a mighty burnished mirror that reflected the Maori village, with its sloping roofs and the romping children on the banks. "Good-bye, Mochau, I must go home now," I said at last, and the old chief, Mochau's father, looked up as he squatted with his back against a tree and said, his tattooed, wrinkled face smiling: "You stay in pah till to-morrow?"

"All right," I replied; and then Mochau's eyes shone with pleasure, and her bunched hair flew out in the soft forest breeze as she ran across the patch into the whare to peel the potatoes and boil corn-cobs for supper. After supper the kind old chief and his pretty daughter sat by me on the slope; the moon shone over the lake and was reflected in the still water, wherein the gum-trees stood upside down in a shadow world.

HALF-CASTE MAORI GIRLS

Sitting on the grass, with her chin on her knees and her romantic eyes staring straight in front of her, Mochau started to chant to herself. "Come on, Mochau," I said, "tell me some more fairy tales." She laughed, then grew very earnest, for she always imagined she was the heroine of the tales she told. Then, facing me and looking into my eyes, she began:

"Long, long ago out of the sea rose the head of a beautiful youth, Takaroa. His eyes were two stars, which he had stolen one night out of the sky. Running up the shore, he looked on the land and clapped his hands with delight to see the beautiful trees and all *horahia te marino*" (so peaceful); "and as he stood looking, the water dripping from his body in the golden sunlight, he said: 'Where is she? Where is she?' Then all the warri flowers on the big trees suddenly heard and looked down, for they had turned into the faces of beautiful girls, and they opened their mouths and cried together: 'I am she! I am she!' Then the beautiful youth of the sea looked up at them closely with his wide-open eyes, and said: 'You are not beautiful enough, not any of you; she whom I love has eyes made out of the sunsets, and the stars all shine in the dark night of her hair; so go away, go away.' And all these beautiful girls cried bitterly, and shrank up and were only flowers again. Then the boy from the sea, Takaroa, shouted once more: 'Where is she? Where is she?' and all the caverns along the shores and the mountains echoed back sadly to him: 'Where is she? Where is she?' Then Takaroa lay on the shore in the deep grass and cried to himself and fell asleep.

"In the morning, when the great sunrise was shining over the sea, and all the mountains inland were on fire with golden light, he was awake, and, jumping up, he lifted his hands to the sky. 'O god of the sky, where is she? Where is she?' And at once a little hihi bird came flying across the forest sky and, sitting on the pohutukawa tree just above the beautiful youth, started to sing sweetly on its twig. Takaroa listened, and looked up and said: 'Are you my love?' And the little bird started at once to swell, its feathers all puffed out, and it grew and grew; then lo! out jumped a beautiful girl!

"Oh, so lovely she was," said Mochau, as she stopped and looked at her imaged face in the moonlit lake; for, as I told you, she always would believe that she was the beautiful heroine; then she continued: "Her hair was like the tangled forest with the stars shining in it, and her eyes more beautiful than the sunset. 'Oh, oh, you are my love, you are my love; sing to me, sing to me,' the immortal youth said; and side by side they sang together. Then he plucked a bamboo cane and made a magic flute, and she sang and danced. 'Oh, how beautiful you are,' he said as he looked upon her lovely body. And she said: 'Do you love *me*, Takaroa, or my body?' And he said: 'Oh, Tamo mi Werie, I love you, not your body, but your beautiful eyelight.' Then all day they danced and sang together.

"Then night came, and he made a lovely soft bed for her, and she lay down on the grey moss and curled up her warm limbs. The beautiful youth lay down beside her and kissed her red coral lips and said: 'Oh, my love, place your arms round me.' And she said: 'I dare not, oh, I dare not.' But still he pleaded, and he was as beautiful as was his voice, so she relented and put her arms out and sighed; and he clasped—a little bird! Oh! how he cried, and cried, for in the grey moss was still the impression of the beautiful girl's body; and though the little bird had flown away, he still kept looking down at the grey moss bed and crying out: 'Oh, come back to me.' But the little bird came not back, and he was alone with the silent night; and all around him the old giant trees, with gnarled trunks, sighed and moaned in the moonlight with deep, windy voices as the wind blew through them; for they were the stalwart warriors, the long dead tattooed chiefs who had once lived in the world of love and grief."

Then Mochau looked once more into the lake water at herself, and the tears were in her eyes; and the old tattooed chief's eyes blinked in the moonlight as we sat together and looked at each other. I cannot show you the surrounding forest and the deep stillness of the waters, or paint the moon that shone over the lake, or Mochau the Maori girl's romantic eyes and face.

Presently Mochau looked up into her father's face and said, "Parro, tell us a tale also"; and immediately the old chief, who longed to outrival his daughter, for the Maoris seem to live chiefly that they may dream of far-off battles and tell weird legends, began and told me how this world got into our Universe.

"Before the very beginning of things a mighty god was walking across the clouds in the sky. He had not slept for thousands and thousands of years. So he put his giant feet against some stars that twinkled between his toes and, with his head pillowed on the roaming cloud, sat and rested; and his shadow moved across the sky like a mountain-man wherever the cloud moved along, and obscured the fixed stars in its passage. On and on he went for thousands of years, resting, which to the mighty god was only like a tiny rest of one minute. Then he suddenly said: 'Oh, I do feel tired'; and as he slowly rose to his feet and obscured all the Milky Way he yawned, and lo! out of his mouth, to the mighty god's own surprise, jumped thousands of tiny boys and girls. Round and round the god they swam in space, with gleaming eyes and laughing voices; and then, suddenly growing tired, they too cried: 'We are tired, give us something to sit upon.' The old god sighed, and on his breath came all the stars of the lower firmament; and he shed tears at the thought that he had become sleepy and yawned, and made boys and girls come, and those tears made the great seas beneath him! Then, as the children cried again, the great earth heaved up silently under him also, and he threw the moon into the sky. Still the children cried out: 'Oh, we are so cold!' So he tore out one of his eyes and threw it into the sky, and lo! the great sun shone and warmed them! Then they said: 'Oh, dear god, we are hungry.' And the god sighed again and touched a fleecy cloud, and out jumped thousands of woolly sheep; and from his new clouds of moonlight he plucked bunches of glittering wings; and birds soared, singing across the new sky. Still they cried: 'Oh, dear god, we want something else, and then something else.' And the great god became terribly fierce and shouted the thunder; then the rain fell! Still the children were unsatisfied, and the god said: 'All right, you shall grow old and ugly'; and when they understood what that meant they cried loudly to the god for forgiveness. So he relented and said: 'Though you must grow old and ugly, you shall have little children to take your place.' And they clapped their hands for joy. But still they were unsatisfied; and he got fierce again and said: 'You shall fall asleep, and your bodies turn to flowers, and trees, and dust.' And then at last they felt a little more satisfied; because, when they found that they had to leave the beautiful world for ever, the stars, the flowers, the trees, the ocean and the sunsets became sad and seemed more beautiful to look upon: and so the first old Maori men and women got very ugly and crept into the earth to die quite satisfied!" Thus finishing, the old chief licked his dry lips and sang me a chant, as he lived on in some past age; and Mochau looked at him tenderly and sang softly with him. They looked like two children together, and not father and daughter at all. They lived in a dreamland and cared for nothing else, for they lived within themselves.

Eventually I bade the Maori world farewell, and arrived at Christchurch, where I was forced to stay for two or three weeks, for whilst gazing at a derrick that was hauling up a huge coping-stone I slipped and sprained my ankle, and was laid up for a week, and thereby got into low water.

In the house in which I was lodging there was also staying a retired actor, who was, like me, *in extremis* through the lack of the essential wherewithal. This old actor was an amusing man, always cheerful and a good companion. He was a man of about sixty years of age; and when I sat on the side of my bed and played my violin to him one evening his eyes gleamed with intense pleasure. "Bravo, youngster!" he said, and in his extreme delight his clean-shaved face wrinkled up with happy thought. "Fancy you talking about being hard up when you can play the fiddle like that." Immediately he unfolded a plan, which was to give concerts in public without any preliminary expenses; in common parlance, we agreed on the spot to go "buskin."

The idea of playing in the streets of a city was not congenial. It lacked all the romantic troubadour element of my previous experiences in the little bush towns up country. But nevertheless my companion's cheerfulness and optimism gave me courage. He had a remarkably good voice, and in our room we rehearsed all the songs that he knew. Together next night, with our wild harps slung behind us, we sallied forth. My comrade had brushed his antiquated tall hat up till it shone with renewed prosperity. He had also cut out of paper a pair of new white cuffs, for he had a great belief in looking respectable. "My boy," he said, "we must let them see that we are not allied in any way to common plebeian street players. How do I look?" Then he gazed at himself in our looking-glass with pride, while I told him that he looked the last kind of man to be singing in the street. I meant what I said too, for he had a very distinguished look, and his speech had the intonation of bygone polish in it.

In the heart of the city, by the kerb-side, we started the first open-air concert. It was after dark, and the well-lit street was thronged with people, who generously dropped coins into my partner's tall hat; for as soon as he had finished singing he went into the crowd, as I played on. Whether it was my comrade's melodious voice, or my violin-playing, or our respectable appearance, I know not, but I was astounded at the money he collected. After each "pitch" we retired into a bar and counted out the proceeds and shared alike.

My comrade smacked me on the back with delight as he continually had another drink. "Don't you think we had better finish now?" I said, as I noticed that he was getting a bit excited; but he would not hear of such a thing. At the next pitch, by the arcade, he started to shout out, going through his old parts; he even opened his mouth and went through Hamlet! The vast crowd that collected to watch his antics stopped the traffic, and the police moved him on. "We had better get off," I said to him, and to my great relief he agreed.

Just as we were turning a corner an aristocratic-looking old gentleman came up to us and, touching me on the back and saying, "You play the violin rather well for the streets," got into conversation with us. He invited us up to his residence, where we had a good supper, and my friend entertained our host with reminiscences of better days. We were invited to stay the night, and left next morning as guests. I did not go out with my friend any more, but at once sought for a post.

I eventually secured a good orchestral job as violinist. I also got into "society," and played drawing-room solos at a residence where the hostess was a person of very high standing in Christchurch. One day while I was playing a violin solo to her daughters in the drawing-room the door suddenly opened and a loud-voiced lady swept into the room, bringing a pungent odour of scent with her. She looked at me hard for a moment, then put on her pince-nez and once more surveyed me critically, saying: "Dear me, how you do resemble the young man who was playing a violin in Queen Street with *another* awful man!" I do not recommend violinists to go "buskin" if they can do better and wish to rise from the vagabond state. If they do they will be recognised long after they have forgotten the incident themselves.

To have even your ability recognised is sometimes distressing. I remember being awarded the first prize in an amateur violin solo competition at Bathurst, in New South Wales. I played Paganini's *Le Streghe* and his violin concerto in D. I was awarded the first prize by the adjudicator; then someone recognised me as a professional and I was immediately disqualified. I remonstrated, but an old programme was produced, whereon it was stated that I had been special Court violinist to the kings, queens and high chiefs of the South Sea Islands! I think that is the only time in my career that my position as first violinist and composer to royalty has ever been recognised! also the only occasion when the musical and critical ability of the royal houses of the Southern Seas, through choosing me as their Court violinist, has ever been acknowledged.

Many things happened during my New Zealand wanderings, and one incident stands out in stronger, yet sadder, relief than many of the others as I dive and grope back, deep down in the silent waters for my dead sea fruit.

You will admit, I am sure, that I have not gone into rhapsodies over my virtues, but verily I believe the worst of us are better than we seem!

One day I was resting against a tree by the track. I was on my way to Wellington, to reply personally to an advertisement that offered a good salary to a violin dance player. It was a long, weary road and I was very tired, but happy, for I had about a sovereign in my possession. I had been reading my Byron and Keats's *Ode to a Nightingale*, to which I had written music, notwithstanding that the ode was the utterance of music itself, for when we are young we rush forward to paint the cheeks of the gods and teach wise old "bush-fallers" philosophy. I was feeling lonely and poetical, which, in the worldly sense, means slightly insane. The world seemed to have a glamour of poetry about it after all. The grandeur of the sombre forest bush seemed a part of me as the old gnarled giant trees stood silently in the gloom, like wise old friends staring at me, who would protect my homelessness if they could. The sun was blazing hot, and, just as I was thinking that I only had the silent butterflies for companions in a magic world of bright flowers and wise old trees, a tired-looking girl came round the bend of the track. As she was passing me she looked quietly into my face and smiled. I had never seen her before, so you may guess a good deal about that smile, and not be far wrong in thinking that Mrs Grundy's unprivate opinion is a correct one.

It was a wan smile, and as weary looking as the feet of the owner of the smile as they dragged along the dusty bush track as though they cared not where they led the wretched body. I looked up and returned the smile, for the eyes of the girl were brown and earnest-looking. She came straight up at once and sat down beside me! "I suppose you haven't a shilling or so to spare, sir?"

I looked at her kindly, I am sure, and, with the quick intuition of her sex, her manner immediately changed. She saw that I returned the smile in a spirit of woeful fellowship only. She was a good-looking girl, about twenty-four, two or three years older than I. Her hair was glossy and thick, and to this day I remember her fine brow and the look that lighted up her face. She had a pretty, yet weak, mouth, but the star shone on the dim horizons of her eyes. As she looked long and earnestly at me, I got up and said: "I'm off; I've got to get to Wellington"; and away we went along the track side by side. I asked her a lot of questions about herself and she answered me truthfully, telling me that she was a three-quarter caste Maori girl. I should never have noticed it if she had not told me so. Her father was an engineer and had been killed in an accident, and her mother had taken to drink and gone to the devil. I saw by her manner and by all she said that she wanted to impress me with the disadvantages she had had in her brief career; also that she regretted that first familiar tell-tale smile. I looked much older than I was, for I was tall, well made, with thick bronzed hair, grey eyes and sensitive, curved nostrils and lips. Indeed I possessed all those physiological defects that have made me what I am! For to get on in this world one should have square nostrils and a protruding, bull-dog jaw, and eyes with a mental squint that can scan north, south east and west of one's world of prospects all at once.

Yet I was happy enough, untrammelled, and out of the grip of conventionality—that relentless old man of the sea could not cling to me. My soul roamed at will, like a riderless wild horse, across the plains of life. And as I was romantic, and the glamour of Byron's gallant corsairs sparkled in my head, attuned to the tenderness of Keats, I spoke of the beautiful sunset and the goodness of God, and gazed down on the frail derelict beside me trudging along in her dilapidated shoes. How I remember her earnest eyes as she looked up at me! Most assuredly the great poets are really the sad, truthful Bibles of this world. For the tenderness, the atmosphere, of their inspired minds still sighed out of their graves into my heart, like the scent of the flowers growing over them. Her voice became soft and sighed with mine, and, God knows it's true enough, I was never so proud and religiously happy as when that "bad woman's" eyes gazed up into mine with admiration—my eyes indeed! Oh, we men, who write as though *she* would do that which we would never do!

Presently we saw the wooden houses of a township ahead, and as we entered the little main street, ignoring the curious looks of the stragglers who were leaning against the verandahs of the few shops, sheltered by their big-rimmed bush hats, I took her into an eating-house, where we ate together. She became very silent, and when we started off again, down the main road, I noticed that tone of respect in her voice that we give to those who we think we realise are better than ourselves. So I started to sing cheerily and made her laugh.

We arrived at the outskirts of Wellington at dusk and stood under a lamp-post. I gave her several shillings; she refused to take them at first, until I said: "That's all right, I lend it to you." She clutched my hand, looked up at me quickly and then hung her head and cried like a child. I soon cheered her up and made her promise to write to me, saying: "I am a musician and can make plenty of money!" "I thought you were something great like that; you've got the look in your face," and she looked at me as though I was some wonderful being. We were standing outside a third-rate theatre, and I asked her if she would like to see the play. As she said she would, we went in, the "loose street woman" and I.

When we came out I said good-bye to her, and she got on a car to go to some friends. She seemed so happy as she looked back at me. She did write to me, and I gathered that she had obtained a situation in a boot factory. They were neatly written letters, and ah! how I recall the soul, the woman part of those letters, and what they really meant; but suddenly they ceased. How I pray that her life after that was a happier one than that of the gallant corsair she met on the bush track in New Zealand long ago.

As I look back I see again the weary face of that neglected girl; her eyes are looking at me. I did not love her then, but, strange as it may seem, I love her passionately now. Her shabby skirts and the bit of dirty coloured blue ribbon round her throat are sacred memories to me, and the old dilapidated shoes are shuffling a dusty song on the weary track, a song so unutterably sad that I think Christ must have composed it. I think God gathers all His beauty from grief; that, enthroned in loneliness, He gazes eternally across His stars and across His dark infinities and sees some Long Ago! For not in the vastness of things, or the mighty ocean of space, can we see or feel so much of Infinity as we can see in the derelict eyes of the friendless; as I saw, and see now, in the tramping Maori girl of my spiritual passion.

Ah! how I love the memory of those imaginative boyish days. I often wonder if many boys were, and are, as I was, and see the strange things that I saw. My earliest recollection is of the little bedroom at the top of the house where I slept when I was six or seven years of age. On moonlight nights I could see the poplar-trees swaying to the wind outside my window as I lay alone in bed. Just beyond the trees was a stable, and its chimney had a large cowl on it. That cowl was shaped like a helmet and had ribbed marks on it, like deep wrinkles on an old man's throat, and as the wind blew it turned slowly and majestically round. I used to peep from the sheets out on the moonlight night with frightened, awestruck eyes; for my childish brain firmly believed that it was God's head moving against the sky—watching me whenever it turned towards my window!

I told my mother about it, and they all assured me that it was only a chimney cowl, but still I did not like the look of it, and I was delighted when they shifted my bed into another room. At another time I stole some green apples off a tree in our garden and got very sick and ill. My dear mother made me promise to steal apples no more; and she said to me: "Though I cannot always see you, God can, for He is always walking about everywhere."

"What is He like?" I asked, and then she described Him.

Not long after that I was going up a lonely lane near our house when I suddenly spied some green gooseberries in a long front garden. Being a born vagabond, I opened the gate and crept in, and kneeling down by the bushes I stole a pocketful of the unripe gooseberries. Just as I was bolting off an old gentleman with a long white beard, who held a walking-stick to help him along, quietly opened the gate, walked in and looked at me with solemn eyes. I stood before him trembling like a leaf, quite certain that God stood before me! I hung my head with shame and said: "Oh, God, I am so sorry, please forgive me"; and then I saw a kind look in God's eyes. I promised never to steal again. He let me out of the gate; and I rushed off home, thrilled with excitement. I almost burst the door open and, rushing up to my mother, shouted: "I've seen God! He's such a kind old man. He's given me a penny!" Sometimes now I think that God is dead, that He has died of sheer loneliness and grief over the sad lot of His lost children.

I have often wondered what I have lost through embracing scallawagism with its visionary splendours. Probably, were it not for that, I should be the proud possessor of a brick house in a decorous suburb, and oh! vast ambition, wear a white collar and cuffs. And, who knows, be pushing my lawn-mower, hiding my sarcastic grin over its ostentatious hum—as I watch my envious neighbour cut his grass with shears!

Even so, I think the greater prize is in being able to sit over the hearth fire or the camp fire with one's comrades, revelling in the realism of the "Not Permissible," turning the Universe the other way and singing the reminiscent vagabond's Excelsior—Onward to the Past! Ever back to some happy past, back to the miser hoards from the glorious Past to the loaded wine cellars of dreamland's infinity. To uncork the bottled dead sunsets, foaming champagnes of forgotten forest moonlights and blazing camp fires, bubbling laughter and friendly eyes. Drink deeply to her lips of other days, renew the old vows, clasp her tightly, gaze in her eyes ere the desert wind blow her from your arms—as scattered dust! And, if she be old, if her face, her loveliness, be changed to the wrinkled map, the sad parchment whereon Time's hand ever toils to write creation's grief, kiss her passionately, dip her in the bath of old cleansing imagination, rewhiten her limbs and make her beautiful! Watch her happiness! Make the only future man ever knew, or ever will know; gladden and become rich with life's old wine of the beautifully unreal! Friend, shut your eyes and look at the past; see sunsets and sunrises, the mirrored blue days of silent skies, soaring birds, ancient cities, nations and their histories, empires of splendid chaotic violence, laughter, love and intense tragical drama. Now shut your eyes and look at the future—can you see one moment of its reality? No, you cannot. So make your spiritual creed some dim, long-ago remembrance of your own happiness, and cherish and make the old the new! Make yesterday, and to-day, and to-morrow shining planets that came, and are coming from the illimitable past to swim into the happy skies of your ken. And let the lawn-mower's triumphant, respectable humming go by!

Probably we vagabonds are mad, and the great majority who laugh at sentiment are the really sane ones. How strange indeed if, after all, the poets are wrong, and the great and glorious aim and end of the Universe is— affluence, with flabbiness, grand pianofortes, Brussels carpets, retinues of wooden servants and gold! Gold! Indeed, for all those things we vagabonds must hold the candle to the devil. For alas! the body cannot live on sunsets and the memory of sad derelicts, dead sailors and forgotten heroes. But mentally we are wealthy. We have explored the gold-fields of the universe and struck a rich vein. It is rough gold, truly, but perhaps our Creator never meant it to be reforged and rehallmarked after He scattered it among the stars. Certainly it has always appealed to me in the rough state, more so than in the polish of strange, unmusical voices, high collars and a great lack of appreciation for shabby men. We vagabonds are not conscientious judges of worldly greatness. We are strangely biassed in favour of those lost outcasts who drift on the waters of infinity, singing chanteys to the wandering stars, and not caring so long as "God's in His heaven—all's right with the world!" What matters if men are happy? Yes, even though "they fall by the roadside and die," with no obituary notice and the "cause of little crape," as one of my critics said. He and I, I think, would tramp the world together if we had a chance to live our life over again. We may live again; I sometimes think I have lived before. And what greater truth is there in the hearts of men than their own belief in all that they believe?

CHAPTER XIV

Memories and Reflection—A Picture of Robert Louis Stevenson—German Appreciation—Of Norman Descent—A Cannibal's Execution—An Australian Sundowner—A Voltaire of the Southern Seas—Types

DREAMING over New Zealand days and the many types and characters I have met destroys the continuity of actual events: my thoughts digress for a moment to various experiences and pictures which my memory has recorded. Memories, in the perspective of dead Time, vary with our moods. Sometimes the figures and events stand out vividly, and at other times are illusive, and seem some sad, intangible thing far away in the background of life.

The old bushman's red beard and twinkling eyes; the squatting savages by their huts; the sensitive mouths and wondering eyes of the native girls; old scallawags; beachcombers; the noise of sailors on ships in the bay; Horncastle's jovial face aglow with joy and drink; the palm-clad shores, and Apia's primitive town, seem far-off dreams. I can still see Robert Louis Stevenson in Samoa; his tall, bony form, attired in white trousers, shirt and old shoes only, stands on the beach. His hand is arched over his watching eyes, his loose scarf blows out behind him to the gusty trade wind, as he stares seaward at the fading schooner that takes some friend away for ever. He looks like some memorial figure, the statue of a half poet, half pioneer gazing with aching eyes across the sea. The wind stirs the wisp of dark hair on the high, pale brow; the head is hatless and perfectly still, but the fine eyes are alive and full of far-away thoughts. Now he moves away and goes up the shore, and does not even see the smile of recognition on the face of the trading ship's skipper, who passes with a Samoan sailor and one other. Like the memory of some tragical living picture it all flashes across my mind. I could think it all unreal, some far-off rocky, beautiful unknown isle, set in the seas of my imagination, as I paint the stars, the skies, the breaking waves, the ships and the sailors coming into the harbour, or once more going seaward. At other times Samoa's Isles come back vividly, and just as a sailor, far away at sea, stands on the fo'c'sle head and watches the big clouds shift on the horizon as they break and suddenly reveal blue tropical skies over the outstretched, unknown continent's shores of singing waves and palm forests, so I see the past, and the figures move. The winds stir the trees, and the magical, musical voices of savage men and women sing and laugh, in a world that is now *The Arabian Nights' Entertainments* of my boyhood.

As you can imagine, I have met many strange types of men and women in my travels, types both good and bad. I tramped many, many weary miles in the Australian bush when I was fifteen years of age. Often I tramped alone, when I could not get a congenial comrade. I was sometimes very lucky; and my reminiscences of those good comrades are the lights that shine down the dark tracks far away as I remember their eyes. One was a man of about thirty years of age. He was exceedingly cheerful and full of song and devilment. I can still see his refined face aglow as he sits under the scorched gum-trees smashing swamp mosquitoes on his hand or singing his favourite songs in a quiet, manly voice. We stayed together for two or three days at a sheep station, where the boss was a German. He was all right. But there were two German women and a son there too. When I played the violin to them, and turned around for the welcome and expected applause, they said: "Vell, dat vash little nize"; and then they shook their Teutonic square heads and, with their eyes and hands lifted to the shanty roof, said: "But, O-ez! you shoulds hear zem play that tunezz in Germanhy—O-o-o-o-e-z-z-z-z-z ze diff-er-enze!"

Then my boyish blood warmed up and I said: "Germans can't play the violin. Paganini wasn't a German. No German ever played except by science."

"Mein Gott! Mein Gott! O, haves you never vash heards Vons Kriessburgh? He play that same tuenz vich you just now play so—phoo!"—here they shrugged their shoulders with disgust at my performance—"like dis," and the two German women, who had faces like pasty pumpkins with glass eyes stuck in them, and the son, with his big moustache twirled at the ends, lifted their hands and eyes to the roof to express the ecstatic memory of the German's violin-playing. Their mouths went "O, o-ez-e-z-z-z-z-z-ez," emitting a strange sound that faded away in complete exhaustion as they sank down on to the three chairs like three puppets. Not only violin-playing, but everything, was wonderful in German art. If one said, "What a nice picture," or "What nice butter," they'd raise their eyebrows and sigh out that old crescendo, "O, O-e-z-z-z," and say: "Have yous *never, never* tasted German butter?" It was the same with eggs, beef, pork, men, boots, girls or any d——d thing!

My congenial comrade went off to New Zealand, and I ran across another one, who was most uncongenial for a time. We were tramping across the bush-lands, looking for work on stations and secretly hoping that we were not wanted. My friend was a short, thick-set, thick-necked fellow about two years older than I, with a slightly elevated, protruding chin and a mouth that talked from morn till night about his ancestry. I forget now whether he said they were descendants of Julius Cæsar's invading horde or of William the Conqueror. Anyway our friendship was one incessant argument.

I was just on six feet high, full of health and independent strength, and I found that I was supposed to walk beside him with my head hanging for shame because I was only a "common Englishman." We were on a lonely bush track; ragged gum-trees fenced the broken sky-lines for miles and miles around us. The only onlookers were parrots and cockatoos, like vividly coloured leaves overhead. There was no sight or sound of human habitation in that vast, sombre solitude as we tramped along together. A feeling of grim exultation seemed to suddenly seize me. Once more I swallowed another pill of insult, and I looked down sideways at my blue-blooded companion. I thought of my ancestral forefathers, and wondered if *his* ancestors had robbed my ancestors, and ravaged their lands and castles—my possible birthright!

He did not know what I was thinking of as he talked away. His short legs strutted along the track with the toes turned up, his nose and chin also inclined skyward, as once more he reminded me of my plebeian origin. Suddenly!—— Well, I'll not tell you all, for why should we be proud of the animalistic strain that sometimes dominates our natures? Why be proud that suddenly a bolt seemed to fall from the blue, and one of the reputed descendants of the first Kaiser Bill got his deserts, and lay with his back in the dust, his Imperial nose and semi-conscious eyes staring half vacantly up at the Australian sky, while plebeian, old pioneer England, with a swag on his back, tramped away and faded on the horizon—triumphant—alone!

Ere sunset darkened the sky I lay ambushed in a clump of wattles by the forest, then peeped and saw my comrade coming slowly down the track with his toes turned down. I repented and thought: "Even if it's true, he cannot help being the descendant of bloodthirsty ravishers, who killed old men and robbed my country's churches. No, even he cannot help himself." So I crept out and told him I repented, and once more we tramped along as comrades. So silent was he about William the Conqueror that you would have thought such a man had never lived. He admitted that night, as we sat by the camp fire, when I had explained my feelings to him, that his descent was only a family rumour. Hearing that, I truly forgave him, and we lifted the billy can of cold tea and drank a united toast to the memory of Caractacus and Boadicea, and death to all descendants of the first great bloated Kaiser Bill who dare prove to us their murderous, cowardly ancestry!

LAKE ROTORUA AND MOKOIA ISLAND, N.Z.

I met yet another gentleman of ancient emigrant blood in Tahiti. He was a gigantic old chap, a chief. I slept in his hut with four American runaway sailors, who were waiting with me for the next boat to call, so that we could clear out. Night after night that old chief would sit and tell us of the wonderful earlier days, when he was the great king of the inland dominions, loved by all the tribes for his bravery and justice, and had had a special envoy sent out by Queen Victoria to represent her appreciation to the one true Christian monarch of the Southern Seas.

He had fine eyes, and they flashed as he told of these old days, and his tattooed frame swelled majestically over many a wild memory. He even shed tears as he sang to us old far-off songs of dead heroes, mighty chiefs and tender maids he had eaten at the cannibalistic festive board. One night we returned to the hut and found that the great monarch had bolted off with all our possessions; even my last shirt had gone! Two weeks later he was caught by the gendarmes; then we heard that he was a ferocious cannibal of low origin, and that they had been trying to catch him for twelve months. He had killed a native boy, strangled him in the forest, and eaten him. Before we left we heard that he had been shot by the French Commissioners. About six weeks after, while I was walking along the beach at Apia, I met him. He ran for his life, before my friend and I got a chance to recover from our astonishment and run in the opposite direction. The hired native sharpshooters had deliberately missed him, and the old scoundrel had fallen dead till nightfall only!

Another time I met an old dilapidated sundowner, a real specimen of the Australian bush-lands. It was miles up country where I first met him, sitting under his gum-trees by a creek making his billy boil. He gave me a hot drink and I gave him a tobacco plug; and as the billy boiled up again he said: "Where yer bound for?" "Anywhere," I answered. "Wall, yer better come with me to Coomiranta Creek, ten miles off the western track, by Wangarris Yards; we can get plenty tucker there; and then on to the Sandy Hills and across Dead Girl's Flat into Hompy Bom, that leads across Gum Creek into Dead Crow's Paddock, two miles or more from Dead Man's Hollow. Then strike the gullies by Riley's ranch, and there we can get another stock of tucker. He's a real all right 'un Riley is, and not too bad either."

And so he rambled on, as he wiped his grizzly grey beard, a beard so thick with spittle and tobacco juice that it acted as a kind of fly-catcher for him; the buzzing insects flapped their wings and struggled with their tangled feet in that awful hairy web till they were swept into Eternity by his brushing hand. Indeed his companionship was greatly esteemed by me, for as we tramped along under the sweltering sun I walked beside him untormented by the mosquitoes and the myriads of hissing flies that like a swarm of honeybees kept on his side, following his monstrous bushy beard as we travelled south.

His whole life was centred on the various stations by the known tracks and the grades of generosity in the hearts of the overseers and stockmen. These sundowners arrive at the stations at sunset and appeal for work just as the day's work is finished and bolt off at daybreak into the bush, with their old brown blanket on their backs. Stolid old men some of them, they are real derelicts of the old days. They look like grey-bearded figure-heads of ships, fixed on weary, ragged bodies, as with their pipes in their mouths they pass and fade across the oceans of scrub, spinifex and sand, buccaneers on the high seas of Australian bush. My old sundowner hardly ever spoke as we wandered along under the gum-trees, as the magpies sat on the twigs and chuckled, and bees moaned in the bush flowers of the hollows. We arrived in a bush town of about twenty wooden houses and two shops that sold all humanity requires. I played the violin, and he was delighted when I gave him all the money which he collected in his vast broad-rimmed hat.

"I say, matey, chum up with me," he said, as his long-sleeping commercial eye opened and stared at the money. But I didn't chum up with him; I was not built for a sundowner. I recall how he always said his prayers after he had tucked his blanket around his body and laid his head on the heaped bush grass. He was old then. I suppose he's long been dead now, and lies somewhere in those far-away bush-lands.

I've seen some strange types in my time; but what are those types compared to the normal tribes I've seen and played to, laughed, loved and squabbled with. Little brown children clothed only in moonlight and sunlight, singing cheerfully by the South Sea breakers under the dark-fingered coco-palms. Sad little faces, some like deserted baby angels, looking up into my face—my children! Dishevelled, strange old bush mothers, crooning to their buds of humanity, tiny brown clinging hands and moving mouths at their kind, softly feeding brown breasts—my mothers! Old tattooed chiefs and grim-looking kings; rough-haired semi-savage girls; and youths jabbering in strange tongues, with hushed, secret voices, over the terrible white plague that had entered and stricken their primitive city of huts; the white-faced, fierce-looking invaders from across the seas. Ravishers of their maidens! The scum of the Western cities prowling about the villages that had become the hotbeds of lust and sin's terrible paradise. Missionaries, with melancholy, hollow voices, who seldom knew anything of the intense inner life of humanity and the great philosophy of happiness. Superstitious, bigoted old chiefs cursing the white man's Bible. Philosophical old brown men with high brows and keen dark eyes reflectively nodding their heads. South Sea Oldenburgs striving to convince grim South Sea Spinozas. Stalwart, dark tattooed Schopenhauers shouting about wind-baggery.

I can see again the ironical heathen chief sitting by his palatial hut. He is clever, a Voltaire of the Southern Seas. His strong face is tattooed; grim-looking are his little eyes as he grins and looks at the Marquesan coat-of-arms which he has invented and placed at his door—a large empty rum barrel and on top of it a Christian Bible!

I see the pretty Samoan girl, Millancoo, with lovely dreaming eyes and thick bronzed hair, with a red and white hibiscus flower stuck in at each side. Her brown limbs and figure are the perfection of graceful beauty, dressed only in a little blue chemise. She eloped with a "noble white man" to the Gilbert Isles, and committed suicide when he left her, ere her first-born could creep to her bosom and taste the only milk of human kindness it would most probably have ever known.

Earnest-faced Tippo, her sister, sits on the slope. Happy as night with its stars is she, with six little dark, plump children with demon-like eyes romping all round her. She has married an uncivilised nigger from Timbuctoo! O happy girl! How the natives chided and sneered at her at first for not marrying a great white lord as her sister did!

Beautiful women, and men also, I have met in strange places. I have found them in the hovels and among the scum of life, and sometimes in the palatial home of affluence. Convicts of New Caledonia in the calaboose or toiling in chains, breathing, yet as dead as dust, with hollow, sad eyes, corpses from La

Belle France—my poor brothers! Old men and women begging by the kerb-side in the far-away civilised Isle of the Western Seas! The old man in rags, a skeleton on tottering feet, shivering, going down the cold, windy, main road of the lighted suburb, singing, with a palsied old mouth, some song that God composed ere Christ came. He is my beloved comrade; bury me with him, so that the flowers over us may twine in our dead dust and find mutual sympathy.

I have seen multitudes of commercial burglars, wealthy villains, who fought so valiantly to save their own lives that they have received the commercial V.C. for valour—and penniless, profligate angels, fighting side by side in the battle of nations—that battle wherein the bullets cause mortal wounds, though many years pass before they send the bloodless corpses to heaven—or hell.

I have seen old, ragged, hideous, long-dead women still sitting by the attic's hearth fire, sipping the gin bottle—sweet-fumed opium for their spectral dreams. As they stare at the embers burning in the red glow they see their own girlhood faces smile once more back into their bleared eyes, with remembered beauty, happiness and glorious faith. Old *roués* too dream somewhere—the men who made the vows to those drunken old women and never kept them—may they sleep well, but never wake!

I have heard the majestic cathedral organ thunder its rolling music to the roof as the beggar passed by the massive, nail-studded door on swollen feet, rubbed his cold skeleton hands together and spat viciously. No food in his body, and his soul—well, why should he worry about his soul?

I have seen the great shocked multitude open their eyes aghast, and heard the tremendous crash, the clatter of the hail of stones, when the voice said: "He that is without sin among you, let him first cast a stone at her." O wonderful goodness! O icy, stony virtue.

Ah! not only in the wild Australasian bush or in the Southern Seas is the great drama of life enacted; the great drama that makes your heart cold, and the old warm belief become encrusted with icicles, as you dream over the strange lot of the wandering, lost children.

I've laid me down deep in the bush to sleep,

And wrapt my body in the sunset's blaze.

Then wondered why He made sad wings for days

To fly away—and all our world to weep.

Like to a myriad birds blown round sunset

In song, I thought I watched God's careworn Face
Brushed by bright wings—the unborn human race
Who did not want their mortal birth—just yet!

I heard the growing flowers cry in the night,
And trees—that whisper of old cherished things.
And still the startled, hurried rush of wings—
It was the stars sighed out—upon their flight.

O Troubadours, O Stars, what sing you of?
O wandering minstrels, is it to God's plan
You sing?—or to the exiled heart of man
Who pays with death's blind eyes and cherished love?

But still the children cry upon the plain
Beside a grave; and still the cheerful king
Grows fat; and sad old men say: "Anything,
O God, except to live this life again!"

CHAPTER XV

The Lecturer—The Italian Virtuoso—Disillusioned

Before I left New Zealand I secured an engagement to play the violin at a concert hall where the district assembled to applaud the talent of youthful pianoforte players and maidens who had cultivated voices. I was engaged to play violin solos, accompanied by the piano, and to perform suitable tripping melodies for old feet when the parents danced after the entertainment.

One night, when I was hurrying back to my rooms after the dance, sick at heart (for, believe me, I do not tell you of my many aspirations and the disappointments of those days), I heard a wheezy voice behind me call: "Hi! you, Mr Violinist." I immediately turned, and an old gentleman with a benevolent, cheerful face stood puffing and smiling at me. "Pray excuse my interruption," he said as he bowed; then he continued: "Ah, my dear boy, you are a real musician and play your instrument as though you have a soul; you remind me of my own youthful days, when I played the violin, by special command, to Queen Victoria." Hearing this, I at once became inwardly attentive. I had several manuscript songs that I wanted to get published, and no publisher in New Zealand or Australia would look at them unless I paid for the expense of engraving, so, not knowing what influence the old fellow might have, I speedily got into conversation with him—not from ambitious motives only, for he seemed a kind-hearted and intellectual old man, and therefore commanded my respect as well as my hopes. Inviting me into an hotel, he offered me a drink, and seemed very much surprised when I asked for "shandy gaff," which is a mixture of ginger-beer and light ale. I flushed slightly and reordered whisky at his suggestion, and, though it tasted like kava and paraffin oil mixed, I bravely took sips of it, while the old chap told me of his violin engagements and the praise accorded him by the musical critic of *The Times* and by personages in the royal courts of Europe. As I listened, and nodded approval and surprise, I observed him carefully.

He was innocent looking, with a cheery round face and eyes that were small, but vivacious and blue; his hat was neither a tall hat nor a bowler: it had a small rim, which gave it that clerical contour which seems to be worn especially to allay any suspicion that might fall on its owner. I would not reflect upon the appearance of this gentleman so much if it were not that his appearance helped him enormously. I am not going to be hard upon him either; notwithstanding his sins, he was at heart a kindly man; but Nature had mixed his dough with too much yeast, so that his aspirations to do well rose far beyond the range of his intellect and solid, commercial honesty. This was a fact that helped me considerably; for this commonplace failing of our race, shown in him, put me on my guard in the future and saved me much pain and many misfortunes in after days. I do not mean to be sarcastic in the foregoing remarks, though it may sound like it. I only intend to convey to those who have not experienced much the fact that all individual types of good and bad men you meet in civilised lands are just teachers in the university; that you must face, if you are not blessed with wealth, and go off to seek it. They give you experience, and make you a critic of your race, so that you can know and appreciate goodness, if in your lifetime you are fortunate enough to meet it. They also teach you to be lenient in your judgment of others, and by comparisons and pondering over their sins you will recognise your own.

Though the old fellow tried to impress me with his greatness, and praised my many virtues, I instinctively felt that I did not possess them. I also noticed that, though he told me that he had just arrived at Christchurch to give lectures to increase the funds for orphanage children, his fancy waistcoat had been brushed to death and looked shabby. This fact damped both my hopes and vanity; for I perceived that his praise of my violin-playing was inspired by very much the same feeling that made me repeatedly nod polite approval over his erstwhile fame in the royal courts and concerts of Great Britain. In short, we were both hard up for something that we needed, and saw that we could help each other by being polite and awaiting events.

I was young, and he was grey and old, and possibly had been a really good man in his day, till the soulful melody of heart-beats, called life, had gradually resolved itself into a minor key, and that drama of grey hairs and a wheezy voice that praised my youthful melodies in that saloon bar off the main road in Christchurch, New Zealand. He fingered about in his pocket, and I at once ordered him another drink, and inspired with bravery, through his shabby waistcoat, I boldly called for shandy gaff and pushed the whisky aside. We were now, by observation of each other's deficiencies, brothers, and though Queen Victoria's praise of his talent still lingered in my memory, I noticed that he gave a sigh of relief as I paid for the next drink, and at once I felt that we were at last equals. I will not weary you with any more details, but on the way home that night he walked beside me, and I agreed to be the solo violinist at the lectures which he was about to give in various halls that he was hiring. I was not to get a specified salary, but was to receive, which was better still, he said, shares in the collection and in the tickets sold, after the bulk of the proceeds had been put by for the New Zealand orphanages.

Next morning he called at my rooms at the time appointed. By daylight my clothes did not look as affluent as they did by gaslight. In a moment he noticed this and without any overture said: "Put your hat on, my boy, and come to my tailor's and get fitted out." I was astonished to hear him say this, and, not thinking my prospective abilities in his service might deserve such kindness, my best instincts got the momentary upper hand of those inclinations which are usually the strongest in men who have endeavoured to earn their livelihood by musical accomplishments. So I at first demurred, and then, overjoyed, went with him to his tailor, who lived not a half-mile off. He even bought me india-rubber cuffs, and the day before the first lecture came off I looked as well dressed as anyone in the district.

On the morning before the first lecture at the Suburban Hall I strolled down the main road and to my astonishment saw my name in large type on big white bills. If I remember aright, this is how the advertisement went: "Signor Safroni, the celebrated Italian violin virtuoso, has kindly consented to perform at the Orphanage Fund lectures"; and then followed an account of the lecturer's philanthropic and stirring speeches on behalf of helpless children. At first I felt annoyed at this being done without my permission, for I had a kind of suspicion that the old lecturer thought more of himself than of the orphan children, and I did not want to be mixed up with anything that was likely to look shady, both for my own self-respect and my youthful principles. I at once sought my new employer and told him, as delicately as possible, that I did not care to be billed as a celebrated violinist from Italy, and, moreover, not so very far off was the very place where I had been playing. "My dear, dear boy," he said, opening his eyes as though with amazement, "you call yourself a violin-player and are afraid to be billed; you must be mad!"

"Well," I answered, considerably mollified by the force of his arguments, "your bill says: 'The Right Honourable S. Middleton will take the chair.' How can I be both? And I know nothing about taking chairs either." "Leave it all to me; all you've got to do is to play the violin and make money," he said; and I went off, feeling a little guilty of ingratitude, for I certainly had a good suit of clothes on, and my expectations, financially, seemed very good.

Before the concert night my employer canvassed the streets, and indeed the whole district, and sold some hundreds of tickets. Girls even stood at the mission rooms and church doors and sold his tickets; they were given special permission by the clergy, because of the noble cause which my employer lectured upon.

When I arrived at the hall at the opening hour I saw a vast crowd waiting by the door. The old lecturer was with me and rubbed his hands as we went round to the back entrance to prepare for the concert. His personality was of the masterful kind, but, mustering up my courage, I at last said to him: "Shall I have to take the chair and make a speech?"—for I was still a little suspicious of my dual personality as an Italian violin virtuoso and the Right Honourable S. Middleton.

To my intense relief he patted me on the back and said: "Play the violin as well as you are able and I will do all the rest." My feelings were relieved, and the thought of how much I should get from the shares of tickets sold cheered me up considerably. Before I proceed I may as well tell you that though he professed to lecture for the benefit of little children and was deeply "religious," for he prayed so fervently before meals that I also prayed, out of sheer respect for his religious earnestness, as far as I knew he never paid one cent to any fund; neither did he pay for the halls that he hired, nor for the printing of his preposterous bills, nor for anything that became his.

There was a special dressing-room in this hall; it was like a box, and just at the side of the stage door. When the old lecturer was ready he gave the little door-boy twopence and told him to open the entrance to the hall and let the crowd in at the front; while the professor at the back groomed himself before his little pocket mirror and I combed my hair.

My heart began to beat a little faster than usual, for I heard the audience starting to stamp and cheer with impatience just behind the small door in front of me. The old rogue said hastily: "Go in and take the chair and I will walk in behind you." "Perhaps you had better go first," I said, and stepped aside. "No, no," he responded quickly, in his masterful voice, and, not wishing to appear nervous the first night, I took a bold plunge and suddenly appeared before the vast crowd of bronzed faces that made up that New Zealand audience. Had it been an ordinary solo engagement I should have had something to do and so have been completely at my ease. But when the vast crowd rose in a body and cheered me, thinking that I had appeared first to make a preliminary speech, ere the great philanthropist lectured about cruelty to orphan children, and all the other lies on his bill, I felt very ill at ease, and could only bow repeatedly and gaze at the little door, hoping my employer would step on the stage. He did not appear, and I think I must have bowed several times after the last clapping hand had ceased among the smiling ladies in the front seats, who were gazing upon me with evident approval, and at last, bewildered, I stooped to open my violin-case. I was about to let the lecture go to the winds and start a solo when suddenly the door opened at the side of me and the professor stood bowing to the audience. They rose *en masse* and cheered him, as I nearly tumbled over my violin and sat in the little chair which was the only furniture of the platform.

I felt like one in a dream as I sat there twirling my fingers, watching the old fellow as his arms swayed and lifted with his grey head toward the ceiling, and in fervent tones he told the audience that the Right Honourable S. Middleton had been suddenly taken ill, and that I had kindly consented to take the chair, as well as perform solos on the violin. I have found out since that this ruse is a commonplace excuse for a one-man lecture and entertainment; it saves expenses, and is practised at lectures and concerts throughout the world. He was really a clever professional liar, and the way he held his arms aloft and passionately pleaded for the helpless children touched the audience as though it throbbed with one large heart. It is a memory that I think would make the most credulous nature become sceptical when listening to shabbily dressed men who appeal for charity beyond their own immediate requirements. Though he had bought me a new suit—on credit I found out afterwards—he did not trouble much about his own clothes, but depended on the pathos of his voice and his grey hairs. I felt suspicious of the genuineness of his orphanage appeals, but as I sat there listening to him a sense of intense shame came over me, for I, as well as the whole audience, was touched by the pathos of his phrases and the descriptive figures which he gave of poor little starving orphans that had appealed for bread. Then, with his hands lifted to the ceiling, he held the whole crowd spellbound as he described a dying child's last look and words in a London workhouse.

As he finished a great sigh echoed through the hall, as though it was one sound from a thousand hearts that were bursting with emotion. His voice ceased and he turned to me, and as I lifted the glass of water to his lips I noticed that he had tears in his eyes; for his imagination had carried him out of himself and touched him as well as me. Then I stood up and played a solo, after which I extemporised an accompaniment to a sacred song which he sang; for though he was old and sinful his voice was mellow and sweet.

He told me he was the last living member of the Old Christy Minstrels of London, and from his manner and general conversation I still believe that assertion of his was a true one. I asked him once to play the violin, but he would not do so, though he could play the banjo well.

I have never been so cheered by an audience as I was that night. I was called and recalled. I do not believe it was so much for my playing, or for the opinion of Italian royalty and the Queen of England on my "wonderful" playing—it was on the programme—as for my being thought a friend of that old lecturer on dying orphan children. For before we played the National Anthem he told them that I had consented to go with him through New Zealand and play solos purely for the sake of helping unhappy children, and that I was to receive no salary. I did not know how true it was when he said that, but I often think how fortunate I was not to have been arrested with him; for, though I was quite innocent, I believe that we were both liable to penal servitude for giving those charitable concerts.

Before the audience dispersed the lecturer made an extra collection, notwithstanding the fact that each member of the audience had paid one or two shillings for admittance, and given sixpence for a programme!

At the hall door, after all was over, he interviewed many of the ladies who sought a personal introduction; we also received many invitations to call at their homes, and my old employer seemed quite touched by the many sympathetic phrases they poured in his ears. When we were alone he stood under a lamp-post and counted out the collection, and though I lounged by him, and gave many hints, he did not offer me a portion, so I asked him for my share straight out. He had promised me some money just before the lecture. "I dare not give it to you," he said. "I must first pay for the hall, the printing and the amount due to the orphanage; then, rest assured, my boy, you shall get your share."

Next day he got fearfully drunk, and I became convinced that he was not genuine, though the night before I had left him thinking that I must be mistaken in my suspicions. The very boldness of his bills and his plans would have disarmed older men, and I was then only about twenty-one years of age. I had given my other job up and so, for the time being, I was compelled to stick to him. He rebuked me for not saying grace before my meals, and I discovered that he really was religious in the common sense of the term; we even had arguments together because I would not agree with all he said. He was extremely happy and sang to himself all day, rose at five o'clock every morning and splashed water all over the room as he washed, while I complained and begged for another hour's rest. I felt envious and yet sorry for him, and myself too. When a man dimly realises his abjectness in the flesh he has begun to realise his divinity; the night of his mind, that was dark, becomes unclouded, and the stars glimmer forth only to sadden him. He does not feel any longer so ready to criticise the dark of his neighbour's mind, which is still happy in that night of intellectual blindness which is such a blessing to men who inherit the heavens through an acute squint. My swindling old employer rejoiced in this squint to an abnormal degree; he really did believe that he was a pious and good-living man. When I refused to work for him, and told him he was a rogue, he was so shocked that I even relented a little, and took his proffered hand when I said good-bye. He seemed to value my opinions, though he did not agree with them, and I honestly believe that, had he not had his religious aspirations to fall back upon, he would have fallen back upon himself and been a really good man.

When he left the district his creditors came down on me, and I had a lot of trouble to prevent myself being arrested. The tailor who had supplied my suit of clothes stopped me in the street; I lost my temper, and we nearly came to blows, and I was almost locked up. Next morning I called upon the tailor and told him the truth; he apologised for his remarks and refused to take more than half the money due for the clothes, which I paid him. I never saw the lecturer on orphanages again; and as it was years ago, and he was old then, I feel that he must have given his last lecture, closed his stage door for ever and gone away.

CHAPTER XVI

Homesick—Off to England—At Colombo—The Stowaway—Home Again—The Wandering Fever returns—Reflections—Outbound for West Africa—On the West Coast—King Lobenguela—A Native Chief speaks—The Jungle—King Buloa and the Native Ceremony—An African Caprice—Music—A White Man among Wild Men—Nigeria—A Native Funeral—Night in the Jungle—Gold Mines—The African Drum

ABOUT this time I became homesick and tried to find a berth on one of the homebound boats. I eventually secured a job on a tramp steamer, the s.s. P——. There was nothing exceptional on the trip except the monotony of the ship's routine. We called at Hobart, Tasmania, and after experiencing stiflingly hot weather crossing the Indian Ocean eventually arrived at Colombo. The natives came clambering on board and attempted to take possession of all our portable property. They are a dark mahogany-coloured people, a cheerful-looking folk. All their actions seem to be guided by a strong commercial instinct. Loaded with bunches of bananas, and baskets of oranges and limes, they ran about the decks, bargaining for old shirts and cast-off clothing. Over the vessel's side floated their outrigger catamarans, swarming with dark, almost nude men and women. Swimming in the sea were their children, shouting, "I dive, I dive," as they looked up to the passengers on deck, who threw pennies into the sea. As the coin reached the water down went their heads and up their legs, as like frogs they all dived down into the depths in a mad race to secure the coveted coin, which is never lost. At the moment when it seems impossible for them to live so long under the water the calm surface of the sea trembles at the spot where the coin was thrown in and up come a score of frizzly heads from the ocean's depth, and the winner holds the prize between his teeth.

About a week or so after leaving Colombo we entered the Suez Canal. It was night. As the boats enter the canal a searchlight is fixed on to the fo'c'sle head to illumine the narrow waterway that flows ninety miles across the desert. It must be an impressive sight from the desert, the steamer going across like some mammoth beast, with a monster eye in front and the port-holes pulsing light in the iron sides as the steamer moves along.

I remember one incident that happened before we passed the canal that night. I was standing by the starboard alleyway dreaming, and watching the stars glittering over the desert, as the engines took the steamer along at about four knots an hour, when a rustling noise behind some barrels startled me. It was quite dark, and the decks were silent, for most of the passengers were asleep. Wondering what on earth could be stirring in the gloom, I leaned forward and saw two bright eyes looking out between some casks, and a soft voice crying out said something to me in a language which I did not understand. It was a pretty little Arab maid, a stowaway, who had crept on board at Ismailia, where we had stopped for one hour. I lifted her up tenderly; she was as black-skinned as night and only wore a tiny loin-cloth. She raised her bright eyes and was crying; but I took her along the alleyway and down below, and by kindness reassured her. We gave her a good feed and then, tired out, she fell asleep in my bunk, and I slept on the sea-chests in the cabin. In the morning she danced to us in our berth and caused us great merriment. We sneaked her ashore at Port Said, where she had friends; she had stowed away so as to reach them. We gave her plenty of food to take off with her, and we were sorry to see her go; she was only about seven years old!

Three weeks after leaving Port Said we arrived in England and berthed at Tilbury Docks. The atmosphere of primeval lands, shining under tropic suns and glorious stars, faded to a far-off dream as the dull, drab-grey of English skies drenched the wharves and the shouting dock labourers.

As the days wore on once again the roaming fever turned my thoughts to the sea, with all the splendour of its grand uncertainty, its devilish irony and vicissitudes. Though the glamour of romance had faded, yet my wanderings and turbulent experiences had completely unsettled me; indeed they had unfitted me for the humdrum commercial existence which I should have had to follow had I made up my mind to settle in my own country, assume respectability, and hide, as beneath a cloak, my inherent vagabond nature. The feathered quill pen at the desk would have fluttered to fly, held by my sympathetic hand.

The old wandering fever still gripped me. I was always wanting to be off into the uncertainty, to be buffeting round the capes of unknown seas, exploring for the marvellous unexpected, standing on the decks of imagination, under the flying moonlit sails of glorious illusion, singing wild, mad chanteys over wonderful argosies of schemes that could never be realised!

Yes, to be ashore on some far-away isle, clasping the savage maid in your arms by the coco-palms, gazing in the delicious orbs of the Universe—infinity in beams of eyelight. To breathe the present, yet be alive in the past, far away down the centuries of the modern dark ages! To walk by primeval forest and tumbling moonlit seas where they break over coral reefs. To rest by camp fires and huts, talking with bush women and men, and girls with sparkling eyes, eyes clear as heaven with her moon and stars. To be back in the splendid aboriginal darkness of—as it was in the beginning.

Yet alas! as I dream the faint, immodest blush of dawn tints the distant sky-line. It is the birth of grief and beauty; awakening sunrise is agleam in her warm eyes; her sandals are dipped in fire and the stars are in her hair. Onward she creeps, in the beauty of her maiden nakedness, cloaked in glorious, unreal tinsel and grief. Blushing like a goddess she comes, treading the sky! The glorious, wonderful harlot—Civilisation!

It was a grey day when I next found myself outbound, going down Channel on a tramp steamer for the Canary Isles and Sierra Leone. I had often wished to go to West Africa, and so, when the opportunity came, I did not hesitate.

I will not dwell at any length on the events that preceded my arrival on the West Coast, but will briefly give my impression of things as they appeared to me in those days.

You cannot, however imaginative you may be, imagine you are elsewhere than on the Gold Coast. The atmosphere of the moist jungle, the barbarian hubbub of excited native voices, the beating of the tom-toms in the far-off villages, the toiling natives, driven by the loud-voiced white overseer of the gold mines, continually remind you that you are in the barbarian paradise of unconventionality.

For miles and miles the primeval jungle stretches; and standing on the hill-tops you can see the far-off native huts looking like groups of peg-tops against the sunset.

On the higher slopes, by the gold mines, stand the bungalows of the white men. They are comfortable inside and well furnished, sheltered from the blazing sunlight by mahogany and palm trees. The white men who are employed on the mines loaf about near them and the Gold Coast natives supply their wants. For a brass ring, or a piece of sham jewellery, they can purchase native labour, and for a pound or so buy dusky female slaves, whom they call "Mammies." Virtue is not the most prominent characteristic of Gold Coast natives.

As the white men sit in those bungalows by night they can hear the native drums beating far away, and watch the lizards and scorpions slipping across the moonlight of their bedroom walls, and, maybe, hear their comrade in the next bungalow raving in the delirium of fever. Malaria, black-water fever and other things often end the exile's career. At night the living can dream and think of home, and watch from their bungalow doors the little white stones and crosses glimmering in the African moonlight in the hollows where the homesick dead white men lie asleep.

SETTLER'S HOME, GOLD COAST

Though the gold mines lay all round, gold was not the essential requirement. A bottle of English beer, placed on a post by a bungalow or graveyard, would make a dead white man sit up and grasp it. Missionaries had been on the Gold Coast for years trying to reform the natives, who many of them had embraced Christianity. They often asked us mysterious questions about the white man's land, as though they were puzzled and could not fathom the meaning of it all. They had a faint idea that England was a land of some beautiful Golden Age, where sin was unknown; otherwise, why did the white men come across the seas to preach to them when the natives were so contented with their lot, and wished the missionaries to hell? So spoke King Lobenguela. He was a powerful fellow and when he walked looked very majestic, as he trailed his heavy blanket behind him. He lived in a palatial kraal and had a multitude of slaves, who washed his feet continually. He had embraced Christianity, and went off across the jungle to the mission room three times daily, and all day on Sunday. He was a typical specimen of African aristocrat and spoke fairly good English. His one intense wish was to see

English royalty, and confer some honourable degree upon them for bringing to his dominion salvation and Sacramental rum, which he drank by the barrel. The one ambition of the chiefs seemed to be to take the Sacrament. There they are out there, with all the old instincts very much the same, notwithstanding the introduction of Christianity. When the white races have educated them, and equipped them with scientific weapons of warfare, who knows? They may assert their individuality, and strive to get their stolen countries back again. The truth is often spoken in earnest! It is as well to remember that in those vast African territories many millions of fine native men dwell, with a muscular power and patriotism equal to that of the peoples of civilised lands. The moving finger of Destiny has always suddenly pointed to the hour of mighty events, with an ironical grin at our unprepared consternation.

The West African bush-land is the wildest under the sun. Nothing but short bush jungle and vast forests meets your gaze as you wander on from sky-line to sky-line in your caravan, and, as a ship passes islands on the trackless South Seas, often you pass a native village and hear the tom-toms beating away at their mysterious sound codes.

In those isolated villages, far beyond the outposts of civilisation, you will sometimes come across a white man who dwells alone with his memories. Sunk to a semi-barbarian state, they live with the natives, who have a deep reverence for them and their superior knowledge. They live on mealie broth and nut milk, and dress in the native style. When the white stranger from far off is seen approaching the native village he is carefully scanned through a telescope by the white exile ere the latter shows himself outside the native kraals.

Men of the civilised Western cities do not dream of the sad dramas of life that are hidden away from their knowledge far beyond the outposts of advanced civilisation. London audiences cheer and weep in the theatres as the curtain drops before the footlights over the mock-hero's grief. But oh! if they knew of the great unknown, the sorrowful dramas behind the awful curtain of reality.

While I was on the coast I made the acquaintance of an elderly tourist who was gathering material for a book of experiences. He was extremely fond of music, cheerful, and a keen observer of character. When he proposed to me that I should accompany him on his travels I was very delighted and at once agreed. We went by boat round the coast—he paid all my expenses—and visited a host of villages, finally going as far as Bamban and Krue, and many places whose names I have now forgotten.

I remember many incidents of those early days, especially a white-whiskered old chief whose name was Tamban. He was about seventy years of age, and had a wrinkled, wise-looking face and a bald pate. He loved to sit by his kraal, wrapped in his big brown blanket, and speak native wisdom.

He was dead against the white men, and at heart was a genuine old heathen, and no fool either. Though he professed to have embraced Christianity, and possessed a Bible, he had sold many square miles of his dominion to white men, over and over again signing the documentary deeds, with many expressions of loyalty and blessings on the great white Queen. It was afterwards found out that he had sold the same land to scores of different white speculators, who opened syndicates in London and sold shares to the unwary.

When he was in liquor he would reveal the true thoughts that burnt silently within him and longed for utterance. "Heathen, me! forsooth, ah! ah! measly, white-faced goat!" he would shout when the missionary approached him. "Bring forth the mealie broth and rum, that I may toast these white skunks speedily to their hell!" And saying that he would turn his dark, wrinkled face to the blue tropical sky and lift his war-club, and off rushed his womenkind from the kraal to do his bidding.

Then he would turn to the white missionary, who stood with his broad-brimmed Panama hat tilted forward to hide the grin on his lips, and thunder forth, his big black lips fairly flopping with drunken passion: "Who is this white God that you prate about? Liar! Show me this one shadow that is better than my fifty gods! Show me Him, and I will crush Him as I do this struggling flea!" and saying this he pulled his dirty blanket the tighter round him and then held up to our gaze a flea between his thumb and forefinger. Then, with a sneer on his lips and much blasphemy, he would continue: "Give up my fifty gods and trust to one indeed!" and then down he would crash his club, as all his old wives, squatting by the kraal, quivered in their skins. "Ah! ah!" he said, and his bright eyes winked humorously at the harem queen, a dusky beauty as black and bare as starlit night swathed in a wisp of vapour; "pass me the bowl full, filled to the rim, mind you." Then he would smack his big lips together and mutter: "Tribesmen, the white man's rum speaks more truth than his God of lies." The foregoing gives a pretty fair example of the real character of those old native chiefs and kings, who still cling to their old beliefs and yet profess Christianity in much the same manner as they do in the islands of the South Seas.

My friend and I were always on the move, sometimes riding and at other times walking. We tramped along jungle track for many miles and often passed natives who came by us in their primitive caravans. We would wave our hands to them and watch them go out of sight; for the tracks wind along by deep gullies, swamps and impenetrable forest lands.

We hired two hammock boys. I was pleased, for they carried my violin and my friend's camera; also a load of photo plates and curios. South Sea Island heat is wintery compared to the dense, muggy atmosphere of the West Coast. By night a white mist creeps out of the primeval jungle glooms; and at dawn the sunrise looks ghostly, as it gleams across the glimmering slopes and gullies, and sparkles a blaze of forked chameleon light on the jungle world. Far away the natives are beating the tom-toms in the hidden villages as you walk along like a man asleep and scratch yourself; for each night was a nightmare of restlessness: though we wrapped our feet up and sealed all the holes in our mosquito nets, we did so in vain. The mosquitoes got at us somehow, and their bodies were bloated with our blood long before dawn. Ants, too, abound, and they are as big as half-a-walnut shell, and go moving along in vast battalions, attacking friend and foe alike. There are centipedes also, and when one rises from one's extemporised bed they rush off on a thousand legs to hide from the sudden blaze of light.

Thick grass ten feet high, and fern-trees a foot higher, grow on the jungle slopes, and at dusk they are afire with crimson and yellowish blooms, tropical orchids and flowers one has never seen before.

One evening at dusk we arrived at a village called, I think, Kafolo. King Buloa ruled the dominion, and the priests consulted Ju-Jus. The Ju-Ju is a hideous idol, carved to satisfy the heathenish ideas of the African natives, who still worship wood and stone, as the Islanders did in the South Seas years ago. Polynesian Islanders are educated gentlemen compared with the usual run of West Coast and Nigerian natives.

As we crossed the river by a bridge of logs that divided the village from the jungle, we sighted a tiny city of huts. We waved our hands and approached slowly, with a little apprehension. The King (or high chief), dressed in an old pink striped shirt, came out of his kraal and welcomed us. His face looked like a black, gnarled tree trunk carved into human shape, till his thick-lipped mouth opened with a smile revealing three or four remaining teeth. He held over his frizzly head a large white umbrella, a present from some trader, which intensified his dusky shade. Out of the huts under the jungle palms came the ebony-coloured population—good-humoured-looking men, women, girls and piccaninnies. The King invited us into his palace. The skulls of fallen foes ornamented the door. We stepped inside the royal kraal and were somewhat surprised by the comfortable surroundings. Native tapestry, made of fibre and woven grass of various hues, covered the walls, and the floor of the first apartment was hidden by thick matting, on which squatted several ebony-coloured females, who belonged to the royal harem. As we entered they started jabbering and rolling their dark eyes. Chairs and tables covered with matting made up quite a decent amount of furniture, evidently purchased from traders. A Ju-Ju, surrounded by empty gin bottles, stood in the doorway of the next room. It had fierce-looking glass eyes and a face that looked half human and half crocodile. We expressed delight at all we saw, for we were alone there and felt that by being friendly with the chief we were keeping on the safe side. Then the old high chief stood erect and had his photograph taken; he was as pleased as a child with our attentions. I played the violin to him, and he was greatly delighted as I scraped away; his eyes glittered with pleasure and curiosity. I made him hold the violin, and he made several scrapes; his fat lips widened with fright until they reached his ears when the strings wailed. That night, as sunset smudged with a yellowish gleam the misty, heat-laden horizon, and a myriad creeping insects came forth to hum and buzz, Mr T—— and I graciously accepted King Buloa's invitation to attend a village ceremony. He made signs to us and said, "Much good you like see," wrapped a large brown blanket, red striped, about him, the very sight of which made us perspire, for the heat was terrific, and majestically slinging one end over his shoulder walked in front of us, to lead the way to the jungle ballroom.

I saw a sight that night which outdid, in grotesqueness and lewdness, anything which I had seen in the South Seas. The royal opera box was a square-rigged set of bamboo poles lashed together with strong native fibre. Mats slung over the cross-bars made comfortable seats, elevated about six feet, whereon Mr T—— and I sat, and the chief with crossed legs in the middle.

Four native girls had just reached maidenhood and had been sold to four respective husbands for so many bullocks. It was the custom to confer on such maidens an honour which, to Western civilisation, was one of great degradation and shame. Afterwards the girls were brought forth to stand in the middle of the cleared jungle, so that the whole tribe could gaze upon them as the festival dancers whirled round them. There they stood before us, revealing a similar timidness to that seen in a young bride at an English wedding. The King started the applause by striking a huge bamboo rod on the side of the primitive opera box as he drank large bowls of palm wine. He was soon drunk, reeled and shouted: "Fu Fu, Ki Ki!" The glimpsing moonlight streamed through the palms on to the maidens' faces and on to the dark hordes of shrieking natives who whirled around them. Those erstwhile maids stood embracing each other, then unclasped, chanted and clapped their hands in rhythmic motion, and then, to the delight of the assembly, imitated every gross gesture.

My friend kept close to me and I to him as the besotted King slipped off his seat and fell on to the next rung, still shouting: "Ki Ki!" One of the maidens was really handsome for a negress; she had fine eyes, full lips and a well-rounded figure of light mahogany colour; the curves of her body resembled a Grecian bronze. She stood for a moment perfectly still in the moonlight, with one knee timidly crossing the other, ere she turned to show her comeliness to the admiring audience! As they sang the native orchestra crashed away on tom-toms and wooden drums. Some plucked strings that were stretched across gourds; others blew, with their big black lips, at bamboo flutes. They played out of tune, but the tempo of the primitive strains suited the dance exactly. "Mvu! Mvu!" shouted the King, and then he made signs that I should play. Without a moment's hesitation I held the violin to my chin and played like a happy barbarian, though my heart thumped with apprehension.

Again they danced as I played on, and through my brain flashed reminiscences of my tribal solos in Samoa and elsewhere. Suddenly the circling ring opened and from a hut close by came the dancers for the second act. By the throne they ran, dressed in grotesque festival costume, painted in hideous lines of white from head to foot. They looked like hordes of skeletons from the tribal cemetery jumping round living maidens. So rhythmically did they whirl, and so fantastic was the sight, that they seemed monstrous puppets strung on wires pulled by some mysterious hand in the dark jungle; for often they would stop perfectly still, and then in the moonlight once more whirl away. How the audience of men, women and children stared and clapped as they squatted on their haunches on mats; and they encored just as they do in the music halls of London town when the ladies in tights whirl and jump before fascinated audiences.

There I sat with T——, gasping with curiosity as the King thumped, and playing on, far happier than when, dressed in an evening suit and tight, high collar, I fiddled in city orchestras, playing every night the accompaniments of the poor hits of the day to affected stage voices.

Notwithstanding the apparent lewdness, their innocence almost sanctified the smiling scene of dark faces, and I realised that it was but a custom truthfully expressing primeval man's original idea of the beautiful. So we were not shocked, though we drank deep from the whisky flask to steady our nerves ere the head chief sucked at it.

The tribe encored me, and I played again. To my surprise they got hold of the wild chorus of the Scotch reels and whirled around, shrieking it! They had musical voices and, I believe, good ears. The melodies they sang resembled wild laughter in song; the tom-toms banged and the flutes screamed between. This is the mirth music as I memorised it:

Reproduced by kind permission of Messrs. F. Pitman Hart & Co., Ltd., London, E.C.

Next day we were taken round the village and entered many of the native homes. They were snug enough, with sleeping-mats and bamboo furniture, and many boxes with little mats on them. In the corners were maize, yams, kolanuts and gin bottles; the chief ornaments were the skulls of dead relatives. Comfortable kraals they were, though the furniture seemed scanty and reminded me of the homes of struggling authors, poets and musicians in the large cities of the world. But these were happier homes; for the heads of the families were unambitious, save that they prayed for copious rains to fall on their yams and mealie patches. The richer natives wore ornamental garments and had honours conferred on them, such as foot-washer or mosquito-squasher to the King. Real poverty seemed unknown, and decrepitude and the complainings of old age ceased with the blow of a war-club.

Artists engraved pottery, and musicians were much appreciated. Poets were applauded, and in all the villages I came across were looked upon as exiled gods. When they spoke their wisdom and native lore were listened to with rapt attention, as though the great god Abassi had spoken: a strong contrast to the neglected poets of civilised lands, where poetic voices cry in the wilderness to deaf ears. William Watson, Robert Bridges, Chesterton, Blakemore, and all the other voices of modern music would have found a large measure of appreciation in that land, had they been born there; for it was an El Dorado for poets. As for John Masefield and Kipling, they would have stood on stumps and sung till all the coast villagers, through sheer poetic delirium, put out to sea for other lands and wild, poetic adventure.

Lovers of Wagner would have rejoiced to hear the strange primeval music, music that expressed the true barbarian note of joyous or wailing humanity; and after hearing that which I heard they would more easily have understood the deeper meaning of the celebrated *maestro's* compositions.

I played several solos to the King next day as he sat in his hut-room, and he touched me with a dead king's thigh-bone on the neck, and so gave me the equivalent to a British knighthood. We were taken before the favourite harem queens; they blushed and smiled, showing their white teeth, as T—— and I bowed and gesticulated our appreciation of their dusky beauty.

With all their apparent sins they seemed deeply religious. We knew not what their creeds expressed, or on what mythology they were founded. We only knew that Abassi and Sowoko were great gods, and their subjects were life and death, as in all creeds they must be. Their Ju-Jus were hideous enough to express the agony and ultimate end of all we know and all that is born of flesh. The Ju-Jus they knelt before were as deaf to their appeals as the images of the Virgin Mary and other idols of Catholic and Protestant high churches are.

When we left King Buloa we wandered on mile after mile and continually entered other countries; for you cross frontier lines at every river and swamp, and come across tribes who speak a different dialect and worship off-shoot gods: the Akanaka tribe, Egbosh, Apiaongs and many others. On the rivers sailed dug-out canoes, long enough to hold from twelve to fifteen natives, and smaller canoes wherein ebony youths paddled their sweethearts and sang the latest tribal hits.

All the villages were familiar with white men, for traders came long distances, from Sierra Leone or the Gold Coast, and from Calabar, to bargain for copra and palm-nuts and many other things.

Slavery was in vogue, and rich chiefs bought young girls and youths and took them into their homes. I saw a witch scene, much like the scenes I had seen in Fiji; hideous old women and men consulted the Ju-Ju, then haunted the credulous natives with lying stories and prophecies of good and bad things.

I played the violin to several tribes, with the special idea of seeing how my music appealed to them. Some were curious only, and others seemed to enjoy the melodies. A native girl from Sierra Leone sang as I played, and had a really fine voice, with an earnest note in it. I think the West African natives, on the whole, have good, musical ears and a genuine love for music, greater than that of the English people. I have heard native military bands perform, and heard no difference in the playing when compared, of course, with amateur bands in Great Britain.

THE FIRST MOTOR-CAR IN A GOLD COAST VILLAGE

In one native village we discovered a white man living. He was about fifty years of age, and very grey and sunburnt. At first he was reticent, but T—— got him on some interesting topic, and I played the fiddle, and then he opened out. I cannot tell his name or what he said. He was not hiding, but was sick of life and wished to end his days out there with those wild men. I can still see his blue eyes gazing at us, among the black ones, as the natives stood by their village huts and waved good-bye as we tramped off.

The population of Ashanti was very mixed. Moors, Mohammedans, negroes, Arabs and many more, who had emigrated across the Sahara to the West Coast in ages past, had left their types in the blood of the natives.

We went to Accra, Akamabu and Sekondi, where we stayed with an old chief who was about eighty or ninety years of age. He had white whiskers, and was shrivelled up like a mummy, but he was a most interesting man and spoke good English. He had fought under King Osae Tutu, the Ashanti king who in 1822 defeated the British, who in turn revenged themselves in 1826 on the Pra river.

Finally T—— and I took boat for Lagos and arrived on the coast of Nigeria, where we saw native life and tropical bush that differed very little from that which I have already described. All the villages were similar, and their semi-barbarian population lived under their old customs, modified to suit the requirements of the British Commissioners. The natives all seemed prosperous and fat; rent and clothes did not trouble them, so they traded, and kept the proceeds for their immediate requirements. The bush was dotted with mahogany, ebony, camwood and yellow-wood trees; rubber and oil-palm were cultivated.

Long stretches of dry weather prevailed, and then a thunder-storm came along and seemed to shake the very mountains; the natives put their gourds and calabashes out and the deluge filled them in five minutes. Rivers that were tiny brooks rose in half-an-hour and tore along in foaming, swirling torrents, washing a village away. T—— and I saved the life of a native child as it passed us on the thundering flood; it was still in its sleeping-basket and looked up and yawned, only that moment wakened from sleep, as we grabbed it and pulled it ashore. The naked mother came flying towards us, waving her arms; when she saw her baby, and realised we had saved it, she embraced us and wailed with gratitude. We blushed, and after the storm T—— got his camera ready and took her photograph. She was extremely self-possessed; indeed semi-savage African women lack the virtue that white women have— their colour does not reveal their blushes.

One day we saw a native funeral; I think it was at a village called Awakar. We were walking along a jungle track some miles from Ediba, on the Cross river, when we came to the village. It was the evening, in drought weather, and we smelt the village as we approached the clearing. The village orchestra was in full swing. Drums, native pipes, clappers, tom-toms and bamboo rattlers, horns made of elephant tusks, all were being used, and made, as you can imagine, a weirdly impressive combination of sounds. A chief was being carried to his last resting-place. We were deeply interested in the scene that met our curious gaze. Wailing old men carried the coffin slowly along, and kept spitting, for the weather was muggy and hot. The chief had been dead some days; the coffin lid was unfastened, and we could see the dark, frizzly hair of the dead chief's head at one end and the toes at the other. Myriads of winged insects and flies buzzed above the body and the procession as it moved along. The head chief, who was just behind, kept drinking *tumbo* (palm wine), which an ebony girl handed to him; and they followed him with a large calabash full to supply his thirst. T—— and I kept to the windward of the procession, and puffed vigorously at our pipes, and holding our noses we walked just by the side of the native military band, that played the death march behind the group. Right ahead of the procession, just in front of the hearse of wailing natives, walked eight elderly, stalwart chiefs, who carried a monstrous Ju-Ju. Its hideous, half-human face, with big glass eyes, stared backwards at the coffin and the procession as the whole group moved along. "Give me a pull at your flask, T——," I said; immediately he handed it to me and then took a gulp himself. Presently the procession stopped at the far end of the village before a large hut. We made inquiries, and found it was the corpse's late homestead: the custom was to bury him under the floor.

As they stopped, the sweating hearse of twenty mouths spat, and they lowered their grim burden before the hut-tomb. All the mourners commenced a weird monotone of melody, a melody that had bars in it resembling an English hymn. As we stood at the end of the village watching that heathenish burial, and the high priest lifted his hands and chin up to the big Ju-Ju's wooden face in earnest supplication to the gods for that dead man of his diocese, the scent of the jungle blooms came in whiffs to our nostrils. Sunset was fading, and as the coffin disappeared in the doorway, and darkness drifted over the whole scene, I seemed to be standing in the dark ages, alone in some vast dream of life's sad drama. But the jungle bird in the mahogany-tree started to sing sweetly, and then reality stole over the village, and I heard the wails of the mourners sorrowing over the blight of creation; real sorrow it was, and for all its grotesqueness the same as the sorrow of the civilised races. Still the bird sang over my head; it was a jungle nightingale passionately pouring forth melody as the native voices afar died away; and I dreamed on till T—— touched me on the arm, for it was getting late and we did not wish to stay on in that particular village.

We slept that night in another village called, I think, Eko. I shall always remember it because of the look on my friend's face as I shaved him. We only had one razor between us, and that was rusty. T—— was terribly scrubby and he said: "Can you shave, Middleton?" "Yes," I said; and I lathered his smiling face with a mixture of fat and swamp water for twenty minutes, to make up for the razor's bluntness, and then started on him. He was a handsome fellow, but as I pulled the hairs out in batches his face twisted and contorted till he looked like a Ju-Ju, and the tiny black piccaninnies of the native village jumped and screamed with joy to see the white man's terrible grimaces. "Be brave," I said, and away came the skin of his chin. Then he performed on me; but I was younger, and only suffered half as much as he had done as he scraped the down from my cheeks.

A few weeks later we bade each other good-bye. I promised to write to him but lost his address. I never saw him again, but I have not forgotten him, as he will see if ever he reads this. I have seldom had a more cheerful or intellectual comrade in my travels than T—— was, and I am sure he created fame by his facial contortions among the village children in the African village Eko years ago.

You are never really lonely in the African bush, for as you tramp along the bush tracks with your swag—a flask of whisky and insect powder wrapped up in your mosquito net—strange things follow you, singing and blowing tiny flutes in your ears as they circle round your head, a dancing ring of tiny bodies on wings. Some of them hum at sunset, and if you feel poetical you can fancy you are out on the lonely track, with all the stars singing round you, as like some burdened creator you mumble to yourself and move along with your myriad satellites following you. At night you are not companionless, for the festering heat makes you feverish and imaginative. As you lie down to sleep, after closely fortifying yourself from all living, creeping things, the African moon steals up the sky and noises sound in your ears. The hideous Ju-Ju faces that you saw yesterday in the native village emerge, grinning, from the jungle, to peep and dance all round you; some of them bend over you, put their wooden mouths to your ears and whisper: "Englishman, Englishman, go home to your people before you are dead." The fat lizards, gliding up and down the moonlit mahogany tree trunks, swell to a monstrous size as you watch, and jump right through your head; but pale shadow faces creep out of the jungle, faces with blue, kind eyes, and you recognise your own memories as caressing fingers, made of homeland dreams, touch your brow and at last you fall asleep.

I have often rested by the track in the lonely bush while birds puffed their throats and sang to me some sweet refrain that winged my heart overseas to England; and often at sunset a bird would sing a strange song that made me feel as though I had been dead for ages, and the sounds of the native drums in the distant village came from ghostly battalions of the Pharaohs, calling me across hills of sleep. My dreams have made me one of the wealthiest travellers on earth. If I can take my best dreams to my grave I shall be happy enough, for I shall own my own heaven and the memory of life's hell will pass away.

I remember once when I was tramping the Australian bush alone I fell asleep in a hollow, and my dead brother, who was lost overboard at sea whilst going out as a sailor to Australia, crept out of the gum clumps just by my camp bed and lay beside me. I was happy, and put my arm round him all night long; but I felt very miserable when I awoke and tramped on alone at daybreak. I tell you how I felt, because men feel as well as see when they travel the world.

If we could only creep across the years, and gather in a harvest of our boyish dreams, and live them all again, how happy some of us would be; now our days rush away like the waters of the rivers to the sea: we still call the rivers by the old names, but the singing waters of yesterday have gone for ever.

Our dreams are spiritual and beautify our brief existence. When we cease to dream we are truly dead; the memory of yesterday's dream gilds the hollowness of to-day as flowers sadly beautify old graves. I have often met the dead walking the streets, avaricious skeletons without real eyes, and have touched their cold hands and felt the chill of death. I have also met the living where I least expected it—in savage huts, in wild lands, where the inhabitants gave me their primitive food, with brotherhood or sisterhood breathing through their kind eyes, and then cried and sang as I played my violin to them. A bird singing at sunset, up in the banyans or coco-palms, would appeal to their wild brains; its tuneful throat expressed the voice of some infant goddess of their innocent mythologies: the winds stirring the forests, the noise of waves, all were voices calling to them from shadow-land. When the forests of those isles have disappeared, and the spires of the cities rise everywhere, the thundering wail and crash of the Fijian cathedral organ will fail to do that which the small bird did with its tiny, tuneful throat.

I have written of the seamy side of native life, both on the Gold Coast and elsewhere, but as in everything else the bright side of the sorrow is also there. Years have changed many things and the advancement of time has swept much of the dross away. The name of "The White Man's Grave" now sounds as primitive as "King of the Cannibal Isle" in Fiji. Where once the swamp mist lay yellowish in the hollows, sparkling atmosphere now shines; drainage is plentiful, so the evils have departed. The gold mines are run on advanced scientific and medical lines; forty miles from the coast are the Abbontiakoon Mines, and the Abosso, Broomassie, Anglo Ashanti Gold-Fields, and many others. Right up to Nigeria, with its tin mines, all is now healthy and cheerful. Elevated bungalows stud the heights round the mines; they are well drained, and as you enter the tent door of those dwellings, half hidden by jungle bananas and palm, you see the white man living in comfort and cleanliness that would often outrival the homes of his native country. The mine-owners pay excellent wages to the whites, and the natives are ruled by fines and kindness; to whip a native, or to strike one, is a dangerous offence.

The gold mines are a blessing to the West Coast natives. The wages they receive provide them with plenty for their primitive requirements; but they have to be strictly watched as they dig, for they hate work and will try all possible subterfuges to save digging to the proper depth.

Gold is found almost everywhere, but not in payable working quantities. The country is chiefly owned by native kings, who sell their territory to the whites who go that way prospecting. I have met men in London who owned large tracts of jungle-land in West Africa, wherein gold, four ounces to the ton, lay. They showed me the deeds, signed by the native king. But the next day I have met another man who owned the very same land and did not know the other owner; for those artful native kings sell the same tract of land to every white man who wants to buy it. So it is well to be careful in buying shares in Gold Coast mines, though the mines I have mentioned are equal to any in the world, and are equipped with the latest machinery. The managers from London go out there at frequent intervals, and the whole business is worked by educated white men. But for the black-faced natives and the surrounding jungle and bungalows it might be in London's highest commercial centre. Indeed men employed by them are better off than in London, for they give splendid wages, palatial bungalows and medical attention, as well as paying fares out to the coast, and home again when their employee's time is up.

The bungalows are all on elevated country and are consequently healthy, and now, wherever mines exist on the Gold Coast and in Southern Nigeria, you come across smiling Englishmen enjoying the wild jungle life and smoking by the bungalow doors, while natives rush about waiting on the Gold Coast potentates—for such they are. Often they go motoring, and the delighted natives go with them in the white man's wonderful train. When they reach the outlying villages the whole population rushes forth to see the car tear along the jungle track, and if the hooter sounds their black bodies fly off into the jungle in all directions, the piccaninnies too, all frightened out of their lives.

Often one hears the tom-toms and native orchestra playing in the distance. The music drifting on the hot night wind across the jungle is impressively weird and carries one away back, back to the barbaric ages.

The African natives for centuries have had a kind of mysterious wireless code. Warnings of the approaching enemy are drifted on the winds, from tribe to tribe, travelling through the medium of drum sounds, a tone code of quick taps and slow booms, for hundreds of miles down the coast and across country. If a great chief dies mysterious drums beat and are heard miles away in the next village, where the villagers beat their drums in turn and pass the sounds on; and so it goes onward, to fade with the sunset into the last friendly kraal of the dominion.

[From the Author's Military Band Entr'acte, *Night in the Samoan Forests.*]

CHAPTER XVII

A Negro Violinist—Sierra Leone—Some Violinists—Wagner—A Sea Chantey—Old Memories

WHEN I got back to Sierra Leone I was glad of a rest and stayed at the English hotel for a couple of weeks. At Freetown I heard a negro play the violin really well. He held the fiddle to his breast, instead of to his chin, and played Raff's *Cavatina* and *La Serenata*, very expressively. I complimented him on his playing, and discovered that a Hungarian violin-player had given him a course of lessons. He played African dances and melodies wonderfully well. We had a glorious time, that negro violinist and I.

In an old bungalow by a native village where soldiers and white men congregated we gave concerts night after night. The men came from far and near and joined in the sing-songs; our small, extemporised orchestra played homeland songs; the exiles shouted themselves hoarse. We made up part songs and put our own words to them, and the natives came from the village and peeped into our bungalow with delighted eyes and ears as we scraped away. It was there that I wrote the melody that is now the trio of my military march, *Sierra Leone*. This is how it went in the original setting; a few years later I made a military march trio of the strain and sold it to a London publisher. I heard it performed by Sousa's Band at several commemoration festivals in New York city.

Reproduced by kind permission of Messrs. BOOSEY & Co., London, W.

I have heard many violinists, among them Joachim, whom I heard when I was a boy. While on a ship in the East India Docks I obtained leave from the skipper for a Saturday afternoon off, and full of excitement went to Sydenham and heard the great violinist perform at the Crystal Palace. To tell the truth, I was disappointed. He played a Viotti concerto, stood like a statue, and his fingers and arms moved with the ease of machinery. His bearded face was raised toward the ceiling the whole time, as though he saw some beautiful sight in the sky above the palace roof. It struck me as a very refined and intellectual-looking face. His playing revealed perfection in the trained artistic sense, but lacked the fire and emotion born of the singing stars.

I heard Sarasate play at his villa near Biarritz. His nostrils dilated and pinched in as he played, and he had all that Joachim lacked (when Joachim played in public), for he was a spiritual player; you could have thought that the angels were wailing and fingering his own heart-strings. M. Ysaye played rather like Sarasate, but seemed more conscious of his own ability, which destroyed the atmosphere of the public performance which I happened to hear.

Kubelik I have heard twice, at Bournemouth and in New South Wales. He performed with Joachim's machinery-like ease; his double-stopping revealed the perfection of the performer's ear and the dexterity of the fingers that seemed to outdo the player's own heart; but it struck me as cold playing, as if the player's command over technique was greater than his musical temperament.

I have often heard it said that the marvellous technique of Paganini is to-day the technical equipment of all violin virtuosos. I doubt it. Certainly they are not mentally equipped with his way of playing. When you look at Paganini's compositions you see something that is the outcome of *one* personality, the white heat of genius who first discovered the musical gold mines in the depths of the violin. What must the man have been whose genius was so intense that he invented that which all others imitate and call their equipment? Paganini could not leave his playing to posterity, but a true critic can look at those individual compositions and dream of the tremendous passion that inspired the *maestro* to leave us those fugitive echoes of his playing, for that is all they are. Paganini played like an inspired, deep-feeling barbarian; his style was not artifice and did not represent, by artistic bowing and phrasing, the niceties of polite emotion and the artistries of civilisation. We have no compositions as he played them. He stood before his awestruck audience and extemporised melodies, chords, sparkling arpeggios and staccato and cadenzas, that were all half forgotten when the intense musical fury of his heart ceased and the magic fingers were silent; and so we have only hints of his style. His imitators scrape out phonographic records of his published compositions and say they are equipped with Paganini's art.

I heard an English violinist, Henley, in London. I was off to Jamaica next morning and only heard him by accident. A friend of mine said: "Come in this hall." We went in, and I was astonished. I thought at first that the violinist whom I saw playing, with Joachim's ease and Sarasate's passion, must be some foreigner; but he was an Englishman. His double-stopping was superb, with a passionate fire in it alien to Kubelik's temperament, I should think. Altogether he was really the most artistic and passionate player I ever heard, Sarasate excepted. While he played I realised that note that tells of genius, which makes you feel that the performer's violin and fingers are imperfect instruments, are not as great as the heart that is trying to express its depth of feeling upon strings.

I went abroad after that. I have not heard since of Henley the wonderful violinist. He was English, and I suppose London's fashionable musical world positively refused to go mad about an Englishman when so many German and Austrian violinists were about.

I heard "King Billy," the Australian Aboriginal King, play the violin by the kerb-side in Sydney. He was the world's worst "great violinist," made a squeaking row and thought more of the cash the Colonials dropped in his tin pot than of the melody which he performed.

RIVER SCENE, WEST AFRICA

An artistic public performance on the violin is widely divided from the poetry of violin-playing in solitude, out of sheer love to express the performer's feelings and relieve the tension of sorrow and joy that is oppressing him. When I was a boy, staying at Leichardt, in Sydney, I heard someone playing the violin and accompanying his playing with his own voice. The sound came from a little wooden house on a flat. I stood still and listened. It was dusk. On the window was a bit of scribbled paper: "Room to let, cheap." That gave me a good excuse, for I was intensely curious to see the man who played and sang so beautifully. I knocked at the door and was asked in, and I got in conversation with the player. He was a Norwegian with a handsome face, but unshaved and worried-looking. His wife was about thirty years older than he was, and as he played to me she sat near and her old wrinkled face beamed with delight as I praised his playing. He played by ear and was self-taught. I could easily see that. But he was a great violinist. He expressed his very soul as he played, in a weird, peculiar style, Norwegian melodies. I felt greatly drawn toward him as he played and sang to me, looking past me with steady, dreaming eyes as he extemporised sweet strains. He had hard, rough hands, through working on the roads. I saw him night after night. I thought at first that his wife was his mother, and I said, "Your son is a real musician." When he smiled at me and said, "My wife, not mother," I felt very uncomfortable.

He took her old wrinkled hand and led her into the little kitchen and kissed her tenderly. I suppose Norwegian women age quickly, or they had fallen in love with each other when he was quite a lad; but it was beautiful to see their sincere, sweetheart-like affection for each other.

He secured a job on the Broken Hill Silver Mines, packed up and went off to Melbourne. I never saw him again. I often think of him and his clever, handsome face as he sat breathing heavily and playing and singing to me. He would have been better than Joachim and Kubelik if he had had their technical equipment and no road stones to break and ruin his hands. I cannot remember any special feelings when I heard the great violinists, Joachim, Kubelik and Kreisler, except curiosity and momentary admiration, but the memory of the stone-breaking Norwegian's playing is as vivid to-day as then; and when I think of it all the poetic atmosphere of his playing still haunts me. So if it's true that Time is the great critic of poetry and music, then assuredly, as far as I am concerned, my Norwegian friend was the greatest violinist I ever heard.

It is difficult to define art. I suppose anything that appeals to the best emotions in men and women is art. A good deal of what is known as art to-day will soon be cast on the rubbish heap of the mediæval ages with the old ideals and idols. People move in the realms of art as they do in frock-coats; it must be just *so*, and must have three buttons on the front only; if it has four buttons it's not art. Art should be natural and oblivious of fashion, and, like true religion, beautiful in rags and tatters, pale-faced, walking the streets of humanity, singing with the birds and stars, and looked down upon by affluence.

Do the thousands who hear Wagner understand the depth and meaning of the music as Wagner thought they would understand? Do they hear the barbarian note in his music that tells so well of the savagery of the German people, the barbarian shriek, the exultation over the fallen and the tramp of bloodthirsty warriors driving the helpless victims of the fallen cities before them? I do not think so. It's fashionable, and to have heard Wagner is to be in the fashion, and so off people go and hear and see "Wagner." Most of them would more thoroughly understand and enjoy a phonographic record of a Solomon Islander's cannibalistic dance, accompanied by living pictures of the scantily clad native men and women, beating their drums and whirling round the blushing bride, clad in half a coco-nut shell and her hair only. Their funerals are conducted with the same austere art that makes them all go and see Wagner.

I like Beethoven and Mendelssohn's concertos, also Schubert's music, indeed all the really good classical compositions, but my memory of the old chantey, *Blow the Man Down*, as I heard it sung, and sang it myself, with crooked-nosed old sailors as we rounded Cape Horn, with seas crashing over the decks and the flying scud racing the moon, the old skipper on the poop shouting, muffled to the teeth in oilskins, his grey beard swinging sideways to the wind as the full-rigged ship dipped and rolled homeward bound, is something of music, singing and haunting my soul, that will only die when my memory dies. I can still see the crew climbing aloft and along the yards, their shadows falling softly through the moonlit grey sails and yards on to the decks. Melodies from the sails aloft, gliding under the stars, still sing beautifully to me as I watch the sleeping sailors, far out at sea, in their tossing bunks. Then they stand by the galley door, with their mugs for the hot coffee, while the chief mate tramps away the night to and fro on the poop, humming *Soon we'll be in London Town*. Then, as I dream, the sails crumble in the moonlight, the decks are awash, sink and disappear; sailors are struggling in the moonlit waters. Their white hands are tossed up as they sink, one by one; and now daybreak steals over the sky-lines that fence that vast grave of wandering waters.

Often memories play on the strings of my heart as I stand listening to the great orchestra of the winds fingering the giant forest boughs, or to the noise of seas on the moonlit shores.

CHAPTER XVIII

My many Professions—I turn Poet—On a Tramp Steamer—"Shivering Timbers"—Modern Seamen—Struck by Lightning—I leave the Ship

I HAVE been almost everything in my travels. Stow-away, sailor before the mast, bandmaster on a mail steamer, wet-nurse to Samoan twins,[13] bushman, boundary rider, woodcutter, sundowner, post-digger, snow-sweeper in North America, painter, deck-hand, "shilling-a-monther" in a liner's stokehold, messroom steward, native overseer, private grave-digger, author, violinist to South Sea kings and chiefs, solo violinist and orchestral violinist in the large cities of the world, music teacher, song-writer, cornet-player, composer of music for military bands, actor and singer, trader, canvasser for crank patents and medicine, banana planter in Jamaica, nut planter in the South Sea Islands, gold miner in Australia, violinist to Geisha girls in Japan, and the leader of numerous splendid schemes that mostly failed. Glorious schemes they were; but you can never be sure of anything except that you will be certain to attend your own funeral.

> 13. Their mother, a native woman, was drowned by the upsetting of a canoe. A Norwegian sailor and I found the infants, screaming, in a hut on the coast. We secured a ripe coco-nut, and opening the eye-hole in the shell, we placed it in turns at the mouths. They both tugged away and pressed the shell with their hands as though they were at the breast! and soon went off fast asleep. In the morning we gave them into the charge of a native girl, who took them both away to the dead mother's relations.

I have also been a poet. I wrote a little volume of Australian lyrics which are all burnt now. I was so pleased with the first proofs that I put them on my bedroom mantelpiece, so that I could see them ere I slept and directly I awoke at daybreak. The reviews in the newspapers and journals thrilled me. "Full of sincerity, spirit and impulse." "Marvellous descriptive ability." "A real barbarian poet of the South Seas." I thought my fortune was made, and I could not sleep through thinking of coming fame and fortune. I thought surely such reviews in the newspapers will sell thousands of copies of my book, and I was very happy over my bright outlook. It was summer-time. I became restless, and with the reviews in my pocket I went off, walking very fast in my excitement. I soon arrived in the country at a beautiful spot.

A windmill on the hill-top whirled its big black hands as though trying to catch the winged music of skylarks in the deep blue morning sky. By the lane-side stood a cottage for sale. The very place for me, I thought. I will buy it and write there. What glorious poems of Australia and the South Seas they will be! The bird singing in a clump of firs just by my future front door rippled out notes as though its little body would burst with joy. I took an old envelope from my pocket and started to write a lyric—how happy I was—even the lyric was good!

A month later I wrote to the publisher and said:

"DEAR SIR—Will you kindly send me a cheque in settlement for copies of my *Australian Lyrics* sold. I would not trouble you before the quarter, but unexpected calls on my purse have arrived at an inopportune moment."

Two weeks later I received this reply:

"DEAR SIR—In reply to yours of the 16th, no copies of your book have been sold, and we would call your kind attention to balance of £2, 10s. overdue for binding, and £1, 18s. for corrections in proof, etc., and 9s. 4d. for postage in sending out review copies."

So ended my volume of poetry, though I must add that the publisher turned out a good sort. I would sooner deal with publishers, some of them, than with stokehold bosses and concert managers. Music and book publishers cannot publish authors' inspirations that do not sell and keep the author as well. I wish they could. As for the reviewers of my poetry, they made me feel the happiest of aspirants for four weeks, and I feel grateful for that four weeks of greatness.

I think it was after a voyage to the Cape that I stayed in London for a week, and then secured a berth on board the s.s. *Port Adelaide*, a tramp steamer. We called at Las Palmas, and then went slap, bang across the world for Sydney. It was a monotonous voyage. We had a stowaway on board; they sent him down into the stokehold. He had been a London street arab and street singer, was a jolly youth and sang *The Ivy and the Myrtle were in Bloom*. Then he came round with the hat and got tobacco from the amused crew. The sailors encouraged him to tell his experiences and were delighted to hear how he carried parcels for passengers at the railway stations, and often bolted with the parcel if it looked valuable! He would finish, and then take his tin whistle out and blow it, do a jig and sing some mournful street prayer.

We had very bad weather after rounding the Cape, "running the Easter down." There were four passengers on board, and one died of consumption. He lay on the hatchway for two days and nights: the weather was so bad that we couldn't stop the ship and decently bury "It." He was canvassed up and weighted with lead, and seas came over the body all night long; we crept by it on deck like frightened shadows. When it was calmer the captain said the burial service, and then all the crew, standing round the tied canvas length, said "Amen." Then gently, with the chief mate, I pushed it forward into the grave of wandering waters and heard the awful plomp as it touched the sea.

At once the bell in the engine-room rang full speed ahead, the engines started banging and we were off again.

About a week after that we sighted a full-rigged sailing ship bound for New Zealand, a Shaw Saville boat painted with white squares. She was doing about twelve knots and coming right across our bows. The main-mast was snapped off by the main-yard and two of the boats were gone; she had been through some terrible weather. She came dipping and rolling by, so close that as we looked over the side we saw the apprentices wave their hands; we all waved back as she passed by, dipping her flag to us, and we saluted back with ours. I felt a choky feeling as I watched her pass, with her broken spars and torn sails, flying away towards the mist of the sunset, the figure-head with hands stretched in prayer at the bows. The white-crested, curling waves lifted their arms and plucked at her sides as she went rolling and pitching by. There was something in the sight of that beaten ship that inspired me with more tenderness than anything I have ever seen at sea.

I would often sit in the dim, oil-lit fo'c'sle as we swayed and dipped along. The tiny round port-holes lifted to the fall and rise of the bows, revealing the tossing blue moonlit seas outside. In that roaming home of merchant sailormen, at regular intervals, came the steady-drawn, thundering music of the steamer's onward plunge as the screw urged her across the world. From the middle of the deck roof swung the oil lamp, its faint beams showing the outlines of the huddled sea-chests on the deck floor and, all around, the narrow coffin-sized bunks wherein lay the sleeping or wakeful crew. Some snored, their bearded mouths wide open; others smoked and made ribald remarks, as Jim English the boatswain, a typical sailor of the old school, yarned of long-ago voyages on windjammers. A real old shellback he was, and the only sailor whom I ever heard use the expressions "Shiver my timbers!" and "Avast there!" I had voyaged in many sailing ships and tramp steamers, and mixed with many crews in foreign seaports, but never till then had I heard a living mouth utter those ancient nautical phrases so familiar to me in my old sea novels. "Stow yer gab," "Holy Moses," "Who the hell?", "Gawd lummy" and "Gorblimy" were almost the only typical remarks in which sailors of my experience expressed their various moods.

This old shellback, Jim English, was about sixty-five years of age, and had sailed the seas before most of the crew were born. Sitting on his huge brown sea-chest, he would half close his eyelids as I played.

"Give us that again, matey; my old mother sang that to me when I was a nipper," he would say as I scraped some old melody out of the carpenter's cheap fiddle, and his thin, wrinkled lips smiled as though he dreamed pleasantly in sleep. I never tired of listening to his yarns as he sat and took bites from his tobacco plug, his kind grey eyes moving quickly as he brought his fist down with a crash to emphasise the main facts of his wonderful tales. At night, when the wind was blowing and you could only just see the outlined forms of the watch tramping to and fro on the bridge, he would sit and tell us eerie things—how he had seen the phantom ship off the Cape on moonlight nights, dead shipmates climbing aloft among the grey sails, singing chanteys.

"Chummy," he would say, "my wife's been dead these 'ere twenty years, but often at night she sits on that old sack by my bunk there, looks at me in the old way and sez: 'Jim, keep off the booze, and don't make the round trip a dead 'orse.' And never a drop have I touched these ten years; and the old girl comes with me and sits there and looks at me with her laughing grey eyes on every trip now."

So earnest was he that our heads instinctively turned as we looked at the sack in the dark corner. We half expected to see his dead wife sitting there staring. He believed implicitly in dreams, for all the dire disasters of his life had been foretold in them. He was a kind of old priest of the sea; he wore an oilskin skull-cap and looked upon all of us as mere children; and we felt like children as we listened to his advice and experiences. He had cures for all our ailments, and was most superstitious. Once while he was yarning and sewing his socks he put one of them on inside out. Suddenly discovering it, he whipped it off, then turned almost purple to the centre of his bald head and said: "Now I've done it, mates! Some cursed thing's sure to happen before the trip's over. I've lost four shipmates overboard and all through them putting their socks on inside out!" As he said this anguish wrinkled his sea-beaten face, and I too almost cursed the unfortunate mistake. The sailors shuffling cards at the fo'c'sle table looked over their shoulders through wreaths of tobacco smoke and wondered. As for me, I believed all he said. My awestruck eyes watched him as he yarned on and fed my imagination till I was a child again. His personality filled me with admiration; I almost worshipped him. I really think if he had mutinied, and secured the old tramp steamer, I should have followed him, as a son his father, and thrown in my lot with him.

Nor do I exaggerate in saying this, for his weird personality took me out of myself and away back. He refired the magic blaze, the still smouldering embers of my boyhood's romance, and I was romantic, almost to madness, as a boy. Old bearded heroes, with unflinching eyes, stared through my memories, and fell, striking that last brave blow for right! Beautiful women, running by the magic moonlit sea-foams of undiscovered shores, stretched their arms seaward as the wooden galleons with reefed topsails stood inland for the shore. Forlorn, lovelit eyes shone like stars through the dead sunsets on the sky-lines of vanished yesterdays, till I heard the windy poplar-trees wailing in the lanes outside my bedroom window and the robin singing on the leafless apple-tree. Once more the stolen candle shone, and the light never seen on sea or land blazed through my eyes as I travelled across magic seas and enchanted distant lands, lands peopled with warriors and the beautiful creations of the torn novel by my bedside.

That old sea priest loved hymns. He was truly religious, and often sat turning the leaves of his well-fingered Bible. *Abide with me, fast falls the eventide* was a favourite hymn of his. I think I must have played it to him a hundred times, so that now the melody to me suggests ships far out at sea; and the old shellback, whom I loved, used to sit on his sea-chest telling us boys of the wooden ships that went down the seas and came back from other lands laden with scented cargoes, and that have faded away into the romantic dreams of this generation.

The remainder of the crew were a mixed lot, not very different from the usual run of sailors on tramp steamers. They were quiet men, and had little to do with the firemen and trimmers, who inhabited that half-fo'c'sle that was portioned off for them. I remember one of them was a "shilling-a-monther," working his passage to the Colonies for his health. He was a fine, broad-chested fellow, but in consumption, and whenever he was off duty he seemed to be busy rubbing his chest with oils. He had quite a dozen bottles at the foot of his bunk, which he had purchased in London from quacks: each bottle held oil that was a certain cure for consumption! We were very friendly with each other. I often helped him and, following his instructions, rubbed his back with the oils till the flesh was red. His little hacking cough would disappear for several days and he would be quite cheerful; then the cough would return and blood-spitting follow, and I felt very sorry for him, especially as, when he felt better, he would hit his chest with his fist and show me that he was at last cured.

Playing cards or dominoes, sleeping and smoking were the usual excitements of the crew. On duty, they washed the decks down with the hose, tramped their watches, rolled ropes, cleaned brass work, and followed the most monotonous life under the sun. After rounding the Cape to run the Easter down they became busy with the sails, which helped the engines, when the wind was fair, to urge the vessel on the lonely voyage. A trip across the world on a sailing ship is very different from a voyage on a tramp steamer. She rides the waves and seeks the winds, and like a mammoth bird thing, with men singing chanteys climbing along the bones of her spread wings, she races the clouds that fly overhead, and seems to sway the moon, stars or sun as she rolls and pitches along.

The crews of sailing ships when I was a boy were a different type of men from the crews of tramp boats. They were real sailors, or young fellows who had taken to sea life to learn to be sailors. A few of the old-time men among them, with their weather-beaten faces and old sea ways, gave that atmosphere to the fo'c'sle that has now gone for ever.

It must have been the romantic dreamer's paradise to go down to the sea in sailing ships before the world was worldly. I can imagine those old sailors, uneducated and superstitious, on the great ocean waters, watching the skylines and the dying sunsets as they dreamed of undiscovered shores, or by night on deck fancied they could hear the breakers beating against the starlit sky-line where loomed the shores of Eternity. Time and science have swept all that away from the sea for ever. To-day the seaman stands on the deck and thinks of the latest trade union grievance.

The ways of the ocean no longer suggest eternity behind the stars, or undiscovered lands afar inhabited by strange peoples. To him the ocean tracks are simply the main highways to New York, London and the Colonial cities, and to ports that are like railway stations of the high seas. Passengers get off at Suez, Colombo, Sydney or Apia and catch the next boat or train as the quartermaster shouts: "All aboard! Make haste, ladies and gentlemen." Rich puffing ladies and gentlemen with their daughters reship with their touring luggage for the next port, and they drag their deck-chairs and pet poodles behind them.

Old-time romance of thought has hardened and petrified into our stone carved, grey terraced cities; but the blue horizons of dreams sparkle on for ever! Yet withal, I have enjoyed two blessings in life. One is to have been born civilised, for I have never wanted to hurt a man or do anything really outrageous. The other is to have been born in civilised times that have enabled me to wander the world unarmed and safe; to have sniffed the tropical winds, seas and flowers of far-off countries, and gazed across primeval plains or on the mountain peaks of lonely isles; to have heard the mighty silence of vast forests and peered into the eyes of semi-savage peoples.

The cook of that tramp steamer was a strange old seaman, who drank gin and seldom spoke. He had a gnarled, stolid-looking face and expressionless eyes, very deep set. The green and flower of his youth had left him for ever; not a sentimental leaf or faded flower lingered in his memory.

He reminded me of the mummified, blackened face of an old native I saw once, who still stood erect, just as he had died, in the hollow of a huge tree trunk in a forest of New Caledonia, a tree wherein he had taken shelter just before it was struck by lightning! Heat had blistered the dead face till it resembled gnarled bark. There was still a glassy gleam deep in the eye-sockets, for though the eyes had gone ants had eaten the back of the head away, and so light crept through from behind, where there was a small decayed hole in the tree trunk. It was very faint though, and as I stood a little way off that awful facial expression reminded me of some hideous living mortal, whose soul slept, mole-like, in the cold, winter sleep of age, dead, yet still alive long after the real owner had committed suicide by strangling all his passions.

It is strange how such sights impress us and cling to our memory, for we meet dead men daily, whose faculties are fungus growths; we see their moving lips, shake their dead hands and wonder on the stony expression of their eyes, eyes that have not even the light of heaven behind them, as it lit up that Caledonia mummy's eye-sockets.

Our captain was a Naval Reserve man who carried himself with incurable haughtiness. He saw life's great drama and the light of creation only by being awestruck at himself and measuring all vastness from the soles of his feet to the crown of his head. The chief engineer was a jolly Scotsman, who tipped the convivial chief steward and so always had a bottle of whisky under his bunk. When he was "half-seas-over" he sang *Ye Banks and Braes* and *Will Ye No' Come Back Again?* as the engines thumped and the tramp steamer rolled and pitched along the highway of the world. We ran into terrifically bad weather, and with the sails set, for the wind was fair, the old engines crashed away as she pitched and the screw blades bobbed up behind.

I have never followed the sea directly as a profession, but I have lived and communed with the hearts of sailors, held their hands in warm comradeship, as well as shared their hardships at sea and ashore. And so I have read them as they cannot read the sea or themselves. To the majority of sailors to have been to sea, say for twenty years, simply means to them, "I've been to sea for twenty years," and means nothing more. To have been able to go to sea mentally, as well as physically, and to have been thrilled by the wild poetry of the wind's songs and the romance of the sea, is to be in a strong sense a sailor of sailors. While the average sailor can still chew tobacco and tell you the names of ropes, women and grog shanties in distant seaports, I cannot even chew tobacco; but I can sit in my little room and watch the thundering seas tossing by my bedside, ablaze with the true light of sea romance, while sailing ships, with their crews aloft singing chanteys full of joy, pass and repass through my bedroom door, outbound for the seaports of the world.

About a week later the albatross that sailed the winds with restless eyes behind us night and day wheeled round and put out for the open sea, for we were nearing the coast of Australia. I went ashore in Adelaide and got two shillings' worth of tomatoes for a treat. The man on the wharf helped my chum carry them. They gave me half-a-hundredweight for two shillings!

Adelaide is a real old Colonial seaboard town. I bought a good violin there and a lot of strings. We left next day for Melbourne, and I played the violin the whole way. In Melbourne the stowaway bolted, and the donkeyman swore all the way to Sydney, for the careful London arab started life in the new land with his "go-ashore boots" and shirts, as well as taking, in case of emergency, about forty plugs of the crew's allowance tobacco. We did not feel sorry for the stowaway in his venture in a new life; he had the annexing instincts of the old British stock, and we all felt he would do well in Australia.

I very seldom made a round trip and so, bidding the old boatswain good-bye, after taking him ashore to hear him mutter for the last time "Shiver my timbers," I left the ship.

CHAPTER XIX

Yokohama—A Japanese Family—Pretty Sarawana—A Tea-house Festival—A Geisha Orchestra—Sun Worship—Stowaways in the Stokehold—Reflections—The Kind Skipper

I STAYED in Sydney for a few weeks and finally got on a Japanese ship, the *Maru*, and eventually arrived at Yokohama. I had never been to Japan before, and after tea I hurried ashore. On the wharf stood rows of Japanese low-caste women, dressed like guys. They had black teeth, and faces that looked as though they were carved out of yellow wood, and voices that went "honk-ki-hong-ki-ko koo ko," as though they had an orange in their throats. Their toes turned inward and their eyes outward, and Japanese flies built their hives in their thick, matted hair. It was hot, muggy weather. I was very disappointed at first, but when I got up into the city and found myself walking among crowds of fascinating Japanese people, all jabbering and shuffling along in clogs, I became interested. I had some dim expectation of seeing bamboo dwellings and Oriental fairyland trees, with Japanese lanterns hanging on them. Instead of which I saw fine buildings, well-lit streets and beautiful parks with lakes in them, surrounded by maple and cherry-trees. Boats were being paddled on the lake by Japanese girls dressed in pale blue kimonos and with hibiscus and cherry blossom in their hair. You can never forget that you are in Japan because of the strange language that hums in your ears as you pass along, dreaming you hear the sandalled, shuffling feet of some old ghostly Assyrian city and the hubbub of the population talking across the silent ages.

Next day I went to Tokio; it was only a few miles away, about twenty, I think. There I saw real old Japan, and went off into the Oriental dark ages. I saw painted, red-lipped beauties with slit-shaped dark eyes and faces like dolls, being carried in sedan-chairs in copper-lid-shaped hats. Fanning themselves, they passed by and were carried to the palm-house and down corridors to their mats. I made the acquaintance of a Japanese sailor; he was a genuine fellow, and took a lot of trouble to satisfy my curiosity. I was introduced to his family; they lived at Suraka, if I remember the name aright. I went into their house, a wicker bungalow, and was greeted with, "O Hayo!"[14] Two daughters in kimonos, pink and orange-yellow, waited on me, bowing and curtseying in Eastern style. The old mother was intelligent-looking; she had a face like a South Sea idol, with kind, dove-like eyes. The room was covered with soft mats, and the walls, of matted panels, were carved with Oriental designs. I felt exceedingly happy as I sat by the Oriental maidens and ate savoury rice and fowl and drank saki. The daughters screamed with laughter as I used chopsticks instead of the fork which they gave me. I slept there that night and went with the family next day to see the sights, among them the

Asakusa Temple, where they worshipped the goddess Kwannon. Beautiful green lands surrounded the Oriental city. Sarawana, my Japanese sailor's sister, shuffled beside me, chatting away in Japanese as hard as her tongue could go, and pointing to the cherry and plum trees in full bloom; the quaint old mother and the others came on behind. They think a great deal of their cherry and plum trees, but as I gazed at them I thought of dear old England. I did not hear the blackbird singing in those cherry-trees; I only saw large crimson butterflies flitting over the boughs, and, on the fair slopes, strange bamboo-fenced bungalows, instead of the country cottages and smoking chimneys of Kent.

<u>14</u>. Glad to see you.

They enticed me to a tea-room festival, where I had a large bowl of tea, the national beverage. I sat cross-legged on a little mat by Sarawana, whose bright eyes sparkled and whose red lips often parted in a cheery laugh, revealing her pearly teeth. Geisha girls played samisens and biwas, and danced in Oriental curves round us. They were mostly pretty maidens, with small white teeth and eyes that peeped beneath their pencilled brows like the frightened eyes of squirrels. They had beautiful hair too, with a bit of the national cherry blossom stuck into it. As they sang and strummed on their stringed, lyre-like instruments they seemed perfectly oblivious of all around them; their oblique eyes seemed to gaze on something miles away.

Sarawana had been a Geisha girl and played for her living as I had, and so we became comrades. Next day I took her and her sister down by the river. It was a beautiful spot; the banks were smothered with cherry and plum trees, camphor woods and bamboos. "Why are you so sad, Sarawana?" I said as I sat by her side. Her sister sat with a Japanese lad among the bamboos just by. "Me litee Samaro, and he dead"; and then she sang a little Japanese song, after wiping her eyes with the big sleeve of her blue kimono. We were quite alone, only the little yellow birds twittered in the plum boughs overhead. "What does that song mean, Sarawana?" I said, and then she told me, in pidgin-English, its meaning.

"Unblown the cherry blossom blooms

Are hid in the cold of dead lips, weeping to blossom,

And crescent moons of coming springs

Are pale for ever in thine eyes—O my love,

Kwannon sits on her throne, Samaro,

Pale as chrysanthemums waiting thee

As camphor trees sigh over thy grave,

O my Samaro."

"Did you love him much, Sarawana?"

"Me litee him as the birds the boughs; the river cry of him: 'O my Samaro!'" Then I tried to comfort her. "Laugh and be happy, and come on the river in a pleasure junk," for as I spoke a Japanese boatman beckoned us, laid his rowing-poles down and started to bargain with me. Then Sarawana answered: "Me litee you-ee; Geisha girl want be ap-pee little while."

"Of course," I replied; and then she said: "Samaro dead, but he know me good-ee and white man know-ee too!" Then she lifted her pale blue kimono and revealed her tiny, clogged feet and ankles as she stepped into the junk; and by my side, singing melody and words that I could not understand, she went down the river. I thoroughly enjoyed myself, sympathised with the sad little Geisha girl, and admired her modesty and poetic tenderness for the dead youth that she loved.

I saw many Geisha girls and Japanese women of all classes, but they were not all like Sarawana, and so I tell you of her. Japanese men and women are very much like the white races; just one difference marks their characters with a ray of spiritual light: the girls, boys, women and men of Japan are poetic, everything about them is a symbol. A butterfly sat on Sarawana's hand: it was a kiss of her dead lover, and when it flew away it went back to his grave to kiss the flowers and make him happy.

The birds in the plum trees sing old love vows; their wings fading in the sunset are the beautiful thoughts of the dead or the living flying home to heaven again. Japanese eyes shine with tears of joy as they think of those things at which English girls and boys would toss their heads back and scream with laughter.

I did not return to my ship, but stayed at Tokio till my money had all gone. For a while I stopped with my Japanese sailor friend; he was a generous fellow, and invited me to stay with him and his people as long as I wished. I taught Sarawana to play some easy melodies on my violin, and I was surprised at the quick way she picked up fiddle-playing. She taught me to play one or two Japanese tunes, and I sat outside her bamboo bungalow and played as she sang, and the cherry blossoms dropped on us from the branches overhead.

I will not tell you all my experiences at Tokio, but I made a bold bid to get a living out of my violin and secured several good pupils. A Japanese lady of note was one of them; she was connected with the Mikado's Court and had relatives in Tokio. She paid me well, and I made good headway with her, and she was exceedingly kind to me. I also had a few Englishwomen as pupils, and went to Yokohama to give two of them lessons daily.

Sarawana persuaded me to get up a kind of Geisha orchestra. She played second fiddle and the cymbals. I ventured forth to a grand festival with my Japanese Geisha troupe. When it became known that I was friendly with the Geisha girls I lost my best pupils, though there was no harm in anything that I did. Sarawana's mother was pleased with our venture, and was delighted when she saw her daughters dressed up in brilliant kimonos and decked out in sashes of rich yellow and blue, with red flowers in their hair! I thought more of the novelty of it than I did of the money I might make. How romantic it all seemed as we marched along, laughing, under the white-blossomed cherry-trees in far-off Japan. I did not know that professors and teachers of English ladies should not go about with Geisha girls. However, I enjoyed myself, and my memory of Sarawana and Tince, her sister, as I called her, and her Geisha friends is sweeter to me than the memory of those pupils I lost.

My Geisha troupe failed, and I secured an engagement as violinist at a missionary hall. Sarawana and her family attended the meetings. I worked there for about three weeks and received a good salary; it was easy, but unmusical, work. I had to play the mission harmonium twice a day, on Sundays three times. The hall was always crammed with converts: old men, young men and girls, some of them dressed in Japanese costume and others in European. Some wore tall hats and white collars; they sang English hymns, though the words were translated into Japanese. The old men and women sang very much out of tune, but looked very earnest; their wooden mouths opened and shut as I scraped away. The mission was conducted by English women missionaries, as well as by men. The Japanese women were very decent people, and when I left they made a collection for me and handed me quite a considerable sum. I composed a hymn and dedicated it to the society, but whether they ever published it or not I do not know; they said they would. When I bade my Japanese friends good-bye they seemed sorry to see me go, especially Sarawana and my sailor comrade. He had a wooden-looking face that smiled eternally, like a carved idol. When he was fast asleep on his mat beside me he still smiled, and so he was a good comrade, for I was subject to fits of depression, and when the little Japanese maid would play her lament and sing of her dead lover I used to wish she was not so faithful.

I was then about twenty-two years of age and had seen much of the world. Very often I would lie awake for hours thinking of things that should have happened, considering the great faith I had in them.

I sometimes thought of going back to England and settling down as a violinist, but then the thought of my country's terrible decorum quashed my longing. I had been a good deal in Queensland and had several good friends there; sad memories, too, of a bush girl's grave by the swamp oak gullies. Sometimes I longed for Australian bush scenes as a lad longs for his own country. I had been to Sydney, Melbourne, Adelaide and Brisbane several times since I first saw them, but things even in one short absence were rapidly changing. As the ships came in crammed with emigrants from all parts of the world the surrounding bush-land of the seaboard cities and towns was cut down and up went thousands of wooden houses. And so old spots disappeared with the bush-land which the Australian hates. If you say to a Colonial "I have been across hundreds of miles of your bush-land with my swag, camping out," he hangs his head with shame, blushes and says: "I know, I know; but we hope soon to cut it all down. I suppose you've seen our towns?"

There is no doubt about it, the majority of Australians born are ashamed of the wild bush-lands, and love the streets and spires and walls of bricks and mortar. Up country it's all emigrant Englishmen, and a few Australians who were born there and so could not help themselves. As for me, I loved the bush and my memories of the bush, and when I went to the old spots and saw wooden homesteads standing on the slopes where I camped by my bush fire I felt sad about it, even world-weary and old as I looked across the few years and saw the hollows and far-off forest trees waving in the moonlight dusk for miles and miles along the shores of my memory.

So I began to think of Australia again as I lay in bed at the Grand Hotel, Yokohama, and dreamt of my old days there. I could not go back to Tokio, at least anywhere near the mission folk, for I had told them I was going straight back to England. I had really intended doing so, but I thought I could get a berth on a ship and save my few pounds instead of paying for my passage. In the end I was left almost penniless and stranded in Yokohama. I lodged for a while at a European's house. He had married a Japanese woman and kept a kind of sailors' lodging-home. I had some strange companions in my rooms; I think they were Moslem, Buddhist and Brahmin men. They were fierce-looking fellows, wore white turbans and had swarthy faces with curly, close-cropped beards. They knelt on little mats and prayed and chanted day and night. I found out after that one or two of them were Mohammedans. Their ancient-looking faces wore an Omar-Khayyám-like expression; from them I heard about Astoreth and Osiris, Allah, Mahomet, and a lot more about Oriental and Eastern creeds. I noticed that they were all very earnest in their prayers, and when I walked suddenly into my room to fetch my violin one evening two of them were kneeling in prayer at the window, worshipping the sunset. They never turned a hair at my interruption, but went on pouring forth solemn, strange words to the dying fires of Japan's horizon. It seemed to me then and now that all the so-called creeds were but one vast monotheistic cry in various dialects, each creed a different expression only, all of them instruments in the vast orchestra of life's drama, playing for the same end—universal, hopeful harmony. The stars vary in magnitude and position, but they are all singing the same earnest melody; for they too are finite, and sing on as those strange men did in the Japanese doss-house at Yokohama.

I strolled along the wharfs at Yokohama harbour with a young English sailor whom I met at the lodging-home. We were both extremely hard up. Alongside the wharf lay the s.s. *Port Piree*, and we resolved to make a dash for it and stow away. She was due to leave at sunset. The funnel was belching forth smoke; the sailors were standing with their friends on deck. With my violin in my hand I walked straight up the gangway, my comrade just behind me. I was well dressed, and the quartermaster bowed as I slipped on deck and asked to see the skipper. "He's in his cabin, I think, sir!" "All right," I said, and beckoning my friend as though he were my valet, I walked across the deck and along the starboard alleyway. We stood by the stokehold entrance and waited our chance. The hatchway to the coal bunkers was open. "Now!" I said. In a moment we had taken the final plunge and disappeared in the ship's bowels. Scrambling across the coal, we huddled close together and waited. It seemed ages before she went, and then we heard the rattling, rusty chain of the anchor coming up and the throb of the winches, and the engines started; we were off. My dear old comrade beside me, breathing in the darkness, was worth his weight in gold. "We're off now, Jack," I said, and he answered: "God knows where to, I don't!" and laughed. We had some boiled eggs and a cooked fowl, so we ate something and then slept. When we awoke the boat was rolling heavily; it was dark, though possibly daylight up on deck. I curled up by my chum and slept again. Three days after we emerged, starving and sweating, choked with coal-dust and looking like two dissipated negroes.

The chief mate said "Hello?" and we gave a grim smile as he said: "I shall have to take you fellows up to the skipper." Up we went and stood on the bridge. The skipper gazed at us through the hot sunshine for a moment sternly. No land in sight as the boat cut across the Pacific at twelve knots. "Put them in the stokehold," he said, and then turned on his heel and started tramping the bridge once more.

By heavens! I was not built for stokehold work. For a week we shovelled coal, and became like skeletons, sweating all our vigour away. Then I played the violin to the engineers, and their chief got the head steward to appeal for my services in the saloon. My comrade had to work still in the stokehold, but I took care that he had good food. I commandeered tins of stewed Californian pears and meat, and built his strength up. He swallowed them down with coal-dust and repaid me with grateful eyes.

For out at sea with sailors a fellowship exists that is almost unknown in the cities of the world. I suppose a ray of the illimitable gets into their brains. The vastness of the ocean, its endless sky-lines, and the ships appearing through them with singing sailors aloft, then passing away, just as stars pass singing something in the uncounted ages of God: these things unconsciously influence their souls and they become children again, forgetting the respectability of civilisation and feeling the humanity that makes men die for each other in the desert spaces and oceans of the world.

Men slumbering in affluence and the tribal pride of some dubious ancestry often appear soulless. Suddenly stricken with some grief or poverty, they reveal something really decent in their natures, something that longed for recognition when the body waxed fat on food and pride—pride in the barbarian deeds of their ancestors, deeds which done now would get the doer ten years in Sing Sing or Wormwood Scrubbs. There's nothing like living on "hard tack" in a tramp steamer's fo'c'sle, or on crab-apples in the Australian bush, or in cities by playing the violin, to bring out the best or worst in men. Sorrow writes the true Bible of the universe and expresses all the poetry of existence.

BOTANICAL GARDENS, BALLARAT, N.S.W.

Though I have seen much of the world and had many downfalls, the atmosphere of my boyhood and its ideals remains. I still have deep faith in God's merciful Providence, in the friendship of men, and in the earnest love of women. The old heroes of my dreaming boyhood still move with me as I travel on; the kindly eyes of earnest men and women shine through the mists of my memories and sweeten with light my dreaming existence; not till I die will they die. I love to hear the laughter of children; their innocent voices and little wails of grief express to me cries from the great heart of music, till I fancy I can see the flowers growing over their inevitable graves. In that feeling I love all men and women; and those who have sinned have my unknown sympathy as well as my unknown love.

Could I have my own way I would lead a vast army to demolish the mighty cathedrals and churches of Europe, and to rob the wealth of the altars, selling the debris and giving the proceeds of the glorious battle in the cause of true religion to the thousands of starving little city children, providing covering for their tiny emaciated bodies. God would be my best friend in fighting for his helpless family and providing comfort for deserted women and fallen men. There is more true unselfish religion in saving a butterfly's life than in moaning for many years in a cathedral pew about your next lease of life.

But to return to my travels and troubles.

I well remember that stowaway trip. The boat was bound for Sydney. We had beautiful weather, and when I was a legitimate member of the crew I did not regret my headlong dip into the stokehold. My comrade and I were treated well, and my violin brought me respect and applause when I played in the saloon concert. My fiddle has always been a dear friend, and wailed passionately on my behalf when I have been in disgrace. I don't think I could find a more trustful and soulful companion if I started off to tramp the world again to-morrow.

As we were flying through Sydney Heads we received a message from the captain. He wanted to see my comrade and me on the bridge. He was an elderly, short-bearded man with kind eyes. "Well," he said, "I shall have to hand you two over to the authorities when we get in. Have you anything to say for yourselves?"

"No, sir," I said; "only we are sorry for stowing away, and wish to thank you for your kindness to us under such circumstances."

He said "Um," and then stopped walking to and fro to say: "Have you got any money?"

"Yes, sir," I said. "We'll go ashore and clear as soon as we get alongside."

"I'll let you off this time."

We both thanked him, and half-an-hour after the chief mate came up to us, and saying, "Here you are," handed us ten shillings each. They do not always do that when you stowaway, but that was my lucky experience. I can assure you that seafaring men are the bravest and kindest in the world; they know it and its ways by instinct. Whenever I hear of a captain going down with his ship a lump comes up in my throat.

CHAPTER XX

Bombay—My Brother's Grave—London Streets—Outward Bound—I play at Government House—Ballarat—Mosquitoes—Sightseeing in New Zealand—A Maori Dance

MY next trip took me to Bombay, where I stayed for a few days at the English hotel by Fort Hill. The tropical scenery struck me as very similar to that which I had seen at Colombo, and the heat as terrific, though feathery tamarisks and palms shaded the tracks. The white population were waited on by the natives. My father was correspondent for *The Indian Times* and my parents had lived in Bombay before I was born. They knew a great many people there. In my pocket I had a letter from home. "If you go to Bombay do go and see Mr and Mrs C——, and whatever you do, dear, be well dressed." I had heard a lot about those great people when I was a schoolboy, so I did as I was bid and dressed up like a prince. When I arrived at the aristocratic, verandahed building I carefully dusted my boots with my handkerchief and knocked. When the door opened, and I gave my name to the native servants, an old man, the great C—— himself, came forward. He was polite to me, and I was the best-dressed man in the house, so I did not begrudge the money I had paid for the loan of the suit at the Bombay tailor's!

Before I left Bombay I went to see my little brother's grave, Gerald Massey S. Middleton. He was buried at Colabba Point, and I discovered his grave at last. A tamarisk tree was growing on it and a few strange flowers. I felt the kinship of that little grave in a strange land; the earth did not hide from imagination's eyes the little dust beneath, which would have been my big brother if he had lived. I remembered my mother and father saying how they had felt when their ship went by Colabba Point, homeward bound for England, and they stood on deck and gazed inland and thought of their child being left behind. I knew how they must have felt as I stood there alone and gazed upon the little stone set between two large vaults. I felt intensely lonely. The Indian bees moaned in the flowers and palms. I saw my mother, a girl in years that day, standing weeping by her lost child; she still stood there in the sunset and shadow as I dreamed. I kissed her, picked a flower and then walked away, the one solitary mourner that had come after many years, and probably the last.

Next day I joined my ship and arrived in London six weeks later, only again to get a berth and go seaward, for the grim respectability of the city soon haunted me with its stony, nightmare eyes. The very atmosphere seemed to whisper: "Englishman, Englishman, are you respectable? Where's your Bible, your rent-book and your marriage certificate?" I seemed to hear that humming in my ears as I walked through London's streets, miserably cold. I shivered, and jumped into a cab at Waterloo and rushed off to Poplar. There was a man who lived there, in Abbot's Road, who was a crack hand at getting berths on the ships for us.

In a week I was off down Channel, on a Shaw-Saville boat, bound for New Zealand and Australia, as happy as a swallow flying South. The music of the sails, bellowing out and flopping to rest, the rattling rigging, the sailors talking and singing on deck, made me feel intensely happy, and yet half miserable as I thought of the ship sailing across the world to a civilised port. I stood on deck wishing there were undiscovered shores where waves sang, never seen by human eyes, and dreaming of old pioneers and heroes of far-off ages. I seemed to realise at a very early age that the light of the Universe, the sun and stars were my religion, and their mystery my unfathomable mistress with divine eyes.

When the tramp steamer, after toiling along for weeks at sea, sighted land I stood on her deck the longest, as the far-off shores shaped themselves, and fancied I could see the old wooden pioneer ships and galleons that discovered them still hugging the misty shore as sunset died. Often when far out at sea I would stand on the poop by night for hours, gazing astern, watching the star-like eyes of the albatrosses, flitting on the restless winds, till they seemed old heroes, my comrades out of their graves, on beautiful wings following the new ships. Then the mate would touch me on the shoulder and say: "Now then, young man, you didn't come to sea to dream." The crew holystoned the decks, the cook swore in the galley as only a sea-cook can swear, and the cabin-boy, who had never been to sea before, said, "Is that New Zealand?" and pointed shoreward. As we rolled along, with all sails set, he stood on his head as soon as my back was turned, for I saw him in the glass of the saloon port-holes. I knew how he felt.

I returned to England on the same ship and then got a berth on the *Seneska* and went to America. A few years later, and I was again in Australia, on the P. & O. liner *Britannia*.

A strike was on, and we lay out in Sydney Harbour for two weeks and used to go ashore in a tender every evening. One night I went ashore and played at a private concert out at Pott's Point, and stayed the night as well. It was a wedding festival, and my host and hostess were kind, Bohemian folk, relations of Sir Henry Parkes. I cannot remember their name. They used their influence and secured me a position to play at the Government House balls in Sydney. I did so well that I got my box off my ship and left.

At Government House I played as a solo my own composition, *The Monk's Dream*, which I had arranged for violin and pianoforte, and *A Soldier's Dream Waltz*, with variations. Among the audience was the present Lieutenant James Ord Hume, who was on a tour through Australia, as adjudicator for the great military and brass band contests of Australia and New Zealand. Hearing me play, and finding that the solo was my own composition, he complimented me, and asked me to go to see him at the Occidental Hotel. I had a very good time there, for he was most hospitable. He was then about to leave Sydney for Ballarat. "Would you like to come on a trip with us?" he said. "Certainly," I answered, for I had a considerable amount of money just then and felt that a holiday would do me good. Mr Hume had not been to Ballarat before and was delighted with the scenery passing over the Blue Mountains.

In Ballarat we had various experiences, and I worked, digging for gold, down the chief gold mine, the War-Hoop Mine. We went outside the town and got into the bush too; for though Ballarat is a beautiful town, with splendid buildings, one can walk in a very short time right into the bush and see scenery equal to the Queensland landscape. The Botanical Gardens are also very beautiful and reveal patches of primeval Australia. We took snapshots of the Wendowee lakelet, because of the pretty little plump Colonial girls standing by the banks; they were nut-brown with the sun.

Mr Ord Hume went out to see a friend who lived in the bush, but we only stayed two nights. There was a stable and swamp near our bedroom window, and when, after enjoying the squatter's hospitality and a musical evening, we went to bed, though we rubbed ourselves with kerosene oil and smoked, the mosquitoes charged down on our feet and faces in Hunnish regiments. At midnight we called our host, and he came to our door in his nightshirt and told us to rub some whisky on our faces and on our feet, and gave us a full bottle of the best brand. Directly he had gone we closed the door, wiped the sweat from our perspiring brows and drew the cork to rub our ravaged bodies.

"Don't you think if we took the stuff internally and then smoked that our breath full of the fumes would keep the cursed mosquitoes off?" I suggested. Mr Hume quite agreed with my suggestion, which eventually turned out to be a most disastrous one for the mosquitoes, for we drank the whole bottle and then went to sleep, and never felt one mosquito bite the night through, nor did we wake till long after sunrise.

I think it was four days before the great band contest, which Mr Ord Hume was in Ballarat to adjudicate on, came off. The whole of Ballarat came to it. It was at that contest that I first became enthusiastic over bands. I felt the fire and go in the Australians' performances; their bands cannot be beaten the world over.

We saw a good deal of life in Australia together before I left Lieutenant J. Ord Hume, a few weeks after the Ballarat concert, arranging to see him later in New Zealand, where he was going to adjudicate at other band contests.

I went as a passenger on a boat to New Zealand, and when I had been a few days in Auckland I saw by the newspapers that Mr Hume had arrived to judge the great New Zealand band competitions at Masterton and elsewhere. I managed to be there. The weather was glorious, also the applause of the New Zealanders as the bands marched by.

I travelled with Mr Hume by train over the Rimnatuka Mountain from Wellington to Masterton. It took three engines to take the train over the rocky ledges and slopes. The grade is one in fifteen in many places. The bush-land and mountain scenery is equal to anything in Australia, for the scenery of New Zealand is wildly magnificent.

After Mr Ord Hume had judged and conducted the massed band performances at Auckland he kindly invited me to join him, and we went off sight-seeing, visiting bush-lands, rivers and hot springs, old tribal battle spots and Maoris in their pahs. Maori guides led us up mountains and across volcanic chasms, and took a great deal of trouble on our behalf. They knew that Mr Ord Hume had specially come across the world to judge the bands, and so they took us everywhere as their guests.

Things had altered a good deal since my New Zealand visit of a year or so before. We went across the bush, on the way to Wanganuis river, and passed through thick, jungle-like forest and scenery that made us forget the world behind. I remember we came across one Maori pah where we got the Maoris to stand and have their photographs taken. I played the violin again, as the thick-haired Maori girls chanted and danced. They have many kinds of dances, and the rhythmical movement of their bodies is equal to the weird beauty of the South Sea Island Siva dances.

Some of the Maori girls are exceedingly handsome, but they fade at an early age. I remember one girl who was both handsome and intellectual-looking; her features were delicate and soft, refined through not being too perfect. She had a clear voice, and I extemporised an obbligato on my violin as she sang in the pah. The chiefs and women were enthusiastic in their applause. One ancient chief was thickly tattooed in engraved, ornamental lines and looked exceedingly majestic. He spoke English perfectly, and I was deeply interested in the many things he told us of his younger days. He was a prince by blood and, like the old chief whom I told you of in a preceding chapter, remembered the days when the rival tribes met in battle, or his tribe resented the white man's encroachment on the tribal lands.

I visited North and South Island and saw many of the geysers. Waimana Geyser is often in eruption and throws up volcanic steam and matter nine hundred feet, and then quiets down. I tramped along in tourist fashion with my gay companion; helped take snapshots, and spoilt a good many! We saw, too, the Waimango Basin, the hot springs and the "Devil's Frying Pan," where one could stand up to one's ankles in fire. We stopped with a guide called Warbuck and had a fine time. From there we travelled everywhere, and camped out for several nights, just for the romance and fun of it. We cooked our potatoes and boiled eggs in the hot springs of the Kerern Geyser, Rotorua.

After that I secured a position as violinist in an orchestra at Auckland and bade Mr Ord Hume good-bye, for soon after he left New Zealand.

I will now return once more to my old Bohemian days. Away from respectability that whitewashes men, back away from the mighty orchestra of moving cogs and wheels, and from the crowds of cold eyes, thirsting for the gold which is necessary to keep them warm in white-collared respectability, back over the seas to the forests of Maori land, to the cry of the curlew and huja in the trees, by the old pahs of Orakan, where Herowera, the old-time warrior, sat by the rushing river waters. His tattooed, engraved face is alive with memories. Once again he tells me of the mighty Rewi Maniapoto and the *esprit de corps* that bound the tribes together in their fierce battles, when Maoris fought as bravely for their rights as the old Britons still do. Still I fancy I hear pretty Rewaro, the Maori maid, singing her chant as she listens to the old chief's reminiscences of mighty deeds and battles of yore. In the birch and eucalyptus trees sigh old winds, and from the mysterious gloom of moonlit Arcadia come soft, weird sounds of Maori musical instruments. I could write chapters about the Maoris and their habits, and their wonderful poetic legends of dead chiefs singing in the forest, and maidens made of sea-foam brightly dancing in the glimpsing moonlight of forest rivers. I have seen Maoris stare down the main streets of Masterton and swear that they could see the rivers rushing along in the moonlight, and the canoes bearing the tribes over the swirling falls, while Maori maids, with their beautiful hair lifting in the winds, danced on ghostly, primeval waters.

RIVER SCENE IN NEW ZEALAND

I have felt as they feel when they see the city spires rising over their enchanted lands, for I can dream as they dream and awake to the same reality. Were I to rise, as a man in a dream, and go back across the years and pitch my tent on the old spot in Queensland where I camped, I should be moved on for obstructing the tramcars, and yet I am still a young man, so you will see how great is the change in a few years. I remember my self-made hut home, fashioned by my own hands, my comrade pulling the thick bush grass and boughs for the walls. How happy we were in that little room as the river sang, travelling onward. Just below we picked the ripe yellow oranges from the deep grass under the scented trees, where often my parrot raced me across the slope and flew by me sideways with its cut wing and won the race as I let it pass. I remember how, before the parrot died, it walked up our cabin walls screaming, with its tongue hanging from its beak; how great was my grief as its tiny jewel eyes opened and closed for the last time. That death was the great sorrow of our hut life, and we buried the poor bird, as parents do a beloved child, by the riverside. We went that same night over the slopes to the camp of aborigines, who cheered us up as they danced the corrobboree, while I played the fiddle under the moonlit gums. The old women were as black as ebony, and they also jumped and beat their hands on their skinny thighs, while old and young men, almost naked, whirled round the smouldering camp fire, with their ribs painted white, looking like hideous, screaming skeletons. We gave them cakes of plug tobacco, and in return they would dance. Sometimes they would just begin and then stop and say: "Me no dance, want more baccy first." I used to answer: "You no dance? Then me no play music." Then their thick lips would flop together, as they all grinned, and off they would start, whirling round in the old brown Government blankets which they wore over their shoulders something after the cavalier fashion of romantic ages. One old fellow had a tremendous head and was the tribal musician; he played a bone flute, the thigh-bone of some ancestor. He blew four notes on it and played them repeatedly; and the dusky forms chanted and jumped round him, beating their black breasts with their hands. This is how the thigh-bone wailed to the lips of its posterity:

Aboriginal.

Those wild black men had creeds and poetic legends of their bush world, much the same as the wild white men. For some historic ancestor's deed with the boomerang filthy old men and women were waited on by the low-caste tribe, who gazed upon their aboriginal gentry with awestruck eyes, and pushed hot, cooked white grubs and eel-like snakes into the big black lips of the aristocrats, who sat by the camp fire and opened their huge mouths in a listless way, their black, protruding bellies heaving in the bloated affluence of their high lineage.

CHAPTER XXI

At Sea in Dreams—In London Town—Off to Bordeaux—Our Chateau—In Biarritz—Old Madrid—I am a Spanish Troubadour—Mercedes—My old Comrade ceases to sing

I am a rolling, rolling stone;

Stern-fashioned in the mould

Wherein God recasts sand and bone,

I glitter with pure gold—

His workmanship, of course, not mine.

So still I roll along,

A sad old stone, half gem-divine,

Gathering moss and song.

God made me; yet I am weak throughout—

I feel this as I roll,

By deep wild waters knocked about,

But like my friend the mole,

Hid 'neath the earth and flowers, I peep

Up through a crack and spy

Another world, from darkness deep

I see a great blue sky.

So on I'll roll and roll; until

On some wild torrent's leap

I fall into the mighty mill,

Sink in the ocean's deep.

To lie quite still as ages fly

'Neath stars up o'er the main,

Till, brought up by the Diver, I

Go rolling on again!

FROM those wild bush-lands I passed away into the cities and on to ships, then again back to the cities and seaports of the world.

I have often thought of the old crews that I sailed with as a boy. I've met them sometimes in grog saloons and sailors' homes in seaport towns of far-away countries; only some of them though—for many went down to the sea in ships and never returned. I have stood alone at night, in the far-off seaport's little street, and heard the drunken laughter of sailormen by their ships at the wharves below as I gazed into the windows of the second-hand slop-shop at the relics. Old binoculars, compasses, oilskin caps and big sea-boots hanging on pegs, in rows, for sale. As I looked a mist crept under the rotting rafters of the dingy, musty, oil-lit room, the old oilskins swelled, and bearded wraiths of dead sailors danced. The big sea-boots tumbled about in a jig by the broken window as I watched, and sounds of long-dead laughter echoed in my ears. Then up the little seaport street, from the bay, came a gust of wind and blew me into the fo'c'sle of a ship far away at sea. I played the fiddle to the dancing dead men and climbed aloft as their hollow voices shouted a muffled, windy chantey. The old skipper, with his hand arched beneath his oilskin sou'wester, looked up aloft and shouted, and we all echoed back: "Aye, aye, sir," and my comrade touched me on the shoulder and said: "Come on, Middleton, you don't want to buy any of those d——d old oilskins."

Once more I found myself off, homeward bound round the Horn, crashing and rolling along, the howling sails aloft singing to the humming winds that we loved to hear, for the harder they blew the sooner we should be in England.

When I arrived in London the autumn rains were falling, and the population of the mighty city of pavements and stone walls moved along under a myriad umbrellas, as old St Paul's at flying intervals voiced forth from its mellow, iron throat the flight of Time.

Some musical friends in the city had suggested to me that I should do a wise thing if I went to the fashionable winter resorts in France. The idea struck me as a very good one. I was told that instrumental players had gone to France, Spain and Italy and come back wealthy. I had seen a good deal of the world, at its outposts, and had not succeeded in making even a portion of a fortune, so I resolved to get out of England without delay. Before I went I felt that I must have a comrade. The thought of old age with its boon companion, decrepitude, had always filled me with a strange horror, as something worse than death, and so for old age I always felt a commiseration and tenderness which gave me confidence in grey hairs, which often got me into trouble, but more often brought advice and sensible comradeship.

When in London, a year or so before, I had made friends with a gentleman whose name was Bonnivard. He had been educated in France, was a clever man and could speak French, Spanish and Italian. It struck me that if I could find out his whereabouts I might persuade him to come with me, for he was a jovial man, and his knowledge of French would help me in my travels. To tell you the truth, too, I was rather short of money and thought perhaps he might even lend me a little towards the expenses of the trip. I was getting older, and experience had taught me that too much money was not so inconvenient as too little. I went off to his villa in the suburbs; the old place had "To Let" in the window. No one in the district knew of his whereabouts, but at last, just as I was almost disheartened and giving up the thought of finding him, I met a gentleman who had known him. He at once gave me his address—inmate, Homerton Workhouse, Hackney! I was very much upset. I knew too well what trials, insults and sufferings my friend must have experienced before he sought a haven of rest in that terrible inquisition, the English workhouse.

I went to Homerton. The officials treated me most politely directly they discovered the reason of my visit. When I told my old comrade I wanted to take him to France, as my guest and interpreter, I was considerably affected by his delight. He had aged since I had last seen him; the old stiff military moustachios had turned white and had lost their aristocratic, upward twirls. Next day they were once more alert and alive with renewed majesty, and the handsome old face, though deeply wrinkled, was boyish-looking with delight. He was a new being in his frock-coat and tall hat, which I purchased remarkably cheaply at a pawnbroker's shop. The gloss of his hat was perfection, and as he smoothed it with his sleeve, in the old way, he laughed almost hysterically, with a schoolboy's laughter, but my ear detected the wizened, high note of age in it, and it made him more pathetic than ever.

The next day, with his dead wife's photograph and his travelling kit in my box, as steerage passengers we went down the Thames together, both happy, on board the s.s. *Albatross*, bound for Bordeaux.

Arriving at Bordeaux, we found it advisable, owing to the state of our exchequer, to live outside in the suburbs, so we rented a pretty little chateau in the Rue V——, Cauderon. The weather was bitterly cold, and we spent a good portion of the day in trying to make our coke fire burn. Every night we walked into Bordeaux and got a good feed in a restaurant; one franc fifty centimes secured us several courses, with a bottle of wine each included. I wandered about Bordeaux a good deal, and went down the leafy pathways of the Botanical Gardens, but could not appreciate anything owing to the cold winds. I had thought to visit spots associated with the old French philosopher, Montaigne, who doubtless in his day wandered over the historic streets where I now walked looking for violin engagements. In my sea-chest at our chateau I had Montaigne's Essays, and I satisfied myself by lying in my bed and reading the deep, innocent wisdom of the great Frenchman. Near where we lived there was a wine merchant and many residents who, I think, worked in the vineyards. From the merchant we got credit, and things eventually became so bad that we lived for some time on wine and haricot beans. At last I secured a course of concert engagements at English and French clubs and concerts.

My comrade and I invited the wine-seller and several Frenchmen to supper every night, and the little chateau with "Zee Engleise gentlemen" in it rang with song as a French harp-player and I played. Long after midnight the noise went on: they all lifted their arms and opened their mouths, while Mr Bonnivard told those chivalrous Frenchmen of his experiences in the Siege of Paris. They were delighted with my comrade's yarns, and he went on spinning them vigorously. I could not speak French, so I could only watch their faces expressing horror or surprise as he fired away.

About two weeks later the smash came. The rent of the chateau was a hundred francs a month and was due; we also owed the wine-seller for about a hundred bottles of red and white wine. It was cheap enough, fourpence a litre.

We could not possibly pay the rent, but we held a hurried and private council and resolved to give our friend the wine-seller fifty francs and send the remainder after we arrived at Biarritz. We dared not give him more, otherwise we should not have our fare. We intended sending the rent to the agent, who was a little Frenchman and lived round the corner, directly we had some luck, and we did do so.

Before we went away we invited them all to a grand supper, which ended at midnight with the stirring *Marseillaise*. We had to be at the Midi station by ten o'clock next morning. The cab arrived; we first went to the agent to tell him we were obliged to leave for the English season at Biarritz and would send the rent on, but he was out, so off we drove. We had no sooner turned the corner of the street than the agent passed us in a small chaise and spied us and our boxes. About five minutes after we saw him chasing after us, about a quarter of a mile behind, shouting at the top of his voice. "Hadn't we better stop and explain?" I said to my companion. But he would not do so; a whole regiment of gendarmes with drawn swords behind us would not have disturbed him, but would have simply supplied more excitement to the splendour of his "La Belle France." He compared everything that happened around him to his life in the Homerton Workhouse, and so rubbed his hands with delight, and shouted in French to the driver, who at once whipped up the horse, and away we rumbled at full speed. I painfully felt that we were not in the South Seas, and began to feel uncomfortable when I noticed that the little agent was gaining upon us. I had come to France to make my fortune, and the prospect did not appear much better than it did when I was seeking wealth in the Australian gold-fields a few years before. I stood up and shouted "Two francs more" in the driver's ear. He seemed to understand, and gave the poor horse another slash, and as we flew by the French people rushed from their villas and shops, thinking a fire engine was passing through the maze of Bordeaux's streets. We eventually lost sight of the agent, caught the train and arrived in due course at Biarritz.

In Biarritz I did well: played at the Casino and gave private concerts at the different clubs and hotels where the wealthy English visitors stayed, the Hôtel de Paris, Hôtel d'Angleterre and Hôtel du Prince. The British residents consisted of titled folk: high chiefs, princes and princesses, descendants of old tribes of blue-blooded lineage. My comrade was worth his weight in gold; his engaging manner enabled him to take liberties with old colonels and the austere English "set" which would have been strongly resented if perpetrated by anyone else. I saw aristocratic old gentlemen flush and clutch their falling eyeglass with astonishment as he smacked them on the back, but they recovered and were amused by his manner, for his appearance and address revealed a personality and intellectual quality equal to their own.

We also went to Bayonne, an old-fashioned city surrounded by crumbling ramparts. They had a splendid military band there and played brilliantly. My companion was so delighted with the change in his affairs that he sang my songs and no one else's as he walked and hummed by my side.

Before we left Biarritz we stayed for a week at the Hôtel St Julien. Mr Morrison, who ran it, gave a farewell concert on our behalf and refused to accept anything for our stay in his hotel. My comrade loved singing, but had no voice for expressing the love. Mrs Morrison heroically presided at the piano as he sang, over and over again, the one song which he sang other than my compositions. It was *The Heart bowed down with Weight of Woe*. Mr Morrison would clench his teeth and drink a stiff glass of cognac, and then, as the old fellow bowed in a courtly way, encore him! Our host was a clever literary man, and had all the kindness and sincerity of a true Bohemian gentleman. My old friend and I were sorry to bid him and his kind wife good-bye. They made us up a hamper of savoury food and told us to write to them if we ever got into a tight corner.

With about five hundred francs in our possession we crossed the Pyrenees, and after a month's travelling, playing at various concerts and Spanish festivals, we arrived at Madrid. We secured apartments in the old Moorish quarter, then sallied forth and mingled with the swarthy population. The avenues and parks were alive with youths and beautiful dark girls with Arab eyes and glorious dark or bronze hair. Groups of roystering men stood about smoking cigarettes. They looked like a mixture of Italian, Moor, Turk and Arab, so reminiscent were they of those races. We wandered by the Puerta de Sol and in the crowded streets near by, and aristocratic, sharp-bearded hidalgos, with large-brimmed sombreros on the heads and cloaks thrown over their shoulders, passed us like cavaliers of the mediæval ages. Till I became used to the scene round me I felt that we walked the streets of some old, lost city; that the sailors of the Spanish Armada still had lovers among the Spanish beauties who sang in groups as they passed us, wearing short, ornamental skirts and coloured kerchiefs loosely swathing their heads of thick dark hair. The Spaniards gazed over their mantled shoulders with admiring eyes, and the laughing, flattered Spanish maidens reciprocated their gallant attention by gazing back with amorous eyes at their handsome figures, with black velvet breeches, slashed at the sides to reveal pink drawers and frills. The *fajas* (sashes) of the men vied in vividness of colour with the gay swathing of the fair, bronzed maids.

We strolled on the banks of the Manzanares river by moonlight and seemed to walk through fairyland, though by day hundreds of Spanish women used the river as a washing-tub, and forests of clothes props and stretched lines blossomed forth with delicate and beautiful undergarments of silk material. The hildagos' velvet breeches and the maids' fajas fluttered cheerfully side by side in the winds among the chestnut groves, and often the cavaliers and dark-eyed maids that owned them lay tucked in bed till the laundress brought them home, so poor were they.

My comrade could speak Spanish fairly well, and kept excitedly telling me so many things that I remembered none of them. In the cheap quarter of the town, where touring violinists and poets generally reside, mysterious smells of garlic and cooking steams killed the romance that hovered about the beautiful terraced architecture of Madrid.

I looked in vain for a position as violinist, but it was not to be had, or the salary was only sufficient to enable one to live on garlic. So I was forced to become a Spanish troubadour and go off serenading affluent hidalgos. Fortunately I very soon replenished our dwindling exchequer. My comrade, having been educated in France, could bow as royally as the Spanish señores, and conducted all the financial part of the business. We went into partnership with our landlady's daughters, who played the guitar and mandoline, and I conducted the troupe. When the festival carnivals began a week later we had a glorious time and made enough money to enable us to live comfortably. I played my Samoan waltz, arranging it for two violins, guitar and mandolines, and the wild barbarian note of the strain was very popular. Maidens, who looked like Arab girls with shining eyes, whirled and swayed in the arms of their Don Juans, as under the Spanish moon my cheerful troupe tinkled away and I played the violin. Except for their artistic gowns and the sashes flapping as they danced, I saw the South Sea Islanders dancing before me; the same abandonment was there. Their musical voices, as they sang the refrain, brought back to me wild tribal dances of the South Sea forest, where a few years before I had conducted the banging war-drums and wedding music for cannibals, high chiefs, dethroned kings and discarded queens.

Pretty Mercedes and Mary, her sister, sang minor melodies in duet style as I extemporised an obbligato on my violin. They then danced the Jota Aragonesa and other dances, and little children romped about and imitated bull-fights, singing wildly all the time.

After the carnival was over my comrade and I strolled about the sleeping city, and visited the old quarter of alleyways and gloomy buildings and hidden dens where suspicious characters met and loose lovers played guitars and mandolines. We watched old priests shuffling along to visit the sick señores, who had fed on garlic and walnuts, and lived in Madrid's East End, but dressed in the blue, open days in majestic splendour and vivid colour.

We went to the many temples of Madrid. They are seldom silent, for up their aisles creep gentle Spanish girls, who come in, cross themselves and kneel in prayer to Jesus and the Holy Virgin. The earnestness of it all would soften the hardest cynic. Old priests abound, and revel in the confessions of those innocent girls as they bow their heads with shame and confess that they have thought more during the week of Don Juan's stalwart, lithe figure than of the Holy Virgin. As they pass one sees them crossing themselves and murmuring their prayers. At the doors wrinkled old women pester one with little boxes of wax matches, walnuts and photographs of Madrid and the Blessed Virgin. If one buys a cent's worth of anything from them they follow on for three hundred yards, calling down the blessing of God, Jesus and the Virgin on one's head.

At night-time, when the moon is high and the olive-trees and palms are windless and still, down the white-terraced avenue goes Don Quixote astride his ass, twirling his moustachios, till far away, with Sancho Panza by his side, he fades under the moonlit chestnut groves. From the forests of alleyways steal appealing figures, with eyes that beg for an admiring glance, and in strange, soft tones wail of sorrows and no food or place to lay their weary heads. Give them a coin and pass on, they cross themselves and mention the Holy Virgin's name, and you realise there is something wrong with the world, for the cry of the Virgin's name sounds sincere. All the cities have that frail woman begging the world to be her husband, because she never secured one good man to love her and rear those bonny boys and girls who wail to be born in the infinite shadows behind her. It is a sorrow that has even spread across the world and reached the island tribes of the South Seas.

Standing on the garden roof of our house in Madrid we could see the country round, a barren country, and looking like the Australian Never-Never Land in a civilised state. It is dotted with dusty tracks and old isolated inns; herds of goats and mules fade far across the tracks, looking like droves of rats in the desert distance.

There are beautiful spots in Madrid, on the banks of the Manzanares, and firs, beeches and chestnuts shade the waters and the slopes by the Royal Gardens.

At night I used to lie in my attic room and listen to the nightingales singing in the chestnut-tree outside my window, its mate piping back approval from another tree at regular intervals. My old comrade lay fast asleep on the next trestle bed, for the Spanish hidalgos gave him cognac, and on the way home from the festival concerts he would clutch me tightly by the arm, as little Mercedes and Mary laughed by my side. In the morning he used to say: "Dear boy, whatever was it that overcame me last night? It's that wretched garlic."

Sometimes when we were short of money we lay on our beds smoking, and he would tell me of the Siege of Paris, his terrible experiences there, and how he ate his share of the elephant and lion steaks from the Zoo. Becoming philosophical, he would tell me of his boyish aspirations, the happiness he got out of them and the worry from the events that never happened. I would say: "Supposing we run right out of money, what about food and a bed?" Then he would cheer me up by saying: "My dear boy, all's sure to be well; we are certain to be *somewhere* and sleep *somewhere* whatever happens." Then, as was his wont, he would lick his thumb and push the old cigar stump into his pipe and hum my last melody—a melody that no publisher would buy—till I, secure in his philosophical comradeship, fell asleep. He never professed or spoke on religious matters, but each night he knelt by his bed before he got in and lit his pipe.

We were very happy in the house of Señora Dolores; she treated us as though we were dear relatives. In her little attic room I spent the happiest hours of my Continental travels. I lay half the night reading my beloved Montaigne's essays. The old French Shakespeare was my best dead learned friend. If ever I was worried and could not sleep for thinking I went to my sea-chest and brought him out. I read some of his essays over twenty times, but they were always fresh, wise and sincere, and I still read them. In that little room I also read poetry's legitimate child, Keats. As my dear comrade slept on I fell in love with Madeline and roamed with Endymion, Lamia and Hyperion. The nightingale singing outside

"Charm'd magic casements, opening on the foam

Of perilous seas, in faery lands forlorn"

as the moonlight glimmered through my little room. I have read somewhere that Keats was earthly. I think if he had lived his intense genius would have fought for the sorrows of humanity, and his marvellous mind made literature and our country even better than it is. It may be centuries before earth, capable of bringing forth such spiritual flowers as his earthliness did, will be born again.

Poor little Mercedes! She crossed herself and murmured the Holy Virgin's name many times as we bade her and her sister good-bye, and I thought of Madeline, and felt sad that the days of gallant knights and amorous warriors were gone for ever. I can still see their eyes shining through sorrow as we said farewell; even the old mother's wrinkled face blushed as we kissed the three.

We went from Madrid to Valencia, where we stayed for three weeks, and then left by boat for Marseilles, and then on to Nice, and finally to Genoa. My comrade was the happiest of men as he tramped beside me; he loved to carry my violin. We started to write an opera together, entitled *The Siege of Paris*. He was delighted as he gave me thrilling, realistic details of all he had witnessed. I tried to place them in lyrical form and wrote suitable melodies round the tragic events. He knew as much about authorship as I did, but I believe, with the help of his clever head and earnestness, we should have amply made up for our artistic deficiencies and lack of literary method.

The manuscript still remains unfinished, as we left it, for not long after he ceased singing my songs. The brief sunlight between the workhouse and the grave faded and disappeared. When I turned away from his last resting-place I was the only mourner, and as I went away into our mysterious world once more I felt very lonely.

So end the intimate reminiscences of my wanderings, most of them experiences up to my twenty-second birthday. Whether I have succeeded in giving the reader an insight into the personality of the writer, such a glimpse as an autobiography is supposed to give, I do not know. Personally, I think it is a hard thing to do in a thorough sense, especially for a vagabond at heart. Each individual is a multitude of struggling ancestral strains, and real active life is manifested in the fight, the fierce hunt to find ourselves; which we can never do, for we die every moment that we live. So all we can attempt in a book is to tell truthfully those things that impressed us deeply at different periods of our life, so deeply that they still remain imprinted on the mind. Also to tell of our experiences for better or worse in this life of ours, where one footstep taken out of the track that we have known and write about would have altered the whole book of our life to another colour.

CHAPTER XXII

I arrive at the Organization—Bones and his Officials—Mabau, the Maid—Chief Kaifa—Mabau in trouble—I advise her—Thakambau's Harem—Chief Kaifa on Christianity—Enoch—Escaped Convicts—Music—Witchcraft—The Hermit Missionary

... While sweetly some

Play on soft flutes and lyres, I, by gum!

Beat with delight the big barbarian drum

Before this drama of the great Limelight

Of stars—and dancing shadows infinite.

THE best part of truth is hidden in the heart of humanity. How different is that which we reveal from that which we think of in silence. Our outward demeanour is civilisation; our hidden inward cravings are barbarism. To some extent these pages will deal with the savage instincts of the natives of tropical isles, and with men who have found refuge in those lands far from the cities of the Western world.

To tell you of the semi-heathen is much akin to telling you of ourselves, for are not the barbarian instincts which we all have within us our own tiny, savage, dusky children? We chide them for their waywardness, but do we not encourage them in secret, as the savage outwardly does, expressing joyously that which we are ashamed of? One has the virtue of truth and the other of polished deceit. Notwithstanding this, I think civilisation the best of all possible things. Truly, however, civilisation is built on a quicksand, and now that the Fijian forest battles and cannibalistic feasts have become fierce and gruesome history the great tribalistic clash of nations, in full swing as I write, reveals more than words the relentless link that binds white and brown men together.

Once when I was wandering in the Marquesan Group I suddenly came across the ruins of an old cannibalistic amphitheatre standing lonely by the forest palms. The stone cooling-shelves, whereon once lay the dead men and women in hot weather, were still intact, but thickly overgrown with moss and sheltered by bamboos; the festival arena and its surroundings of artistic savagery were all gone; the barbarian log walls had fallen. Wild tropical vines, smothered with wild flowers, thickly covered all that tomb-like place, where savages once ate their foes and whirled in the cannibalistic dance, revealing the shapes of the stone edifice, the *pae-pae*,[15] the turrets and log walls. The savage tribes with their sighs and laughter lay dead, silent dust in the forest hard by. I looked up through that amphitheatre-shaped growth. It was night; I saw the stars glimmering through the dark palms as the trade wind stirred them. Now I think those vanished walls were as civilisation, and the green clinging boughs remaining and revealing the amphitheatre's shape sad humanity clinging to the best it has left.

<u>15</u>. Altar.

The simile may not be perfect, but neither is anything that is human. But I must ramble on my way, for I am now well on the road to my reminiscences of Fiji.

Years ago, just off the Rewa river, which is navigable fifty or sixty miles inland, there was a wooden shanty. It had two compartments; the walls were made of coco-palm stems tied strongly together with wild hemp. Situated at a lonely spot, surrounded by primeval vegetation, coco-palms, backa-trees and wild, tropical, twining vines, it was eminently suitable for the purpose for which it was used, for in its snug rooms lived the men who were members of the Charity Organization of the South Seas! The officials did not run the place on Western lines, for it was a true home for the fallen: no questions were asked when suddenly the hunted, haggard, unshaved face appeared; to be hunted was a sufficient reference to enable the applicant to be at once enrolled as a member. Twelve fierce-eyed, rough-looking men, attired in big-brimmed hats and belted trousers, would greet the new arrival, and with the instinct of bloodhounds stare, and reckon up the new visitor's pedigree. If he looked sufficiently villainous and haggard, and pathetically told the woe of some criminal ambition that had been frustrated by the vigilant eye of civilisation, he was immediately given the first grade diploma, a tin mug of the best Fijian rum! If he still possessed any part of the spoil he could have an extra mugful, for the Organization was not a rich one. A little off-side room was artistically arranged; a small looking-glass, brush and comb, and all those things that tell of gentleness and frailness completed its furniture. There it was, silent, clean, tenantless and ready, for often from other lands, with the spoil, the missing man would arrive with the cause of his downfall weeping beside him, and in there she slept!

No one could tell the individual histories of these men. It will be sufficient to say that they were there.

Ere I proceed I must tell you that when I speak of the Organization's whereabouts I mislead you in the name only; the true vicinity characteristically resembles my description. It is obvious that to be faithful to those who befriended me I must be secretive in some of the details which tell of this isle of the South Seas, where men sought, and probably still seek, a harbour of refuge safe from the stern law of civilised cities. To-day this institution exists and still carries on its varied work of extreme humanity. The low-roofed den, the old bench surrounded by the swarthy, unshaved faces of the secretive crew, like bending shadows in tobacco smoke, breathing oaths as the cards are shuffled, has disappeared; but still the game is carried on, though in more magnificent style, for as the cities rise the aristocracy of crime fortifies itself, becoming more guarded and respectable in outward appearance. Be assured that I dip my pen in stern experience for that which I tell you.

When you see these headlines in your daily paper, "Bank Manager Disappears. Officials in the Dock", "Mayor and Vicar Missing," be sure that the head of the Charity Organization of the South Seas has read the Colonial cable in *The Marquesa News* or *Apia Times*, and has rubbed his hands with delighted expectation, and that his agents are watching at the warden gates of the high sea ports of the tropic world. Forest lands, caves and mountain fastnesses and unknown isles of security are fast disappearing from the world as it becomes polite.

Where the bokai feast roared and revelled, and the Fijian war dancers in the moonlight of other years whirled, in bloodthirsty revelry, by the Rewa river, now rise the church spires! Where the ambushed tribe once watched from the jungle with gleaming eyes pass austere university men clad in gowns, with Bibles in their hands, to lecture on Christianity to open-mouthed natives. So things have changed, and the heathenish creeds of the old days faded, and it is my wish to give you one glimpse of that which has been.

It was my lot to stay in the Organization I speak of. A mile off was a small native village, where Mabau, a Fijian maid who helped Bones, the Organization overseer, to keep the rooms clean and tidy, lived. Bones was the descendant of one of those old Botany Bay convicts who, escaping in a boat, put to sea, and eventually drifting ashore in Fiji, made their homes there, and inculcated in the islanders' minds the first contempt for the white race: contempt which, by an age of vigorous striving, missionaries have at last removed. Bones told me much of his convict ancestor, who had been transported from England for stealing a hammer, and so Bones was born in the South Seas. He had a firm, open face, grey, English eyes and a Fijian mouth. He was a fairly well-educated man, and though he looked rough, at heart was kind; he kissed Mabau's pretty face as though she were his own child. In fact Bones in every way struck me as being most suitable for his job of running a South Sea Charity Organization, which was run upon exactly opposite lines to the charity organizations of the Western seas, where the officials have stony eyes and steel-trap mouths. As I have told you, Bones had neither; and as I sat by him and a strange bird in the coco-tree sang to the sunset, I felt drawn to him, and told him more than I would tell most men. It was a beautiful night; most of Bones's friends were away, some at work and some at sea on trading schooners. Bones played the banjo and I the fiddle, and after indulging in some European and native folk-songs he lit his pipe and I strolled off under the palms.

It was on this night that I met Mabau again. Now Mabau was a Fijian maid of rare beauty. She had shining dark eyes and a thick mop of hair; the graceful curves of her bare brown body as she glided 'neath the sunlit palms made many Fijian youths gaze enviously upon her. The Chief Kaifa, her father, sat by his hut door; he had been one of the high chiefs of Thakambau, the last of the Fijian kings. Kaifa was a majestic-looking man; in spite of his thick lips he had fine features, with earnest eyes, and was straight-figured as a coco-palm. As he sat there, dressed in his native sulu, he smiled as I spoke to his daughter Mabau. I knew more of her doings than he thought. She was a true daughter of Eve, for her glance gave no hint whatever that we had met before.

For in my forest wanderings, about two days before the evening I have mentioned, I had met Mabau. She did not know at first that I had perceived her in a lonely spot. She knelt on her knees before a rotting, cast-off wooden idol. Sunset had fired with red and gold the tops of the coco-palms and forest trees; overhead a few birds were still whistling. As I approached, and the dead scrub cracked beneath my feet, the heathen-hearted little maid looked hastily over her bare shoulder and, seeing me, arose swiftly, as though for flight. My voice must have had a note in it that appealed to and reassured the guilty forest child, for I called softly, and then smiled to let her know that from me no harm should befall her. "Why do you pray to that wooden thing?" I said, and then I gave the monstrous effigy a kick. With a frightened sigh she looked up at me and said: "O Papalangi, I love Vituo the half-caste." Then with a blush she told me all, and it seemed that the soul of innocence peered through her eyes and asked for mercy as she looked down at herself and then up to me again, one hand resting on her brown breast. I gazed silently and knew all. The perfidious Vituo had stolen her heart.

"Me killee Vituo; your white God no help me, will he?" she said. I gazed awhile and said: "Yes, He will, Mabau." I would not have told this thundering lie but for the fact that her appealing eyes awoke the best that was in me, and it was my earnest wish to attempt to stay her from inflicting any vengeance on her sinful lover which might bring sorrow to her afterwards.

Encouraged by my kindness, and misunderstanding my gestures as I endeavoured to explain that she should pray to the Christian God instead of to the gods of her fathers, she suddenly lifted her arms and started to chant into the wooden ears of the old idol again. On her knees she went, swaying her body and arms gently all the while in the mystic, Mebete charms. She sang on earnestly, and I gazed, astonished to see the heathen age before my eyes and to feel my ear-drums vibrating to the primeval lore of the South

Seas. Through the forest boughs just overhead crept the lingering rays of the dying sunset, and two golden streaks fell slantwise over the praying maid's brown body, glimmering in her thick dark hair as her head moved to and fro while she chanted her despair.

"Mabau," I said, "where does Vituo live? Why not go and find him, tell him of your love and offer your forgiveness; he will doubtless take you to his arms." In truth I felt this might be, for she was a comely and pretty maid. At my saying this she answered in this wise: "O white mans, I long die and go to Nedengi, or Mburanto the great goddess, who love deceived maids and make gods of children." Then, with a fierce look on her dark face, and with heaving bosom, she continued: "Mburanto will blow the breath of the big wind that will kill him, the wicked Vituo, and then him once dead will love me again, for good is his soul, though his body is whitish and wicked." I saw the depth of her love flame in her eyes, and I answered: "Mabau, go home, and I will pray to the white God for you, and will see what can be done to bring this treacherous Vituo back to you again." At this, with delight, she rose to her feet, her eyes and face shining and expressing pleasure at my promise; her sulu-cloth of woven coco-nut fibre revealed her trembling thighs as, with the impulsiveness of the Fijian temperament, she started to sing and do the equivalent of a step-dance.

As I stood there, and the shadows of night thickened, I heard a voice, and Mr Bones suddenly stepped from a clump of tall fern growth into the clearing where we stood. "What's up?" he said, and I knew then that he had been watching the whole performance. Mabau, who knew him well, started off, with feminine vivacity, to tell him all her trouble. He knew her language, and so she was able swiftly to tell her tale. Now Bones, as I have said before, was a decent fellow, and he listened attentively all the while that she spoke. Then he turned towards me and said: "Vituo is a treacherous skunk, and if he plays her false I will see to it that he gets his deserts. Go home, Mabau, for old Kaifa will be suspicious of your being out this late hour." Off she went, and I had not seen her again till this meeting by her parent Kaifa's home, when I digressed to tell you that, notwithstanding her greeting me as though I were a stranger, nevertheless all that I have told you had happened between us.

The chief, as I said, gave me a friendly greeting. I had seen him once before, when he had called at Bones's homestead and borrowed a mugful of rum. He was a genuine survival of the old cannibalistic days: though he had embraced Christianity as best calculated to serve his interests and requirements, for the Protestant and Roman Catholic ecclesiastics were very kind to him—he had embraced both the creeds—he still, deep in his heart, clung tenaciously to old memories and the heathen mythologies of his tribal ancestors.

By his side sat Mabau, busily weaving a new fringed sulu gown, with varied patterns decorating its scantiness; for it was the Fiji fashion to reveal as much as possible of the maid without her being accused of being absolutely nude. His only surviving wife was a full-blooded Fijian, and as I sat by his side she squatted on her haunches, busily blowing, with her thick-lipped mouth, the embers of a tiny fire that flickered into a thousand stars, to be scattered by her breath, as the evening meal spluttered.

Chief Kaifa could speak excellent English, and as I stayed on, and the hour became late, he told me many things of the old days, of dark beliefs and also of the mighty cannibalistic warrior, Thakambau. As he spoke, and the moon rose and lit the forest, his eyes brightened as the old splendour thrilled him, and Mabau, who sat by us alone, for the old wife had gone to bed in the hut near by, rested her chin on her hand and looked up with sparkling eyes, listening eagerly, and I saw who encouraged her and why she had prayed so earnestly to the old forest idol.

"O white mans," he said, lifting his dusky arms as he spoke, "the old gods watch me to-night, and when I pass into shadow-land I shall be great chief, for am I not still faithful to them? Do I not cling to those who watched over my birth and gave me life?" As he spoke a strange bird screamed afar off in the forest palms, and with his dark finger to his lips he said: "Woi! Vanaka! the dead speak! and they who were unfaithful to men and maids are being punished by the gods"; for ere he finished many screams came to our ears, as a flock of migrating wings flapped under the moon that was right overhead.

Mabau, who had heard this, clapped her hands with delight, and I knew then that she had but little faith in Vituo's promises; for I understood from Bones that he had seen Vituo, and he had pledged his faithfulness to poor Mabau. I say "poor Mabau" because this is no romance that I tell you of, but simply an incident in the sad drama of life that came about through Vituo's unfaithfulness.

Much that Chief Kaifa told me that night, and on following nights that I spent in his interesting company, still lives vividly in my memory, and I think it will be interesting to tell here some things I heard concerning the monstrous deeds of Thakambau ere the awful royal cannibal embraced Christianity.

It appeared that Thakambau had six Fijian maids, who were kept in the royal huts, sheltered and closely guarded by his high chiefs; and though the missionaries had landed in the Fijian Group, and had even made homes on the isle, he managed to keep all that which the old chief told me a close secret. For some time these six maids formed his harem, and they were proud of the royal favour. In time two of them became mothers, and when the babies were six months old the high chiefs came in the dead of night and took them away. As time wore on, and Thakambau sickened of the secret tribal harem, the mothers disappeared one by one also—only a scream disturbed the forest silence. Then the bokai ovens, wherein the dead were roasted, were made hot, and great were the rejoicings of the cannibalistic natives and the tribal grandees who were favoured by being admitted and presented at the Court functions.

At last of the six erstwhile maids two only were left, and one night they too disappeared and ceased to weep, and the harem huts were silent.

Nedengi, the great Fiji god, blessed all those who had joined in the grand festival whereat the maids had been sacrificed; and as the assembled tribe sat in the terrible forest arena, drinking kava and gorging the dead, the Mebete spirits could be heard running, as their shadow-feet sped across the midnight moonlit forest that surrounded the bokai ovens; and the cannibals looked affrighted over their shoulders as they heard the wailing cries of the souls of the dead mothers and maids whom they were eating being pursued by the souls of dead warriors and lustful old gods, who hungered after the shadows of beautiful dead women!

"How terrible!" I suddenly gasped, being unable to control my utterance as the old chief told me these things. Quickly he looked up at me, and swiftly I recognised my mistake, for he was very proud of his dead king and all the horror I have told you. Continuing, I said: "Thakambau was a great warrior, and the mighty Nedengi approved of his doings, and sanctioned them, as the white God does ours."

Though I said that, the old fellow seemed to understand my feelings, and looking at me half kindly and half fiercely, said: "Nedengi did not sacrifice his own son! Nor does he send the helpless, blind souls of his children to the bokai ovens of hell fires to burn in agony for eternity; nor did he hide in the dark of ages. Why did your mighty one God not come before? Why did He send you cursed whites to our isles to shout lies, ravish our maids and steal our lands? Wao! Wao! Why smash our idols? Show me this great white God! Where, where is this Thing you prate about? Where?" Saying this, he lifted his eyes to the skies, and so vehemently did he rattle on, and so many things did he say that smacked of the truth, that for a moment I hung my head and felt as though I were the heathen and he the Christian.

Bidding the fierce old fellow good-night, I went swiftly across the flats, crept into the Home of the Fallen, by Rewa river, and slept.

It was the next day that I met the treacherous Vituo. Bones introduced me to him, and as I nodded my friend gave me a wink and so I assumed more politeness. I was much surprised by Vituo's appearance, for though he was a half-caste his complexion was almost European. Certainly he was of a type which would appear handsome to Fijian womenkind, and from his manner I saw at a glance that he was a mixture of the swashbuckler and cavalier. I pitied little Mabau exceedingly, for she would, night after night, come over to see us, and I knew that she came full of hope that she might meet Vituo, who often came down the Rewa to help the traders, and to take up cargoes of copra and many other things that grew on the plantations which were cultivated and toiled over by the natives.

I stayed with Bones for some days; he was extremely kind to me, and I was glad of the opportunity of getting a rest, and, moreover, the men who lived with him were strange characters and extremely interesting. Often new arrivals came, some with heavy beards and some clean shaven, ostensibly for the purpose of disguise.

One old man, whose name was Enoch, was a quaint old chap and fondly loved rum. I do not know what he had done in his native land—which I believe was Australia—but at night he would shout in his sleep and, suddenly awaking, sit up and gasp, and gaze with relief on the bunks around him, wherein slept the weary heads of the fallen. Now Enoch was very artful, for he found out that I was the rum-keeper and so it was my duty to share out, and night after night I was obliged to get out of my bed and give him tots of rum to allay the awful pain which a toothache was giving him. For several nights this kind of thing went on. I advised him at length to go to Suva and get the offensive molar pulled out, but no, he would not hear of it. At last, after a wretched week of nights disturbed by his groans and appeals for rum, I happened to tell him a joke, and as he opened his mouth wide with laughter I saw to my disgust that he was toothless!

Often I went out into the forest and, placing my music in the fork of a tree, stood and practised my violin. The native children would hear, and come peeping through the tall fern and grass to listen. They became my little friends. I taught them to dance around me, and they screamed with delight!

Several times Mabau came to see us, but Vituo did not keep his promises. She would stand at the Organization door for hours watching the sunset fade over the hills, and then with staring eyes look down the long white track, where once he had so eagerly come singing, to fall into her arms. Bones and I, and even old Enoch, would strive to cheer her up. I used to play the violin and get her to sing with her soft, plaintive voice some of the lotu hymns, and so in this way divert her mind from thinking of her faithless lover. For, to tell the truth, Vituo was now only interested in a white woman who was staying at Suva. Bones knew of this, and told me all about it, and so we all felt deeply sorry for Mabau. In my heart I hated the treacherous half-caste for his heartless behaviour. Time was going on, and Mabau's open disgrace fast approaching, and, as Bones said, it would not be well for her, or Vituo either, when the truth was out. The old chief, her father, still had a huge war-club which was the equivalent of Fijian law, and there was no telling what might happen when her condition was no longer a secret. Poor Mabau! I still remember her melancholy as I made her sing while I played the low notes on the violin, for she could follow easily the chords on the G string, but as the bow travelled up the scale to the higher notes her ear seemed to fail her. It was interesting to listen to her wild voice, which so easily sang melodies in the minor key, though as soon as I played in the major key her voice seemed to grip hold of the notes and slowly drift the strain from the major to the minor.

One night we were suddenly surprised by one of our companions appearing at the Organization door with two new members. They were dark-looking men; one was extremely handsome and very polite, indeed almost courtly in his salutations as he gently brushed the mug's rim and swallowed the proffered rum. Enoch, Mabau and I, sitting on our tubs, watched them intently as they stood side by side and spoke in broken English to Bones, who seemed quite satisfied with their credentials, for they were escaped convicts from Numea. They were unshaved and very disreputable-looking, but after a wash, shave and brush-up were considerably changed for the better, and I discovered that they were as gentle and intelligent as they looked. Reviere, the younger—that was not his real name—had, in a fit of jealousy, shot a rival in Paris, and so had been transported to New Caledonia, the French penal settlement, from where convicts often escaped to live exiled lives in the islands or Australian cities.

Reviere fell in love with Mabau. He and I became very good friends, and though I told him of Vituo and all the trouble, still he gazed upon Mabau as she softly sang with eyes that seemed never to tire of gazing in her direction.

Reviere had been exiled in a convict prison for over five years, and Mabau being the first woman whom he had spoken to since he escaped from incarceration, his infatuation for the Fijian maid was not so surprising as it would have been under normal circumstances. Alas, though Mabau approved of his tenderness to her, and seemed somewhat flattered at his admiring gaze, she did not encourage him; for, notwithstanding the undress costume of the islanders and the looseness of the sexes in the native villages, Fijian maids were as modest as, and if anything more faithful to their lovers than, the maids of civilised lands sometimes are.

Dart Valley, Lake Wakatipu, N.Z.

For two nights Mabau disappeared, and Bones being away on a trading trip, Reviere and I left the Organization officials playing dominoes and drinking rum and went off south of the Rewa river exploring; for we had heard that the natives were having high sprees inland and that the Meke festival dances were in full swing.

It was nearly dusk as we wandered along by the tropical palms and fern that grew thickly by the tiny track which we followed. Going across a pine-apple plantation we once more got on to the native road, and before the stars in heaven were at their brightest we emerged from the thick bush growth and entered a clearing that extended to the native village homesteads that stood under the palms and banyans across the flat.

It was a wonderful sight that appeared before us; for the old chieftains, and native women also, were dressed in war costume, their bodies swathed in bandages of grass and flowers, and as they danced wildly they made the scene impressively weird. The general musical effect sounded like a Wagnerian orchestra being played out of tempo and tune, but the legendary atmosphere was perfect. It also possessed the barbarian note of Wagnerian music, which so wonderfully expresses the German nature and shows that Wagner was a genius for true expression and anticipation.

The moon came up and intensified the barbaric atmosphere that pervaded the excited village. From the hut doors peeped the tiny dark faces of the native children, who applauded with vigour the escapades of their old grandmother or grandfather, who, back once again in the revived memories of heathen days, threw their skinny legs skyward and did many grotesque movements that seemed impossible to old age and the stern decorum which those little children had erstwhile been used to from their august parents. Round the space, to the primitive music of thumped wooden drums (*lais*) and the hooting of bamboo reeds, they whirled; and then suddenly the vigorous antics would cease and all would start walking round in a circle, as the maids, almost nude, except for a blossom or a little grass tied about them, joined in, opened their thick-lipped mouths in unison and chanted some old strain that smacked more of heathenism than of the Christianity which most of them were supposed to have embraced. Under the coco-palms hard by sat several old women who dealt in South Sea witchcraft. I never saw such pathetically hideous old hags as they were. Their faces wrinkled up to a breathing-map of sin and vice as they put their fingers to their shrivelled lips and warned the innocent girls of sorrows to come, foretelling dire disaster, or the reverse, to those who appealed to them for prophecies.

Many of the maidens from the surrounding villages came running up the bush track and delightedly joined in the circling ring of dancers. A few of the latter, who belonged to the low-caste toiling natives, availed themselves of the opportunity to show their figures off, and though the majority of the dancers were innocent enough, in their way, these looser ones swayed about and went through preposterous antics, endeavouring to please the eyes of the semi-savage native men who squatted round as sightseers. Great was their applause at frequent intervals, and deep the pleasure of those women who eagerly sought to please the eyes of prospective husbands.

Reviere and I stood watching this scene; neither of us spoke, so deeply were we interested in all about us. Then I touched Reviere, and told him to look behind him; there sat Mabau at the feet of a villainous-looking old witch who, responding to her pleadings, was doubtless telling Mabau how to win back Vituo's love. There she sat, that artless, deceived maid, rubbing together the magic sticks and repeating word for word all that the old witch told her. It sounded in this wise: "O wao, we wao, wai wai, O mio mio, mio mi"; and so on, over and over again. Poor little Mabau, how fast she rubbed the magic sticks as, unperceived, Reviere and I watched her from the shadows and the old crony picked her two black front teeth with a bone skewer and thought over some new phrase for Mabau and the other maids to repeat after her. Many maids appealed to her and rubbed the sticks, some crossways and some downways, as they thought of the bonny promised babies that would be theirs. Two ugly old divorced wives, who had been foretold new husbands and children if they rubbed the magic sticks the right way, rubbed and rubbed so hard that their dark bodies were steaming with perspiration in the moonlight!

Neither of us approached Mabau as we watched; we saw why she had been absent from us for two nights. We had no doubt that each night she had sat at the black crone's feet, listening to her prophecies and doing all she told her to do with those bits of stick, while Vituo, away in Suva, made love to the young white woman and thought no more of Mabau, who was to bring down vengeance on his head for his sins.

Next night Mabau watched at the trysting-place for the old witch's prophecies to be fulfilled, but found that Vituo did not come as had been foretold, so as she knew of an old and lonely missionary who lived some eight miles from the spot where Reviere and I witnessed the native fête, she told us that she would go and visit the good white man and see if he could help her in her sorrow. Finding out from Bones where the recluse lived, I, being deeply interested, went off the following afternoon to see him. After four hours' hard walking I inquired from some natives, and following a track which was thickly covered with thangi-thangi and drala growth, arrived at Naraundrau, which was situated south-east of the Rewa river and not far from the seashore. There in a secluded spot close by a stream was a small, neatly thatched homestead. As I approached all seemed silent, deserted and overgrown; the trees that shaded the hut-like home were heavy with thick, human-hand-shaped leaves, which intensified the gloom and isolation. I coughed purposely; the door opened, and there, framed in the doorway, stood a tall, stooping, grey-bearded man of about seventy or seventy-five years of age.

"Welcome, my son," he said as I introduced myself, and he noticed that I was tired, for the heat of the sun had been terrific and I was parched with thirst. I had brought my violin with me for companionship and safety; though I had great faith in the Organization officials, I did not wish to tempt their integrity by leaving my instrument behind.

CHAPTER XXIII

Father Anster—Fijian Legendary Lore—Forest Graves—The Blind Chief—Mythology and Love-making—Falling Stars—The Change—A Drove of Native Children—The Village Missionary—A Native Supper—An Old Chief's Reminiscences—Fijian Poets and Musicians—A Tribute to the Humbug of Civilisation

I SAT and gazed round that little lonely homestead by the shore-side at Naraundrau. The scent of the jungle blooms and dead grass crept into my nostrils as soft winds came up from the sea, blew in at the small doorway and fell asleep in the leafy hollows. Opposite the doorway, by his broken coloured-glass window, sat the missionary to whom Mabau had appealed. He had already given her his advice.

He was a venerable-looking old man, with earnest, sunken grey eyes. As his aged, bearded lips moved, and he spoke in a sensitive, musical voice, I at once felt a liking for him, and I seemed to be back in the days of an age that had long since passed away. For this lonely old missionary was the sole survivor of the first white men who had exiled themselves from their native lands with the one intense motive only in their hearts—to endeavour to preach the word of Christ and better the conditions of heathen lands. No ambition in his mind had craved for recognition; he had done his day's work, and there, weighed down with years, he waited sadly, yet patiently, the last act of life's drama, the call of his Creator, to whose service he had devoted his earnest existence. He died, quite unknown to men on earth, for if men do not strive for fame it seldom will come to them, unless they do not deserve it.

"My son, what brings you this way?" he said, and his grey eyes gazed kindly at me.

"Father," I said respectfully, "I heard of you from Mabau, the native girl who sorrows over her faithless lover, and since hearing of you it has been my wish to meet you, and here I am."

Hearing my answer, the old man looked intently at me, and to my great pleasure I saw that I had impressed him favourably. "Art thou hungry, lad?" he said. "No, not hungry, but I am exceedingly thirsty, Father," I answered; and at that he at once brought out, from a little wooden cupboard by his side two coco-nuts, and with trembling fingers pierced the holes with a screw. Very thankful I was as I drank off a tin pannikin full to the brim of the refreshing fruit milk. After that I felt much refreshed and more at my ease, as I talked to my host.

At his bidding I took my violin from its case and played the *Ah che la morte* from *Il Trovatore* to him. As the strain died away, and silently I laid the fiddle down, he crossed his hands over his breast and sat in the gloom, for night was falling fast. He looked like an old, grey-bearded apostle carved in stone as he sat there.

"My son, thou playest well, and I am thankful for thy visit," he murmured; and I was touched and highly pleased, for deep in my heart I suddenly felt a tenderness for the lonely old missionary. I saw by the way he crossed his hands that he was a Roman Catholic. I am a Protestant by birthright, but his sincerity made me feel more attached to his denomination than my own.

As night fell and the stars came out he became more talkative and unburdened himself to me, a fact which I always remember with pride, for he would not have done so if he had not felt instinctively that my heart was in sympathy with his.

Rising and lighting an old oil lamp, he stood it on the window-shelf, and its faint flicker lit up his room. In the corner was a sleeping-mat, for he slept on the floor in native fashion. His furniture consisted of two wooden stools, a small bench table and a few cooking utensils. Outside the door in a cage was a large grey parrot; it looked as old as its master, was almost featherless and seldom spoke. But now and again it would gaze sideways at me and without opening its tuneless beak say in a sepulchral voice, "Good-bye, good-bye," as though it were jealous of my conversation with its lonely master. It was a wise old bird, mistrusted strangers and realised that old age could be tempted and led away from old friendships by the voice of youth.

As we sat there together the moon came out and shone brilliantly over the sea, outdoing the dimness of his oil lamp; so brightly did it shine over the palms that one could easily have read ordinary print.

Taking an old flute down, he started to play upon it, and then with a sigh laid it back on the shelf and asked me if I should care to stay the night. "Yes," I immediately answered. We went out and strolled in the moonlight, and he told me much of Fiji in the old days. Though he was a poor and aged man, with only the moonlit forest flowers as his friends, flowers that would some day blossom over his fast-dissolving dust, the largess of his sincere heart, all that he told me, has been vast wealth to my memories through the years, and his dead voice has haunted my dreams at times.

He too told me of Thakambau; he had known him in his worst days, and spoke with the famous warrior king when he had at length, after many councils with his chiefs, decided to embrace Christianity.

As we strolled under the straight-stemmed palms the silvered moonlit waves splashed over the coral reefs below, and across the waters, like a weird shadow, passed a canoe filled with singing natives.

"Who sleeps there?" I asked him as we passed a mound of earth whereon was a cross half hidden in drala weed. He told me that it was the grave of a white man who had left a ship at Viti Levu and had become attached to the wife of a notable chief. The chief discovered them together by the shore, and after a terrible battle, the white man with a rifle-butt and the chief with a club, the white man fell mortally wounded. In the struggle the native wife was shot dead, and her spirit, the natives say, was carried on wings of fire up through the trees towards the stars that light the shores of that heathen land which was ruled by Mburotu. The missionary told me that he crept through the forest and with his own hands dug a grave under the pandanus palms for the slain body of the white man, and night after night he came and prayed fervently over the man of his race, asking God to forgive and grant to his soul salvation.

I was much impressed as he told me these things, and also by seeing how, as we walked along, he would tenderly bend and touch the tall flowers with his lips. "Under them sleeps the child I loved, or the chief who fell in some bloody tribal fight," he would say; and he told me also that often in the Fijian wilds men, women and children were buried in spots known only to those who loved and buried them.

That same night as we walked along the narrow track by the shore-side at Naraundrau the aged missionary took me gently by the arm and, turning up the inland track, we stood by a native's conical-shaped hut. In it sat an old, almost blind chief, the half-brother of Vakambau, a great warrior who was dead. It appeared that he loved the missionary, and though he would not give up his heathen faith had, owing to the supplications of my host, half embraced Christianity.

It was the habit of the Father to call night after night and pray with the old heathen chief before he slept. I felt very strange as I stood watching the white man and the old Fijian kneeling side by side praying, while three old women squatting in the corner of the den gazed on silently, as though they were carved stone images. They were his servants; being of Fijian royal blood, he would not move himself. Often as he sat there he imperiously pointed to a stone flask wherein was some *yangona*,[16] and at once the slaves of royalty, with machine-like swiftness, filled a stone bowl and held it to his lips. Suddenly starting up, he rushed to the den door and gazed up at the trees, shouting, "Wai, wai, taho mi," then waved his arms, lifted his chin towards the stars and called to the memory of dead warriors and comrades dead with heathen gods. As the Pacific wind sighed softly through the giant backa-trees he bowed his head reverently, for to him so answered the gods.

    16. Native wine made from a root.

I stayed that night with the missionary, and the next day and night also, and heard many strange things. Beautiful were some of the legends of the forest children that my host told me. The stars were the eyes of the fiercer gods, and the falling stars the bright tears of the powerful Muburto and Nedengi's warriors. Fijian maidens and youths prayed to the eyes of shadow-land, and if, as their impassioned lips met, a star fell and arched over them in the vault of night, great was their sorrow, for a god had shed a tear over the grief that would befall the life of the first-born. But if, ere the lovers said farewell, more stars fell, great was their rejoicing, for it was a sign that other gods were pleading to the greater god to stay the evil that was predestined by the first star that burst out of the dark soul of evil Destiny. So, notwithstanding heathenism and the gruesome cannibalistic customs of the old times, much innocence and poetry softened the hearts of the wild native children of those dim lands. It was a common sight by night in the shade of the coco-palms to see love-sick maids in the arms of the Fijian youths, gazing at the skies, yearning for the sight of the vast gods shedding starry tears on their behalf, and often great was their delight to find the foretold grief to their first-born overthrown by the power of other gods. Then the innocent maids gave themselves, body and soul, to the infatuated, delighted youths, and fell with the falling of the stars! When the stars on windy nights twinkled fiercely through the wailing boughs of the bending forest giants, lovers gazed heavenward anxiously, for to them the glimmering stars were the tiny bright legs of their unborn children running happily across the fields of paradise. Often, too, sorrowing mothers would peer up for hours on those windy, starlit nights, as they watched their dead children's bright legs twinkling as they ran laughing over the forest trees in the far-off fields of shadow-land.

As I heard these beliefs of the forest I thought of Mabau, and wondered whether, while she was in the arms of Vituo, the stars had fallen, and in her poetic faith she had given herself to him; and I saw that though the native legends were beautiful, it was sad for the maids; for the stars foretold many things that did not come to pass, and mythology, when applied to morals, brought much sorrow to those that loved.

The aged missionary spoke the language like a native and so, through mixing with the remnants of his old flock for years, isolated as he was, knew all their ways and their passions and aspirations. He told me that the mythology and religions of the South Seas revealed, through their poetic, heathen expression, much that was "new thought" in modern Europe, and that all those things which the great minds of my country had discussed and the nobleness they had overthrown by their doctrine of the "survival of the fittest," a doctrine bringing the whole creed of self-sacrifice and bravery down to selfish motives, had been discussed and expressed in mythology and heathen song by the cannibalistic bards and philosophical savages at the bokai feasts of those heathen lands.

Lands where maidens gave their lives for their lovers, and wives for their husbands, for it had been the custom that when a chief died his wife should be buried alive with him; and so strong was the faith of these people that they met their terrible end bravely, and sang death songs, which could be heard faint and muffled as the tombstone closed over them. It was even then the custom of maids to die and be buried with their dead lovers, their belief being that they appeared before the gods as they died. Those who thought themselves young and beautiful sacrificed themselves, so that in spirit-land they might be ever young and fortunate in their love affairs. Often I saw skeletons in caves, which were the remains of old age; they had been strangled by their relatives to avoid further trouble from the complainings of their infirmities.

On the night preceding my last day with the old missionary Mabau, the native girl, came to him as sunset was fading over the seas. As the shadows crept and thickened around the hermit's home a noise of naked feet in the jungle grass disturbed us. A gentle tap at the door revealed Mabau's dusky face. I understood little that she said, for she spoke in her own language to my host, but I saw by her eyes and trembling lips that she was sorely troubled. After hearing the Father's advice she became calmer, and falling on her knees kissed his extended hand and bearded face as a child would kiss its father; then, without speaking a word, she ran off swiftly into the forest.

The old missionary asked me many questions as to where I was staying, upon which I told him of Mr Bones. Hearing this, he gravely shook his head and scanned me solemnly. "You look an honest lad and well able to take care of yourself," he said; and then I explained to him how I had left my ship at S—— because I could not stand a drunken crew, and that was the true reason for my accepting the Organization's hospitality. From him I heard that a week or so before I arrived a fugitive had appeared at the Organization and the second day after had shot himself. Bones had hastily called on the Father, who delivered the Sacrament to the dying man, who, ere his breath ceased, made his confession. The Father did not reveal the facts to me, but I heard them from the lips of a high-caste Fijian with whom I stayed between my visits to the Organization's shanty. For after the first few days I only called upon Mr Bones as a visitor, taken there through my adventurous spirit, and for the novelty of associating with old villains and seeing the sad fugitives who arrived from the far-off cities of the world.

That night as I lay by my hermit host I watched him as he quietly slept on his sleeping-mat; moonlight streamed through the tiny window hole and revealed his careworn, bearded face. Still as death he lay as the breeze crept into the open door and stirred the few grey hairs above his lofty brow. The beating of the seas on the shore sounded at intervals and died away; the shadow leaves of the palms outside moved gently over the wooden moonlit walls, over his grey-bearded face and crossed hands. I felt that I was back in the Middle Ages, in some mysterious mediæval monastery, instead of in that heathen land of dying crime and bloodthirsty cannibalism, where but a few years before Thakambau, the warrior king, who now lay in the grave not far off at Bau, sailed forth from the creeks below to give battle to rival kings, accompanied by his armada of outrigged canoes. As I dreamed I heard the restless seas below, I saw those primitive fleets of canoes fading in the sunset, filled with dark, savage, patriotic faces, and the stalwart cannibal king leaning on his war-club and gazing proudly as he stood eyeing the canoes of his warriors paddling along to meet the tribal foe. It was almost unbelievable how swiftly change, through the coming of the white men, had overthrown the cannibalistic festivals and heathen customs: at Levuka, Viti Levu and Suva church spires were rising where the bokai feast and fierce songs once broke the silence; from native homes now come the strumming of cheap German pianos and lotu songs sung by mouths that a few years before had eaten those they had loved.

At daybreak Father Anster, the old missionary, rose and prepared breakfast, after which he took his flute from the shelf and played one tune over and over again continually; and the old featherless parrot in the cage tried desperately to repeat the notes through its tuneless beak and, to tell the truth, made as much mess of the melody as my host did; for though he had music in his soul, his lips were unable to express it. There he sat, holding the flute to his aged lips and blowing away; and though I know he must now be dead, hallowed dust somewhere near that spot where I saw him years ago, still I can see him sitting by his little doorway, and see the kind look in his eyes as I bade him farewell and passed away into the forest, with the thought and promise to see him again in a few days.

As I strolled along under the palms and big tropical trees I fell into deep thought; everything was silent, except a few birds singing to the sunset, which they could spy from the topmost boughs whereon they sat. Suddenly I was startled by hearing a noise, and crossing the gullies I went down a steep slope and peeped through the jungle thickets of bamboo beneath the coco-palms to see what was about, and there, romping in the deep fern grass, was a flock of naked native children, tiny wild faces, boys and girls. As I watched my foot slipped. In a moment they all looked up and their bright eyes spied me. Like a drove of rabbits off they bolted, their little brown shoulders and tossing heads of frizzly hair just reaching the fern-tops as they raced away and faded in the distant forest gloom, frightened out of their lives. A stream of sunset out seaward crept through the wind-blown forest boughs and glinted over them as they ran, till they looked like tiny wood-elves racing across fairyland! I never saw such a pretty sight. In fun I ran after them, and two little stragglers left behind, seeing me run, screamed; then through the bushes in front of me suddenly poked the heads of mop-haired mothers and fierce dark men. I had come across a native village!

At first I felt a bit frightened; but as soon as those wild-blooded parents saw my white face and youthful look they smiled, for their instincts are swift and true. I stepped into the village, and soon we were all good comrades. It was there that I met a missionary who lived not far off, and was adviser and preacher to the native village. He was a good man at heart, but extremely bigoted, and when I asked him about Father Anster he yawned and evaded my questions, told me that he was considered a mild kind of lunatic. I did not argue the point, but nevertheless I saw the way the wind blew and thought a good deal. I realised there was no love lost between my old host and the new missionaries, who did not care for hermits who toiled and lived completely by themselves.

The hot season was at its height, and not till the sun had set and the sea winds gently blew over the isle did I feel comfortable. One is forcibly reminded when travelling in the South Sea Isles that the natives in complete undress are utilising their own skins to the best advantage: often I envied them their scanty *sulu* (loin-cloth), as my white duck trousers and shirt flopped and steamed with perspiration as I sweated onwards. I stayed for several hours at the village I had stumbled across. Round the native huts the evening fires blazed as squatting by stone bowls the families ate their supper; dipping their fingers into the steaming mixture, they pushed worm-like stuff into their dark mouths. The toothless old chiefs and mothers were waited on by the children, who often sulkily helped them, hastily pushing what looked like long white worms, that hung from the aged mouths, in between the mumbling lips.

Close by, in one of the conical, thatched dens, loudly wailed a windy harmonium, played by a young aspirant for musical fame. The selling of harmoniums in the South Seas in those days was a paying business: a native would work for three years on a plantation, without wages, to possess one of those instruments of torture, and a family that possessed one obtained a social distinction equal to the Order of the Bath in Great Britain. It was the celebrated High Chief Volka who owned this particular terrible thing.

While the huddled natives chattered and gorged over their calabashes of hot mystery this chief led me round and proudly showed me the sights. Sunset had died, and the stars were beginning to peep through the dusky velvet blue skies that could be seen in many patches above the scattered waveless palms and banyan-trees. Chief Volka was a true survival of the barbaric age, six feet in height, scarred and tattooed from his brow to his knees. He had lost one eye in battle, and the other, through double use, bulged considerably. Leading me into his ancestral halls—three thatched rooms—he stood beside me, as his mop-head touched the low roof, and pointed to a ponderous war-club that hung on the wooden wall. Round it was a grim collection of spear-headed weapons. Standing by my side, with his shoulders majestically lifted and his chest blown out, he proudly told me of the wounds that implement had inflicted, and of the many lives it had, with sudden force, sent hastily to heathen-land. His one eye flashed with revived memories, and then that old veteran of some past Fijian Waterloo told me how his civilised tribe had exterminated the uncivilised foe in a mighty battle, and of the benefit the great victory had conferred upon humanity. For did not the victory overthrow tribal men who ate their wounded on holy days?—thus angering the gods by not keeping them in pickle till the Fijian Lent had passed!

He stood there, drawn up to his full height, his shrivelled but erstwhile muscular arm outstretched, as he told me of the overthrow of tribes on neighbouring isles who had aspired to dominate the whole Fijian Group by militarism. With forgivable pride he took down the huge club that had brought the ambitious leader of the hated hordes to the earth with a smashed skull. It was a mighty weapon, and the bare-skinned youth beside him gazed upon it with awestruck eyes as I said: "And what happened after that victory?" "We had ten years of great peace, many feasts and many wives, and our gods were pleased till came your race and overthrew them." And then he continued in this wise: "Alas, our great civilisation has passed away; revered customs, creeds and mighty histories of my race are forgotten with the old winds. Ah, your white race tramples on our old dynasty of supreme goodness!"

I gazed silently as he spoke and wondered much, for I knew that the foundation of civilisation, and all that is called best, is built on man's attempt to ward off impending disaster. As I thought I wondered how much wisdom lay in his natural vanity, for the warriors of old had died out and the new race looked cute, flabby, and quite devoid of energy. Outside old men and youths smacked their lips and grunted as they nibbled coco-nuts and chewed tobacco; the grandees drank new rum, and the old women and maids of fashion whispered scandal and scratched their mop-heads delicately with one outstretched finger.

Brilliantly the moon shone through the forest trees as I strolled from scene to scene of that South Sea village. By tiny camp fires sat the elder members of the various households; the little children were fast asleep by them on small mats. Some gazed into the fire ash, spat and chewed, others chatted, and on the hill-side sat several groups singing softly so as not to awaken the sleepers. They were strange, weird melodies that I listened to; and as I stood alone in the shadows I knew that I heard in those primeval wails of joy and sorrow the youthful voice of music and poetry as it was ere it attained the artificial development expressed in Europe, tricked out and dressed in all the artistries to suit applauding conventionality. Old women wailed songs that told of dead children, dead husbands or lovers, and all the many griefs that flesh is heir to. I think the sad old missionary with whom I had stayed had awakened in me a note of deeper thought than was usual in my reflection. On my memory are still vividly engraved the scenes of that night; the moonlight over the trees, the stars and the squatting groups of the village natives are all still mine, and the atmosphere is as clear as, yet somewhat sadder than, of yore, like a melody heard again, after many years, in another country. I seemed to know that the wild life and scenery round me was similar to the embryo life of modern civilisation; and there was something real and innocent in that Fijian Arabian night that made the modern world of life look intensely vapid. I still see the women of Fijian fashion, with their legs outstretched before the dying fires, each attired in some sailor's cast-off undershirt or a portion of a white woman's garment. Some strutted under the palms and gazed almost disdainfully upon maidens and mothers who only wore the native grass-weaved sulu. I knew that I gazed upon the first leaders of Fijian fashionable society, society that has reached the zenith of vanity in Europe. I saw budding knighthoods fanning flies and mosquitoes from the high chief's oily body. His eyelids blinked approval as the aspirants to royal favour lifted his fat feet, which rested on a little mat, and blew their cooling breath on them.

Poor relations carried refuse in large stone bowls to the village cesspool. Pet mongrel dogs snapped at the hovering ring of flies and sniffed at the stench as they passed it, whilst the rich relations lolled under the sunlit tropic palms. At the far end of the village, on a stump, stood the fanatic, shouting in Fijian, "Taho-ai-Oa," and shrieking and stamping to entice the straggling villagers to come to his special mission class. Swarthy Solomon Islanders and Indians with brilliant dark eyes gazed at the maids. Under the palms sat the full-lipped youth, Lota-Mio; oblivious of all around him, he toiled on with his rusty nail, carving on a sea-shell the outlines of a maiden's face; the work revealed wonderful talent. Maidens and youths embraced and gazed with shining eyes at each other as the shaggy-headed Fijian poet pointed to the evening star imaged in the still lagoon, for it shone in the fairyland of still waters. They peered over the water's brink and wondered to see their dark faces under the imaged trees that were upside down; then the branches stirred as the mirrored winds blew in the water and their imaged faces broke up and disappeared!

I got the old chief to see me safely on the road home; for though I trusted the Fijians, I did not like the look of the imported Indians, who crept about the village selling sham jewellery and tempting the maids with trifles and trinkets. They were stealthy-looking men, dark and masterful in appearance. Their creeds were slowly overthrowing Christianity, for the natives were weak, and Mohammedanism was more in harmony with their secret cravings and requirements. Also the colour of the turbaned teachers matched their own skins. White men can hardly blame the childish Fijians for embracing Mohammedanism as readily as they turned to Christianity, for in London town the Islamic creed is being preached and is finding numerous adherents, gathered from the so-called high-class Christians, who gain greater comfort from Mahomet than from the sorrow of Calvary.

CHAPTER XXIV

Back at the Charity Organization—Mabau—A Fugitive Bank Manager arrives—How the Organization secured Funds—English Refugees—Departure—Native Burial—A New Sect—With Bones again—Another Fugitive and his Experiences—Galloway's Tall Hat—The Death of Mabau—The Haunted Wreck

I RETURNED once more to the Organization rooms, so tired that I fell asleep without delay, and not until next morning was I introduced to several members whom I had not seen before. My toothless friend was mumbling away to an old "shellback," who in turn was striving to outdo his comrade's experiences on land and sea. "Glad to see yer," said the old salt, as Bones introduced me. I returned the compliment and shook his extended hand warmly. He was the life of the place, and not pleasant life either, for he had an old cornet, and in the middle of the night would lift his face to the low roof and blow some wretched tune on it over and over again. One night there was a fight, for as he played and sang and rolled his eyes to the ceiling a boot struck him behind the ear; one of the members had lost his temper and thrown it. The incident caused a fearful hubbub, the cornet got smashed to bits and one or two of the bunks broken down. Bones came in, pointed a revolver at the fighters and threatened to shoot, and I believe he would have done so if they had not quieted down. They were a rough crew, and I made up my mind to get away from the place at the first opportunity. Many strange things I heard, some of which I will tell you.

Next day as I sat alone reflecting in the Organization's gloomy room I heard Mabau just outside wailing a native chant of love-sickness. She had peeled the "spuds" and finished the domestic duties, for which Bones gave her ample wages.

"What did the kind white missionary say, Mabau?" I whispered softly to her, as Bones and two scrubby-faced villains puffed their pipes and shuffled a pack of cards on the bench.

Looking up with affectionate eyes that gazed at me steadily for a little time and then dropped as she sighed, she answered: "He say pray to white God; go to your people, and if your Vituo no love you quickly find him who will love you." And as she said this to me she gazed into my eyes in an appealing way that made me sorry for her.

"Come this way, Mabau," I said, and she followed me like a little child, till out of earshot she sat under the coco-palms behind the Organization hut. I took her there because I wanted to be alone with her to advise her for her own sake. I liked Mabau exceedingly, for I saw in her something deeper than

I had noticed in most native girls. Sitting by me in the jungle fern, with her chin on her knees, she lifted her eyes to me and sang a weird love chant. "Wail O—Wa—O, Mio" it sounded, as she sang tenderly her beseeching plaint.

"Why do you sing, Mabau?" I asked. "Is it the wicked Vituo that makes you so sad?"

"Vituo I hate," she answered fiercely. "I will kill him, and the white man will be my friend." But I shook my head and told her not to kill Vituo, but go to her own people, and as I spoke I pointed to the forest. Obediently as a child she rose, and before moving away gave me a shell comb from her hair. I accepted it and smiled kindly at her, for I felt sorry for the brown, forlorn girl. Then with pattering bare feet she went down the forest track, wailing. I went back to the Organization room and practised my violin, as I always did for several hours every day, both on land and sea.

I think it was that same night that a portly gentleman looking like a bank manager came down the river from Suva and hastily entered the door, talking hurriedly to Mr Bones. Opening a little bag he gave him a bundle of what appeared to be banknotes, and so placed himself under the protection of the Organization flag. He was fashionably dressed in a tall hat and frock-coat, the tail of which had a singed hole in it, as though he had been shot at at close quarters. Rubbing his hands genially, as though with great relief, he looked round the secluded room and then asked me if I were English, and inquired if many of my countrymen resided in those parts. My reply allayed his anxiety on that point. He had a big, round, clean-shaven, red face; grey locks protruded from beneath the rim of his tall hat, and fitted his brow and neck so nicely that it was easy to see that he wore a wig. His expression was like his hair, false; his was a face that could look jolly and lascivious, or sedate, at will, or even appear deeply thoughtful and religious should occasion require. Intensely preoccupied, he sat looking at newspaper cuttings, and with a vacant stare said "Em—em," as I spoke to him. The natives and the scenery round had no interest for him; some life-and-death business had hastened him our way. He stopped only two nights and then left by the next 'Frisco steamer, bound for some port outside the reach of the extradition treaty. I was glad to see him go. Every time anyone opened the door he started so that it got on my nerves. Once when Bones suddenly opened the door with a crash, on purpose, I believe, he gave a leap and lifted the lid of the emergency barrel, upsetting the mugs of rum and causing the whole Organization to swear as one man. As he jumped in I quickly put the lid on before he could lower his shoulders and head, and crash went his tall hat, while I heard a muffled oath beneath the lid. The emergency barrel was a huge ship's beef-barrel, which stood behind the door, and in it new members of the Organization hid when the overseas police arrived. A cave beneath the floor was a secret known to old members only.

It was a mystery to me how these preoccupied fugitives from justice got to know of Bones's establishment. My mystification was dispelled by one of the old officials, who let me into the secret, telling me more than he should have done, as he swallowed rum and became loquacious. It appeared that Bones boarded the boats as they arrived at Suva, Vanu Levu or Lakemba, interviewed passengers and spotted likely customers. With years of research and experience he had developed a bloodhound's instinct for twigging uneasy fugitives, and by devious artifices managed to give them the hint and let them know that he was the man who understood difficult positions, and was willing to be a faithful friend to all those who yearned to remain unknown.

I also learnt that Bones was not above the ruse of getting a confederate on board the boat, who would pose as a detective and suddenly turn round and scrutinise any suspicious passenger, and so deliberately frighten him into hurriedly leaving the ship. By a prearranged signal, when the native canoes brought the flying fugitive ashore, the Organization officials arrested him! Those who confessed offhand were given the straight hint that their captors were not beyond accepting a bribe and letting the prisoner escape. If they had no money Bones behaved well to them, put them up for a time, then shipped them off at the first chance.

Those who had managed to bring wealth with them gave Bones a liberal bribe, and you can imagine it was no hard job to get it out of them. Men from all parts of the world sought the South Seas as a hiding-place; some came to save their necks, many to escape penal servitude. The Charity Organization of the South Seas was not far behind its namesakes in Europe. It was a paying concern, and though the method on which it was conducted was risky and strange, it was run on lines of truth and charity; stolen money only was accepted, the guilty were punished by being robbed, and help was given to the fallen, who were taken in, fed, and finally guided on the road to seclusion and security. Assuredly it did not reverse its creed, as the organizations of Western seas do, where bent old men on tottering feet tap at the door of charity and, apologising for being old, start to earn the crust of charity by lifting the pick-axe and breaking stones—stones as hard as the hearts of the British officials who waddle with fatness and the wealth screwed out of insane charity-givers.

I could tell many distressing details of that South Sea hospitality; fiction pales into insignificance beside the realities, the tragic dramas of life that came to that old shanty. I could tell you how men fell through the lure of gold, and the temptation to appear wealthy and respectable, in the cities of a civilisation that so often defeats its own purpose; for how often men fall in their ambition to gain the good opinion of those who only *appear* better than themselves.

The unpractical passion of love also brought much wealth to the South Sea Organization's exchequer. I remember one middle-aged gentleman whose manner brought to that degraded forest homestead a flavour of English society. With him, in the tastefully laid-out little room, wept a girl, obviously brought up in English respectability. She was a pretty, blue-eyed girl, but her face had aged with grief and remorse and the thought of motherhood. Mabau was her ever-tender maid and companion. The bond of sympathy that linked the brown and the white woman together expressed something that had an intense note of poetry in it. Mabau's wild intuition read the girl's sorrow and remorse. The two women, so far removed from each other by blood and education, through mutual grief and instinct became equal. Softly Mabau stroked her white sister's face, and she in turn caressed the brown girl, who also was fast approaching motherhood.

I asked no questions of her male companion as he and I together strolled across the landscape. I led him to the native villages, and did my best to interest him and take him out of himself during the three days that he stayed with Bones. We conceived a mutual liking for each other, and he took me sufficiently into his confidence to let me know that they were on the way to South America.

I saw them both off by the s.s. —— from Suva. Mabau carried the white girl's things to the boat. As they stood on the ship's deck they waved their hands to us, and we stood watching the frail girl, clinging to the man's arm, as the vessel moved away and the tropical sunset flooded the seas. We stared till the ship was a speck on the waste of waters. So disappeared those outcasts on the horizon, together with their passion and its fruits, bound for another land, fading from our sight for ever. Mabau cried bitterly. I felt very sad also as we went down the river, and the hut looked more lonely than ever to me after they left.

I only stayed with Bones as a visitor, and several times went off to Lakemba and the various isles of the group, visiting Thombo and the Eastern Isles, also Yasawa, Kandavu and the native villages inland from Vana Levu, in the Bua district. Some of the natives owned profitable plantations, planted chiefly with coco-palms for the produce of copra and food for domestic use.

I often roamed those barbaric lands quite alone, and used to stand and reflect as I gazed through the wooded landscape; the solitude seemed so peaceful, but my dreams would conjure up pictures of the hot-footed, bloodthirsty tribes on the warpath long ago. Swarthy bodies and mop-heads moving through those glooms to charge the ambushed rival tribe, finally bringing their victims to the ovens that fizzled the "long pig."

Where now the cattle roam at leisure, nibbling the covatu grass and milk-fern of the cleared pastures, once towered thickly wooded forest slopes of tropic fern and coco-palms. Patches of those forests still remain. In those old glooms I roamed and spent many happy and exciting times, for among them still stood native villages of semi-savage peoples; many of them clung to old heathen beliefs and sneered as they passed the den wherein moaned the wailing harmonium. Fierce fights often raged among the population, for they were a mixed party, many of them being emigrant islanders from the Gilbert, Ellice and Samoan Groups.

I used to wander about those old native villages, undecided whether to go to Australia or to get a berth on one of the trading-boats bound for Honolulu, and so make my way to San Francisco. The weather was very hot, the thermometer reaching 95°. As I sat in the shade beneath the trees, above my head chuckled peculiar, migratory birds, pruning their wings and whistling to the infinite blue above their topmost bough, which swayed gently to the welcome sea breeze that blew inland. It was there that I saw a native funeral; a Fijian girl had died. I watched the thatched den's door open, as swarthy men, with bowed, lamenting heads, bore on their shoulders the square-shaped coffin. It was sunset and the burying-hour. The whole village started wailing, beating their breasts and naked thighs as they moved on in the grotesque but sad procession. One old woman, the great-grandmother, I think, led the way to the native cemetery. It was a mournful sight, and a novel one for Western eyes, for their grief seemed real! By a lonely forest track the procession stopped, and there, in the shade of a mighty group of banyan-trees, was the grave. Loudly the mourners started to wail, and the old woman and the girls fell flat on their faces and grovelled on the forest turf, wailing a Fijian lament, while the male mourners drank kava from little pots to keep their spirits up. To my astonishment the old woman was lowered into the grave first. She stretched her body out, feigning death so well that her naked limbs and corpulent, brown frame looked stiff with *rigor mortis*. Four powerful chiefs, two at her head and two at the middle, slowly lowered her into the tomb.

Then came forward one who I presumed was the high priest and, standing on the brink of the grave, he lifted his hands towards the skies and called on the gods to take the living spirit of the old woman into the land of death to look after the soul of the dead girl. As the high priest yawned and finished his speech he walked away, and maidens cast flowers on to the living body below. For a moment I thought that the old woman was to be buried alive, but to my relief I saw her dark, skinny fingers hastily emerge and cling to the grave's brink, as up came her head and she leapt out on all-fours.

Then the lid of the coffin, wherein lay the dead girl, was lifted, and the mourners each in turn gazed upon the face and wailed. I did not look, for the sight depressed me, and I hurried away. This method of burial, and the ceremony which I have described, was an old custom modified, a method employed by a new sect, a creed which was based half on heathenism and half on Christianity, similar to the many crank offspring creeds of Europe to-day.

After staying in Suva for two or three days, idling and boarding the few trading schooners in the harbour, I went back to the Den of Mystery presided over by Mr Bones. As I entered the Organization door I saw, through the wreaths of tobacco smoke, the villainous, unshaved profiles of the gay officials, as bending over the long bench they shuffled cards, swore and drank rum. As they welcomed me their fierce, suspicious, wrinkled brows smoothed out again. I had left my violin with them and, though I had been absent several days, it stood on the shelf over their heads as I had left it. They called on me for a solo as I sat down and smoked, but when I responded to their wish a terrible discord began, for the player of the smashed cornet joined in and put my ear out; his time and tune faculties were nil. When I stopped he still blew on, puffing out tunelessness. As the night advanced yarns began, and I heard experiences of those rough men, and truly truth is stranger than fiction. Much that I heard is unprintable, not so much because of its subject and expressive thought as from the fact that in Bones's hospitable establishment I received trust that once betrayed would bring dire disaster on fugitives who are still hiding, or have relatives of high standing in England and elsewhere.

Among others there was one weird-faced fellow there at that time. He looked thin and ill, but had been handsome in his day, and often through his rough accent came a different utterance, that of an educated man. Over his bunk were the photographs of a girl and of two old people. Something in his life had played havoc with him, for secret grief had prematurely wrinkled his brow and face. His eyes were clear, blue and earnest-looking. All the men took to him, for he was willing enough, and when they chaffed him he smiled good-naturedly and revealed the expression that had lit his face up as a boy.

Bones had picked him up adrift at sea whilst he was on a trip to Tonga in a schooner. The man had stowed away on a boat at Sydney that was bound for South America. The detectives had got wind of his being aboard; he had hidden himself between decks among the massed cargo, bales of wool. After the second day at sea the detectives, who were aboard, came down into the hold to see if they could discover his whereabouts. Without water, and with only a few biscuits to nibble at in his huddled confinement, he suffered agonies. It was almost stifling up on deck under the tropical sun, but down deep in the ship's hold he was almost suffocated, and the droves of hungry ship rats smelt his sweating body and viciously attacked him in the inky darkness.

"Often I had half a mind to give myself up," said he, "for the cursed vermin bit at my legs as I beat with my hands to keep them from eating at my face. I dared not sleep; indeed, as I dozed off once or twice I felt them pushing along under the legs of my trousers, and their rough tongues, like tiny saws, licked at the beads of cold sweat that broke out all over me." As he continued, the game of cards along the bench ceased; all hands became still with interest. Mabau, who crouched near my feet, gave a deepening blush as I gazed at her squatting on the floor beside me. She was gazing at Vituo's photograph, which he had had taken in Suva.

Proceeding with his story, as we puffed our pipes silently he continued: "Suddenly I heard a creaking noise forward; the bulk-head doors were opening! Peeping between the bales of cargo, I saw the flash of a bull's-eye lantern; they were crawling over the cargo searching for me! The human bloodhounds nearly trod on my body as they flashed their lanterns over the gloom and crept past me in the dark. In a second I saw my chance. I noiselessly worked my body backwards, as they were searching the cargo right ahead. Half dead I got through the bulkhead door and stood on deck.

"It was night; the stars lit the skies overhead and the funnel belched out reddened smoke that rolled astern. She was cutting across the Pacific at fourteen knots. How I drank in the fresh air as I crept up by the stokehold grating. Hiding myself by the funnel, I gazed up; there was the bridge, and to and fro walked the captain and chief mate. Presently I heard voices on deck; they were back from their search. "He's not down there," one of them shouted. The skipper leaned over the bridge rails. "You are on the wrong tack, I guess," he shouted back. "I wish they were," thought I, and at that moment I heard their footsteps coming up the gangway towards me.

"I held my breath; they flashed their lanterns about; one of them nearly brushed against me as I watched. A pain shot through my head; my God, I was done for! I clapped my hand to my mouth to save myself and muffle the sound. With a smothering throb it came; I gave forth a tremendous sneeze! It betrayed me. In an instant I seized the wooden grating by the bridge gangway and leapt to the lower deck. I heard the crashing and throbbing of the engines, as for a moment I stood by the galley port-hole and resolved on the next step. Gripping the grating tightly, I clambered on to the bulwark and dived into the Pacific! I felt the thunder and swirl of the screw as the revolving blades just missed me, and I was sucked down by the churning waters. Still clutching the grating I came up to the surface and, resting my arms on it, gazed at the ship. She was still thundering on, fading under the stars; I saw her go, racing away. Evidently they had not dreamed that I had jumped overboard.

"The cool waters refreshed me considerably. For a long while I could see the mast-head light of the ship, and then I was alone at sea. Daybreak crept over the world of waters and like a flood of fire the sunrise burst up through the sky; like a speck I bobbed about. Flocks of sea-birds sighted me and hovered overhead, then came down, their legs hanging loosely, as they tried to peek my eyes out! I beat about with my hands. As I got on to the grating, seeing that I was alive, they shrieked and wheeled away.

"The hot sun rose; I became delirious with thirst and, unable to help myself, drank sea-water. At sunset I half fell asleep as I lay on the grating, my legs in the water. I cursed that sneeze that had placed me in such a plight. In the night the moon rose. I was raving with delirium; somehow that sneeze became embodied in human shape; my delirious imagination saw it! There in the shivering moonlit water it swam round me! Nearer and nearer its grinning, demon face came; it seemed frog-like and half human. Dressed in a small red plush coat it hissed at the grating and peeped at me with blue, human eyes! I watched; the Universe crashed overhead. I waited my opportunity. It came. I seized that sneeze by the throat, tripped and squeezed the life out of its vile body, then flung it back into the moonlit waters. Once again it turned and came swimming back towards me, climbed up and grinned at me! Once more I gripped it and threw it over the side. It disappeared, and the dark fin of a grey-nosed shark slowly rose. Reality crept into my brain. I pulled my legs up on to the grating, which was awash with my weight. I waited for death and shouted. I knew that fin was real enough and only a miracle could save me; and it did, for my cry was heard. A passing schooner spotted me across the night, and Bones there threw the rope that saved me."

"Right enough," said Bones, as he knocked the ash from his pipe. Then all the hands filled their mugs with rum and clinked them together, and the contents, with one swallow, disappeared.

Such were some of the various experiences I heard from the lips of those men. Almost everything connected with the Organization had an exciting history attached to it; aye, from pretty Mabau to the tall hat that hung on a peg by the emergency barrel. I think I will tell you the history of that hat just as I heard it from Bones.

It appeared that in earlier days, before Bones had made the hiding profession into a fine art, and one which easily amassed wealth, his means of running the show and replenishing the food and rum casks were not as kindly and humane as the arresting scheme, with the final relief of the victim on getting his bribe accepted—a bribe that often astonished Bones by its generosity, for the shabbiest fugitives were generally the richest and the guiltiest.

Well, to proceed. That immaculate tall hat had brought the Organization in much money. When trading-ships called in at Suva and the surrounding isles Bones would go aboard and negotiate for the part purchase of the general cargo; and he did well; for, though he or his representative had no ready money, they would manage to dupe the skipper or supercargo by giving them a false bill or an I.O.U. from some firm of repute, who knew nothing whatever of Bones and his clever crew. Attired in a frock-coat and that tall hat, they commanded the necessary trust and respect.

Galloway, the Yankee who worked the business personally, managed to get a surprising amount of credit. Scores of harmoniums, musical-boxes and miscellaneous clothes were got hold of through the Yankee's smartness. The whole business was run on fine, strategic lines. After a good deal Galloway would lie low and lend the hat and frock-coat to a confederate. Soon, however, in spite of their care, a breath of suspicion blew across the South Seas. Skippers told each other to look out.

"You see that hole in the rim of the hat," said Bones, pointing his thumb to what looked like a bullet hole; "that d——d place cost me a cool thousand pounds." Then: "You see that 'ole, don't you? Well, when Galloway's pal went aboard a schooner in Lakemba he stands on deck and makes a deal for five hundred clocks—natives would give their souls for a clock—and a thousand tins of meat stuff; in fact almost everything that we wanted. Well, he gives the skipper his I.O.U., seemingly made out and signed by a settler who was well known for his wealth and integrity in Fiji; but, as he stood on deck and signalled to the natives overside to bring the boats alongside to take the first load of stuff away, the skipper, who had previously been done, spied the same hole in that tall hat which he had noticed when Galloway duped him. So he says: 'Before you take the stuff away have a whisky?' and then says, sudden-like: 'You've got your pal's old hat on; what's become of him? I've still got his I.O.U.' Galloway's pal at this looked uncomfortable, and the skipper kept the ball rolling, for he whips a revolver out of his pocket, and as H—— bolts over the side the old curse fires, bang! H——'s ear was blown off. So ended the I.O.U. trade, and H—— left those parts with his ear missing. Then he made a fortune through kidnapping native girls in the Solomon and Marquesan Groups, and got on so well that he purchased a schooner, and ten years ago called this way and invited us on board. As we drank in the saloon aft we heard the general cargo of naked native girls and youths wailing under the floor decks as they called for grub! I took mercy on half-a-dozen girls next morning as H—— got them on deck and paraded them for my inspection. I bought them and sold three to the sailors of a German man-o'-war, and their missionary gave me a good price for the other three."

So Bones rambled on, telling me much which I have left out as being unprintable and, worse—too true to enlarge upon! The traffic in native girls for immoral purposes was common in the early days, and still is to-day, but it is carried on now by more disguised methods; indeed, most of the crimes that were rampant in the old days are worse than ever, for they are carried on with deeper guile, as missionaries, earnest men enough, leave the sorrow and sin of their own lands to spread hypocrisy over the South Seas. For the natives are clever, and with education simply learn the duplicity of the white race; loudly they sing the lotu hymns as they grin in their hearts over the change in things for the better!

Now I am approaching the end of my stay in Fiji. I had my few belongings packed, for I had been promised a berth aboard the *Frigate Bird*, that lay in Suva harbour and was due to leave in a few days. It had been a swelteringly hot day. I had told Mabau that I was going away, and from her learnt that Vituo had completely thrown her over and was much in love with the white woman who had stayed at Suva. Tears gleamed in her eyes as she realised that I should soon be going, and as I sat and played the violin to the men who had befriended me while I was hard up she looked up at me like a whipped dog, with beseeching eyes, and I felt very sorry for her.

At sunset I walked with Bones under the coco-palms down by the river. It was to be my last night. The smell of the decaying ferns and rotting oranges in the jungle grass came in sweet, damp drifts as the cool evening breeze sprang up. In the trees a few birds sang, and from far-off came the sound of the tribal drums beating the sunset out, and the stars to the skies, over the native village a mile away. I had the night before been to Naraundrau to bid farewell to the old missionary. He had crossed his hands on his breast and blessed me, then laid his hands on my shoulders, gazed into my face and said: "Farewell, my son; the blessing of God be with you." I left him as a son would a father, with sadness in my soul for his age, and in my sorrow I seemed to hear a noise beating in my heart—like toiling shovels that day by day deepened his grave.

As I stood by the river slope with Bones we heard the paddling of a canoe, and round the bend came Mabau to wish me farewell. She appeared very excited as she jumped ashore. Early moonrise bathed the pool waters as she stood beneath the palms and to our surprise said: "Vituo is dead; I kill him." As she told us this she lifted her hands to the sky and wailed. We tried to calm her, but it was no use; we only gathered that Vituo, her faithless lover, had died by her hand. Still I can see her figure, mirrored in the water of the moonlit pool, as she wailed, swaying her blood-stained hands and singing a death chant that sounded like this when translated:

"O winds of night I call, I call,

Across the hills of sleep;

Let Mabau to silence fall

For ever into sleep."

Then gazing over her shoulder she rushed off into the jungle, and Bones and I hurried after her. Through the trees we saw her running. Then she reached the sea. "What's she up to?" said Bones, as we sighted the shore. Out on the edge of the promontory, like some carved goddess, she stood, appealing to the skies with lifted arms as she wailed a primitive note of sorrow. Moonlight revealed her stricken, dusky face. Up went her arms for a moment in perfect stillness, then she dived! Bones and I rushed over the reefs; neither of us had time to think that she might take her own life. Stumbling into the shallow water by the rocks, we reached the promontory and the spot where she went in. I dived and Bones followed me. Round and round we swam, moving the liquid depths, as the imaged stars twinkled and faded. "Mabau! Mabau!" we called, then we each dived, scrambled and felt for her. No sight or sign of life appeared; the dark waters had taken her young life away.

An hour later Bones and I crept back to the den, wretched and sad. We did not speak; we still had a faint hope that she might have swum round the promontory point, eluded us and be still alive. I could not sleep, and at daybreak we started off together. As we reached the fatal spot sunrise was creeping over the Pacific. Out on the extreme edge of the promontory we stood side by side and looked down into the clear depths, searching; for on the water floated her ridi, made from a pretty piece of coloured silk, a present to her from the white girl who had stayed at the Organization room. I knew it had been worn to please Vituo, whose despicable conduct had caused his own death and that of Mabau.

Suddenly Bones said: "Look!" and pointed for a moment. I hardly dared to gaze at the spot where he pointed, and then in perfect silence we looked. On the sandy bottom, deep down in the water, by a boulder of red and white coral, was Mabau, her eyelids apart as she stared fixedly up through the clear, crystal depth. The first sunbeams stained the water by her brown figure. The South Seas wild blackbird sang joyously in the coco-palms, and the sails of the outbound schooner that caught the tide faded on the horizon.

At sunset next day I bade Bones good-bye and sailed on the *Frigate Bird*.

For three months I sailed among the islands in a trading schooner and then left it at Hiva-oa, where I stayed for three weeks. I was a bit downcast, and employed my time by hard study on the violin. There was an old wrecked schooner on the reefs, and at night I used to creep down into her hold and practise. I was ambitious to be a great violinist. For a while I was in my element in that ship's hold, and then the natives heard my fiddle wailing and were frightened out of their lives, thinking that the wreck was haunted by evil spirits. I was innocent enough of it all as I played away night after night, until, looking through the port-hole in the bright moonlight, I heard a jabbering noise and saw hordes of natives on the beach, watching and creeping about as I played!

Then a man came aboard the wreck and shouted down the hold: "Halloa there!" and told me that all his hired natives were packing up and leaving for other islands, as they all thought when my violin wailed that the old wreck was haunted by spirits of heathen gods. So I lost my chance of being alone with my aspirations in the South Seas and once more got a schooner and went off to Honolulu and other islands.

I managed, by being careful, to save some money from my ship and musical engagements, for I was abstemious, and devoted my spare time to music and reading. I made several acquaintances among the crews of the ships that traded among the islands, many of whom were young Englishmen who had left the mail-boats and the deep-sea liners to earn more money on trading-boats and see the islands and the Australian cities. I also got to know many German and Colonial sailors. The North German Lloyd mail-ships arrived in Sydney weekly, and the hands would leave and get jobs on the small boats running to Samoa and elsewhere in the Pacific Isles.

CHAPTER XXV

At Nuka Hiva—Gilbert the Astronomer—The Grog Shanty—The Astronomer's Audience—Ah Foo, the Chinaman—Other Worlds than Ours—The Reformed Traders—The Death of Gilbert

ABOUT a month after the foregoing incidents took place, and while I was in the Marquesas Group, I came across an old man who was one of those characters which are often to be met with in the wild, outer spaces of the world. He lived not far from the shore-side, at Nuka Hiva, and was an enthusiastic astronomer. His lone homestead was by the lowest peak of some hills, and so situated that it was eminently suitable for the purposes for which he required it, which were rest, reading and quiet, and unobserved observation of the starry skies; whereat for hours, with hopeful eye fixed at the telescope, he would gaze on cloudless nights.

Night after night, while the traders and natives slept, the solitary old man would sleeplessly follow his hobby. The wild poetry of primeval nature surrounded his hut home; the swinging seas thundered or softly broke over the reefs below, and clumps of pandanus-trees and coco-palms, like æolian harps, caught the wandering winds and wailed mournfully. They were and are wild places, and the scattered isles were as oases on the vast Sahara of the Pacific Ocean. Tao-o-hae was the nearest primitive capital, where strange races mingled and traded. Inland lived the old tribes, the survivors of cannibalistic days. Those old tattooed Marquesan chiefs sat by their conical dens, chewed modern plug tobacco and smoked opium, and looked upon the calaboose as the final resting-place for reflective age. In the villages the natives grew copra and tropical fruits and sold them to the French, who formed the greater part of the white population. They wore the ridi, and still encouraged old tribal customs, and the native women and girls, though modest and virtuous, were often ruined, body and soul, by the Chinamen who sold them opium and did many other things.

Why old Gilbert—for that was the name we knew the astronomer by—had left his native land and lived this lonely life was a mystery that no one bothered about; one thing was certain—he was no myth and was there. We all liked him. Originally he must have been a tall man, but age had bent his backbone and reduced his height by about two inches. His unkempt grey beard gave him a patriarchal aspect, and his deep-set clear grey eyes, fine, lofty brow and kind expression revealed no hint of inward vice. The native Marquesan servant who tidied his one room once a week was old and wrinkled, being over seventy years of age. Photographs pinned on the wooden wall of his bedroom imaged the refined faces of relatives, one of them a sad-faced young girl.

"Solitary Gilbert" was respected by the white community of the district, a community which chiefly consisted of traders and cast-ashore sailors of various nations, and represented the adventurous stock of England, Scotland, and France, one or two Mongolian niggers, and a full-blooded celestial who did their washing and spent the proceeds on Marquesan ladies, who wore few clothes, worked on the various plantations, chatted and chewed.

The traders used to congregate in the grog shanty, which was run by a jovial *libre* from Numea, the convict settlement, tell their various experiences and argue over the latest Marquesan politics or murders, and also express their various views of the local missionaries, who had long since given them up as hopeless atheists. Drinking beer till their teeth floated seemed to be the height of their ambition, though a few hoped to realise by trading enough money to go back to their native land. They were jovial men; some had sailed the seven seas, and some had hurriedly emigrated direct to the South Seas, and only thought of their country in troublous dreams; but all of them positively refused to give up their wild ways, listen to the missionaries and live a sweet and beerless life. Only one man had a magnetic influence for good over them, and that man was the mysterious old astronomer, Gilbert.

I came to know the lonely star-watcher well. Often while I was sitting in the grog shanty, listening to the traders arguing, he would walk in, and talk and lecture them; and they listened with profound respect. When excited by the thrilling subject of his conversation—the stars—his aged lips trembled and revealed the sensitive temperament of a lofty imagination. Something in his manner and in his earnest voice made us all lift our eyes and attention to him.

Every night he would bring his telescope under his arm and, perching it outside on a beer barrel, get the traders, each in turn, to fix their eyes to the lens and gaze at the heavens. We all liked the wise old man, and from him I learnt all that I know of the stars and their travels through space.

Once the old fellow was laid up with a chill and lay for two or three days in bed. I did my best for him as he sat up in his bunk, attired in a red nightshirt, looking ill and solemn, and passing the time by talking philosophy. Schopenhauer was his pet subject when he could not gaze at the stars. He gave me his books, but though I made a great mental effort I only succeeded, after reading the books, in discovering that I knew nothing, that life was nothing, that creation was a tremendous black nothing wherein human eyes continually opened and shaped all that Is! That stars flashed out of the same human consciousness that imagined pain, passion and all the arts and emotions which beautify the imagined Universe. As I knew little at that time of philosophy, old Gilbert found me an appreciative and quiet listener, who did not argue on any point; indeed, I became fond of him and so, through respect for his memory, I am now attempting a short biographical note of his existence.

Music he loved, and I would play the violin to him; old and staid as he was, when I played softly and tenderly some old melody his voice would join tremulously in and, though pathetically toneless, outrivalled a master voice by its sincerity. Poetry he liked, and beyond his table and one old chair and bunk bed his furniture consisted of two long shelves of classical books. Through him my mind was enlarged, till I realised that pianissimo, legato and staccato cadenza and music's mysterious charm, vaguely expressed, but did not fathom, the serious ideals of life; were only as a wailing, wandering wind of the mind, stirring the soul and the flowers of memory, as they sighed through the emotions, a breath on the deep waters of thought.

Yes, that solitary old astronomer friend of my youth, though I did not realise it then, revealed to me that literature and poetry were great and beautiful music fused in the white heat of thought's spiritual flame, and for that alone his memory is ever dear to me.

Notwithstanding his virtues, the missionaries looked upon him as an old madman, and he in turn gazed upon them with intense pity. The storekeeper hard by, who sold everything from a needle to tinned meat, was a "deeply religious" man and trusted everyone but Gilbert. I remember him well; he was determined to be just and right, spoke often about God and divinity, with a voice that rang with the note of justness and sounded like the clink of Government scale-weights. He did well in his store shop, and I think he would have weighed a gift of the widow's mite carefully before she left his premises.

One night he was discovered dead, and Ah Foo, the Chinaman, suddenly left the district; though the crack in the storekeeper's head was put down to a fall, we had our suspicions. The traders cursed the storekeeper's death, because Ah Foo did their washing and they had now to fall back on the native girls, who only wore ridis and grass and could not resist the temptation of such finery, and so often they wore our shirts and collars and under-pants for weeks before returning them, and if they secured admirers they sometimes eloped into the forest with them, and our washing was seen no more! So though the islands were made a paradise by coco-palms, tropical fruit trees, sea-beaten reefs and inland mountains, they had their drawbacks.

Gilbert used suddenly to appear in the grog shanty, quietly sit on a tub, look round, critically scan the rough, unshaved faces of the traders and then say: "Boys, beer may be well, and doubtless has its advantages, but do you ever think of the skies, the vastness of space, with its myriads of worlds, endless sunsets and sunrises sparkling through infinite gloom?" At this they would wipe their mouths with the back of their hands and gaze awestruck at one another, each seeking to hear a reply from the other, for the word "infinity" had something in it that outwitted their comprehension. The oldest and biggest scoundrel of the lot would look the most earnest and, after placing his quart pot on the shanty bench, slowly wipe his bearded mouth and say: "Professor, we do think of them 'ere marvellous things; nights and nights they worries us when we thinks of the vast abscess" (abyss) "called Space." Then old Gilbert, encouraged, would once more proceed and say: "Like unto Thee, space hath no end; and the stars, which are as the dust of heaven, eternally roll out blue days and sunsets for endless myriads of worlds that are sparkling through infinite space. Yet, O men, are thy souls immersed in no more than the fumes of beer!" At this the trader would get argumentative and say: "What's the end of space, and if yer go to the end where would yer fall if yer fell over?"

"O man of beer," old Gilbert answered, delighted to have got up a controversy over his pet hobby, "your thoughts cannot out-travel the range of your intellect; you but surmise an end, because your intellect hath an end; thou art finite and the heavens infinite," and after saying this, which was Greek to them all, he brought forth his telescope from under his coat. Each one outside under the clear tropical skies would glue his curious eye to the end of the tube and gaze at the orbs of space; and so the professor spent his time and gradually induced in the rough traders a genuine love of astronomy.

They all got really to like him and listened eagerly to all he said, and often they ceased their drinking bouts and saved their money when their trading-ships came in from the scattered isles of the North and South Pacific. Many nights down the slopes they went like obedient children, following old Gilbert in single file, as they walked along looking up at the stars, towards Gilbert's observatory. They surrounded him; in a ring, on the lonely hill at midnight, they listened to his lecture, gazed through his old Herschelian telescope at the seaward stars and the moon, and then looked into each other's eyes astonished, saying: "Wonderful, mates, all them 'ere worlds, like this 'ere, and the professor's found 'em!"

Gilbert would stand on the beach, proudly gazing upon his sinful, rough pupils, as the sea-winds stirred his grey beard, and his deep-set eyes shone as they probed him with questions, not to please him, but from intellectual curiosity. Afterwards he granted them all one final drink of rum!

When he died he was buried in the little railed-in plateau, where also lay the dust of exiled white men and a few Marquesan chiefs of the old times, who slept quietly in that silent cemetery by the mountains. When the traders stood by old Gilbert's grave, and slowly lowered the coffin down, tears were in the eyes of even the worst of them. He had made them better men, and through his little telescope tube, which pointed to the heavens, he had put into their hearts thoughts on the grandeur of creation and reverence for God's wonderful work.

So Gilbert lived, toiled and died, the sincerest and most successful missionary of the far South Seas.

CHAPTER XXVI

A Deck-hand on Board the *Eldorado*—A Socialist—A Fo'c'sle Fight—Buying an Island—Apemama—King Tembinok—The *Eldorado* sails—Tembinok's Palace—Seeking the Enemy—The captured Chief—The Hurricane

IN Sydney long ago I shipped as deck-hand on board the *Eldorado*, a schooner bound for Fiji and the Gilbert Groups. The first night out we squared the yards; the wind was aft and the canvas bellied out steadily as we dipped along under the stars at a good eight knots.

On board, as saloon passenger, was a Mr Milburn, a socialistic crank of the theorist school. He was aboard on the outlook for an island which he could buy and which would suit a socialistic colony, and he had got it into his head that Apemama was a likely spot to start his scheme. The skipper, a Yankee with long face and billygoat whiskers, was mostly drunk, and would stand on the poop aft, telling Milburn that the King of Apemama was an old pal of his and he knew for a positive fact that he wanted to sell his dominion. Milburn's blue eyes shone with delight as the skipper listened to him and kept saying: "The very thing, the very spot! I guess you'll be glad yer shipped aboard here when yer see the isles," and then he would smack Milburn on the back, for they were having high jinks in the cabin aft. Milburn had plenty of money and gave it freely to the skipper, who could hardly conceal his satisfaction as he opened bottle after bottle of whisky and gave us cigars.

We arrived in due course at Suva, Fiji. Milburn went ashore and looked around and was delighted with all he saw. The skipper kept close to him and said: "I guess if you like this d——d place you'll go daft with joy when you see Apemama." We only stayed two days at Fiji and then left for the group of islands of which Apemama was one. With fair winds we made a quick trip and soon dropped anchor off the lagoon isle. Milburn, through a telescope, gazed enthusiastically across the lagoon and on to the atolls and groves of distant waving coco-palms; the skipper stood beside him and, as Milburn gazed, smacked him on the back and nudged him in the ribs, saying: "I guess that'll suit you right enough, eh?" He told Milburn to leave the purchasing to him and the isle would soon be Milburn Isle, the socialistic El Dorado of the South Seas.

I instinctively knew that the skipper was on some scheme, and I had discovered that he was the biggest liar on earth and sea, so when he said that he knew that Milburn could purchase Apemama I had my own doubts; but Milburn was a bit soft, treated the skipper with drink and money in advance and had positive faith in his promises.

Later Milburn and I sat on the cabin settee and had a whisky each. We liked each other, for, to tell the truth, we were the only respectable members of polite society on board, for the crew was made up of two or three Americans or negroes, three Polynesians, a half-blood, a lascar and a Dutch American. I felt a bit out of sorts, for the night before there had been a terrible row in the fo'c'sle while the crew were sitting around their bench, shuffling and playing cards by the oil fo'c'sle lamp.

I was standing smoking and watching, when suddenly I was astonished to see them all jump off their feet and start a regular tribalistic battle; one had been caught cheating and they took sides. You never saw such a jumbled sight of struggling figures as the shadows of knives danced on the walls. A white man fell on top of a half-blood, who fastened his yellowish teeth into his opponent's ear; he wouldn't let go, and the white pounded away at his face with his clenched fists, as the half-blood tugged and chewed away at his ear. As the American punched him he cried out: "Yer-rrrr-rr-ip! Yerrr-rr-ip!" and the white man shouted: "You d——d —— —— ——," and many more things, only to be described in dashes. A Chinaman who was shouting: "Kee-Honk! Chow k-rrr—Chrry!" suddenly fell, as an empty hundred-pound beef tub hit him behind the ear. He was buried overboard that same night; and what with one thing and another, as I said before, I was a bit out of sorts and glad of a little whisky for medicinal purposes. Milburn also was a bit shaky. The skipper had shot the tip of the half-blood's chin off and then the matter ended, and all I got out of it was a lost tooth and the knowledge that white men in a passion get purply red in the neck and foamy at the mouth, and that the eyes of the savage races turn yellowish and their brown lips whitish.

The skipper, who had gone on shore, returned at sunset with four canoes crammed with natives, and a solemn-looking old chap with a large, flattish nose, wide nostrils and a wrinkled face expressing chimpanzee astuteness. He was introduced to Milburn, as his half-naked form clambered up the rope gangway and he leapt on deck. To my surprise I heard that he was King Tembinok.

With a retinue of dusky courtiers, dressed in cast-off shirts, in Indian file behind him, he strutted along the deck, gazed almost scornfully at the crew, who were specially mustered to pay respect to royalty, and then looked us all up and down as though we were a menagerie group on show. Royally did he carry himself, demanding little attentions from his retinue, who obeyed his every wish with alacrity. He swung a huge war-club to and fro, as though his whole being itched to find fault and brain the first native who might, to his intense relief, mistake his hurried orders.

"You Misser Milbur, who want to buy island?" he said, gazing up at Milburn, who looked slightly embarrassed as he bowed, while the skipper rubbed his hands together and smiled with inward satisfaction. "Yes, your Majesty, such is my wish, if your dominion is for sale." At this the King bowed graciously and said: "Good isles, much land, plenty houses and coco-palms, but me sell to white man if the money 'nough." "I have come specially from Australia to buy an island, and your land is most suitable, and I have the money to buy it," Milburn answered. King Tembinok bowed once more, till the royal robe of tappu-cloth touched the deck in front of his feet and revealed his bare legs behind him. His beady, intelligent eyes rolled with delight, and somewhat destroyed his majestic bearing, as the skipper bowed him and Milburn into the dining saloon. He turned his head, spat in the tiny calabash that his orderly ever held behind him, and disappeared.

I don't know the exact details of what passed in the cabin, but the King eventually came out on deck blind drunk, with four bottles of whisky and rum, two bottles under each arm. His retinue tied ropes round him, and his big dark lips slobbered and grinned as they slowly lowered his royal carcass down into the boat. The skipper leaned over the side and shouted, telling them to clear off ashore.

It appeared that Milburn had bought the island and given the King a large amount in cash as a deposit, and had also given a hundred pounds to the skipper as commission and for his kindness and help in the transaction.

The sun had set, and Milburn was a bit the worse for whisky, and anxious to get ashore and see the island, which was only natural. The skipper looked a bit uneasy and tried to persuade him to go to bed and go ashore on the morrow, but he was determined, and as the skipper went into his cabin Milburn called the native occupants of a canoe that was hovering by the ship's bows and bargained with them to take him ashore. He begged me to go with him, and at last I accepted the offer, for I also was eager to have a look round, and in a tick I slid down the rope and off we went towards the shore.

With a jerk the canoe touched the reef and we jumped ashore. Before us lay groves of moonlit coco-palms, pandanus and island pines; behind us the silvered breakers were charging and curling over the lines of coral reefs as we tramped together up the shore. Milburn's mouth opened with excitement and pleasure. "Dear, dear," he said, as his eyes gleamed with delight about the bargain he had made. Side by side we stood on the plateau and gazed on the glimmering island landscape, looking at the natives and their children moving about near their den-like homes. I, too, felt some of Milburn's enthusiasm, for the isle seemed a very paradise of peace and quiet. I almost envied the socialist colonist, who, I thought, would soon live at Apemama, and I made up my mind to stick to Mr Milburn, for I saw that he would soon be the reigning monarch and my influential friend.

Not far off glimmered the whitish terraced stockade of the King's palace. "Come on," said Milburn, "we will go and see the King; he's a good fellow and by now will be sober." Saying this he led the way, and the natives, who had answered our inquiries with awestruck eyes, followed us as we passed by the palms and kicked the sand up with our boots, our monstrous shadows gliding across the still moonlit lagoon as we went by. Little native children came with their dark mothers from the native homes among the palm-trees and looked at us with awestruck eyes.

As we strode on Milburn's walk became almost majestic, as he thought of his kingship over that island, and I must admit I felt a bit swaggery too over my prospects. It was excusable, though, in me, for I had had many ups and downs, and all the bread I had cast on the waters had returned to me after many days, buttered with phosphorus paste, so to speak.

Soon we were asking the high chiefs if we could see the King. At first they demurred, and held a council by the stockade gate. Milburn tried to explain to them that the island was now his. "You no savee," he said, as they guarded the entrance and looked at him fiercely and curiously. "No see King," they replied, but Milburn put a silver coin into the hand of the head vassal, and then at once, with much ceremony, we entered through the stockades of coral rock and bamboo posts and went up by the palisade that led to his Majesty's palace bungalows. Four high chiefs accompanied us, with ponderous war-clubs that enforced the laws of Apemama. At the end of the winding pathway, shaded by palms, they all stopped and said: "You want see King Tembinok?" "Yes," said Milburn, showing great irritation at the delay and absurd ceremony that we had to go through to seek the King's presence; for had not the King a few hours before embraced him and departed from the *Eldorado's* decks very drunk? Again we all moved on. Walking through a narrow archway we entered the royal waiting chamber; it was high-roofed for a South Sea palace, and thick tappu-cloth curtains divided it from the room wherein King Tembinok sat. "He does things in style," said Milburn, as we looked round and listened to four Apemama females who sat by the royal doorway, twanged strings fastened across gourds and sang songs that told of love and the mighty deeds of Tembinok's ancestors. "I wonder if he's sober," I muttered, thinking to myself how different and austere all looked from what I had anticipated. Suddenly the leading chief, who was in front of us, said: "Tereoaka" ("white man"). Then we watched, for he turned and said something to us that intimated that the King was approaching. The thick tapestry curtain suddenly divided; my heart beat rapidly. King Tembinok stood before us! At first Milburn instinctively looked over and beyond the King's shoulder, for we had not yet realised that he was the King; then in a moment I saw it all; the old liar of a skipper had brought a dummy king on to the ship and Milburn had been done! Milburn seemed dazed, then once more loudly demanded to see the King! Tembinok stared fiercely at him. I gave Milburn a nudge, but he seemed to lose his head and shouted once again: "Where the hell's the King?" The King, thinking he was mad, in a loud voice shouted a command in his own language; at once all the chiefs raised their clubs and the royal serenading of the palace harem suddenly ceased! I lifted my hands and made rapid signs, and in my fright pointed to my own head, to intimate that Milburn was insane. I thought it the only thing to do, for his sake and mine also. Tembinok seemed to understand me, but he stood before us wrinkling and frowning fiercely at Milburn's manner. He had been disturbed from his sleep. His tall form was robed in a discarded man-o'-war's uniform and his corpulence bulged it considerably. His sleepy eyes still looked fierce as he gazed upon us, and then Milburn shouted: "I've bought this island! Where's the late King?" Tembinok could understand a little English, and on hearing this stared speechless with amazement, then lifted his hand as though to give Milburn a clout. Milburn was a fool, but no coward, and I really believe he would have gone for Tembinok if I had not hurriedly grasped him and shouted: "You blind ass, the skipper's done you. This *is* King Tembinok." Not till I said that did Milburn see the whole situation, and then, to my great relief, he breathed out: "Well, I'm d——d." Then, by gesticulations and pidgin-English, we told Tembinok all, at which he became most courteous and invited us to come ashore on the morrow and look round the palace.

Milburn was almost mad with rage and itching to get back to the ship to have a reckoning with the Yankee skipper. I saw that he was, after all, not the kind of man to be done, and that he believed in getting his money's worth and being boss in his own line, notwithstanding his theories on socialism. We both grasped Tembinok's hand and accepted his kind invitation to call at the palace the next day; and then the high chiefs, wondering at the whole business, rolled their banana-leaf cigarettes between their fingers, bowed and led us out of the royal presence and through the gates of the palace stockades.

We hurried down to the shore; all was silent except a few natives singing as they took a moonlight bathe in the waves. We looked across the lagoon and both stared; the ship was gone! Seaward, like a bird with many wings, fast disappearing under the brilliant moon, we saw afar the *Eldorado* taking advantage of the breeze; for the skipper was crowding on all sail. He had flown!

I will not tell you what Milburn and I said. Heaven will forgive us; it was unprintable. All our belongings were on board too! We were both stranded, and the skipper had made the most profitable voyage of his life. We told the natives to keep a lookout for the next trading-boat and, side by side, without saying a word, but deep in thought, we went back to the palace.

Tembinok had been thinking the matter over in our absence and was in a great rage at being impersonated. He was a wonderful-looking old fellow, with bright eyes, a keen yet half-humorous expression and slightly full lips. He carried himself as though he was the one and only king on earth. He at once invited us to stop till a boat came and gave us a chance to go away. It was well for the skipper that he had gone, for I really believe the ship would have been bombarded that same night by the native King's battalions, so great was the royal rage. We gave Tembinok a description of the sham king, and then some natives, who had come aboard, accepted a bribe and told all; he was a Marquesan chief who then lived on the neighbouring Isle Kuria and was a deadly enemy of Tembinok. A war council was held and things began to look much brighter than I expected for Milburn, who promised to give me a hundred pounds if I stuck to him and helped him get some of his deposit back, and also a bit of his own back off that fraudulent king.

That night we stopped at the palace. Poor old Milburn looked pale and almost cried when he thought of how he had been done, and I could see that he had set his heart on getting the island. Tembinok turned out a good sort; the fierce expression of his countenance had changed to one of majestic benevolence, as he gazed upon us and we humbly sat on mats before him. "You buy island?" he said, and then with a most conspicuous attempt at concealing his cynical amusement solemnly gave orders to his head wives, who sang to him and fanned off the droves of mosquitoes that attacked his eyes and face.

The palace contained many rooms, through which crept barefooted native girls busily attending to the numerous requirements of the head queen. She was a fat, oily-looking woman, of about forty years of age, who put on terrible side and blinked her eyes as we surveyed her respectfully. Two eunuchs kept blowing cooling breath on to her perspiring body, for the little wind that blew was extremely hot.

We slept nearly all next day and then went to see the neighbouring villages; the natives had comfortable wooden homes (*maniaps*) built on posts, open at the sides to let the wind in. We soon tired, and again returned that night to the palace and were then allowed, for the first time, to go over the various rooms. I was astonished at all we saw, for it was furnished well with native and European furniture. It seemed hard to believe that the memory of the King could go back to cannibalism and strangulating festivals; indeed, such things were still practised in moderation. On the walls hung clubs, muzzle-loading rifles and many murderous weapons of savage warfare and law.

A pretty maid blew weird music through a bone flute, serenading the queen, who moved her fat lips in lisping murmurs of melody, while six squatting maidens waved their long arms and sang. On the wooden walls the shadows of the pandanus and palms waved in the brilliant moonlight that lit the palace glooms.

No king in the South Seas lived in such royal state as Tembinok; he reigned supreme in his terraced seraglio and lived a life of luxury and command, a life that to Western minds would seem one of selfish debauchery and fiery lust, but by the code of South Sea morals was one of extreme virtue and moderation amounting to self-sacrifice.

Milburn gasped with horror as a Samoan attendant told us of Tembinok and his ancestors. With their own hands they had strangled wives and concubines who had given elsewhere that which was destined for the royal favour only. In some of the bed-chambers still lay the bones of the victims who had been sharers in the offence, for they were buried under the floor matting. They were generally chiefs who had met their end, through some slight suspicion, from the club of Tembinok or his ancestors who reigned before him. They would creep by night into the supposed culprit's sleeping-room and crash his skull in while he slept. Often down those very corridors, where Milburn and I sat listening, crept, in the dead of night, files of harem wives, stealthily moving towards the woman who it was suspected had given herself up to other than the king. With exultation alight in their eyes they would do Tembinok's bidding, for jealousy of each other was their one pronounced virtue, and seldom was more than one stifled scream heard, as they clutched the sleeping victim on her bed-mat, all their hands struggling in rivalship together to strangle the sleeping concubine who had betrayed their master. As the Samoan from Apia, who was employed at the palace, told us all this, Milburn and I felt a bit uncomfortable about our own presence, and I looked carefully at the revolver which I always carried with me. Then I had several drinks from Milburn's flask, and that and the thought of the hundred pounds he had promised me stifled my qualms; we went off to our allotted apartments, slept close together and, to our great satisfaction, survived the night.

Fortunately I had several plugs of ship's tobacco and so secured the friendship of chiefs of high ancestral standing. I held the plugs tightly in my hand and they each in turn bit off the allowance I allotted them. They seemed very proud men and kept saying, "Me great chief," and giving details of their ancestry, for having no *Peerage* or *Who's Who* they were obliged to remind people, to keep the old names going.

It was a beautiful isle, and next morning I felt glad to be with Milburn there and felt extremely happy; birds sang up in the pandanus-trees, sunlight danced on coral-floored waters, the very fish seemed happy as they leapt in the still lagoons. Milburn said he would like to stay there all his life, and for a while he forgot his sorrows; and well he might, for I knew that if he persevered in trying to get his money back he would have plenty of trouble in store for him. "When I get my deposit back I'll stop and go cruising these seas," he said, and I agreed to go with him.

On the slopes by Tembinok's palace romped the native children, while the Apemama maids sewed dress material into new designs, for the fashion changed and the ridis would be increased by one inch, or reduced, or an extra tassel added. The chief characteristic of Apemama ladies was not modesty, but the bareness of their curved figures served as steel armour to protect their loose virtue; for the rumours of punishments that had been dealt out for amorous crimes made white men and brown men alike regard the maiden bareness with horror.

That day Tembinok and his war council decided to go with a fleet of canoes to Kuria and seek the chief who had aided our skipper in his cruel duplicity. Milburn heard this decision with delight, but, to tell the truth, I must confess that my joy was considerably damped when the council added that we also should go with them to seek and attack the enemy. We did not like to appear afraid, so we asked for a little time to decide, and finally told the high chief to tell Tembinok that we would follow the fleet of canoes in a boat some distance behind!

During the day the sun shone down on the isle in dazzling tropic flame; the whole town lazily lolled and snoozed in the shades of the palms or by the piazzas of their homes, by groves of bananas and pandanus. In the afternoon, to kill time, we went for a row in a native boat across the lagoon and up and down the creeks and shallows of the atolls. The water was as clear as crystal, and we could look over the boat's side and see numerous brightly coloured fish darting and hovering among the scintillating seaweeds that waved gently over floors of sparkling corals; and as we watched it seemed that we looked through a vast magnifying-glass at forests or worlds far away, as branches shone with rich crimson, green, indigo or blue deep down in those depths that shone like some magic world blazed up by rainbows.

To our delight and relief, for we were both deep in thought over the coming battle, before sunset the sails of a schooner came through the sky-line, and before the stars hung in the darkening blue over the sea she was ploughing toward us, within five miles of the immense island lagoon.

It had been arranged that the High Chief Taku and fifty warriors should put off at dusk to seek the enemy. It all seemed like a dream to me; I had to shake myself to realise the position, for it seemed more like some tale from fiction than reality. But it was real enough, for there stood Milburn in the flesh before me, talking to the natives. I found that their great incentive to help us was Milburn offering to buy cargo for them all as soon as the next trading ship called at Apemama. The cargoes consisted chiefly of trifles, ornaments, old tickless clocks, muzzle-loaders, tobacco and artificial jewellery; the latter adorned the bodies of the whole tribe and was the chief dress of marriageable maids. "What's the good of this game, Mr Milburn?" I said, as darkness fell and I saw the natives filling their canoes with ammunition—war-clubs, and old-fashioned muzzle-loading rifles. "Are you determined to go?" "Most decidedly," he replied, "and after I have settled with this case I'll settle with your skipper." "Right you are," I answered.

At dusk the canoes shoved off the silver sands and put to sea. Milburn and I, armed to the teeth, in an old ship's boat, bravely crept behind. It was a clear, starlit night; so bright were the stars that they looked like flowers of flame in the deep, dark blue vault; our shadows glided through the waters that mirrored the heavens as we paddled by. As we passed the schooner, that had anchored at sunset, out came a boat to meet us, and then I saw that Milburn was a careful man and also why he was so brave. He had been aboard and told the skipper all, and arranged for them to watch for us and come and convey our boat across to Kuria. I dare say they all got a good tip from him.

When at length we arrived the natives crept by a lagoon; Milburn and I sat in the boat silent with excitement, as we smoked, kept a sharp outlook and waited results. Taku knew where the enemy lived. The whole horde crept to his hut and discovered him fast asleep, blind drunk; he had just finished up the remaining rum that Milburn had given him on the ship.

As we watched from the boat we saw our army on the shore, struggling along, bearing a burden with them. It was the fictitious king bound and lashed hands and feet. Milburn surveyed him, at first with rage and then with curiosity, and I felt rather sorry for him: he looked so different to what he did when he had scornfully gazed at us on the decks of the *Eldorado*. He rolled his eyes, slowly realised his position and hung his head, looking extremely pathetic as he blinked his eyes like a whipped dog and looked at us appealingly for mercy. Milburn and I went to his hut, discovered nearly all the cash and came back quickly to the boat. "You killee me?" he said, and looked steadily at us. "I say, Milburn," I said, "if you take him back to Apemama Tembinok will club him, and you must remember he's only a native, and after all the skipper's to blame." "I know that," said Milburn; and then I added: "To tell you the truth, I rather admire this old chief, when I think of the clever way he simulated kingship and took us all in." Milburn relented; indeed I think he would have done so without my saying anything. "Unbind him," he said. For a while the astonished natives stared, and then they unbound him, and Milburn said: "You can go." For a moment the chief looked as though he did not understand, then gave us both a glance of real gratitude and walked off majestically, but rather fast, in case we changed our minds.

The natives got their cargo from the schooner in the bay and I received my hundred pounds. Tembinok saw us off; we booked as passengers on the *Bella*, for that was the name of the schooner that came in the nick of time to relieve our minds for the night attack. We eventually arrived at Honolulu.

Twelve months after I met Milburn again in Sydney and he turned out a good friend to me. He never saw the skipper of the *Eldorado* again, for the man left his ship and went off to South America, I think.

I heard of Milburn a little later on as going off to Paraguay on the s.s. R——, which was especially fitted out for taking a modern *Mayflower* crew to start a socialistic republic, soon started and soon ended, for the colony turned out as miserable a failure as when Milburn bought Apemama.

Milburn was not my friend's real name; it seems wiser not to give that here, in this account of our experiences together in the South Seas. One name he deserved, that of a brave comrade and a gentleman.

After my adventures with Milburn I left Honolulu in a large schooner which was bound for Suva. We had only been out three days when a hurricane struck us. A Cape Horn slasher was nothing compared to the weather we experienced. I was standing on deck smoking with several of the crew; some of them were natives. A soft breeze came up and increased till the elements moaned with a steady hum, as the sails bellied out like drums and the foamy manes of white horses tossed away in the sunset; then with a thundering moan the hurricane's breath struck us. The skipper yelled to us. "Aye, aye, sir," we shouted back, for a half-blood and I were aloft taking sail in; suddenly the boat lay over and the rigging to leeward nearly touched the wave-crests.

Darkness slid over the ocean sky, tremendous seas came up, and the schooner backed and shivered like a frightened mammoth thing as the mountains of water jumped down on her deck. I fell forward on my face beneath the liquid mass and gripped the deck with my fingers and teeth! Crash! Crash! the boats were carried away. I heard my chum gasping and spitting sea-water beside me. The sea cleared and the wind shot up my legs— r-r-r—r-r-i-p—r-r—r-r-r-i-p! and my trousers split and nearly blew away. We scrambled to our feet and clung to the ropes. "Hold on, lads," shouted the skipper, and we did hold on too! Scud was flying across the sky and the moon travelling like a yellow racing balloon as the wrack of mist flew under it. The phosphorescent blaze that lit the tossing foam of the travelling mountains of water around us made it all look like a ghostly scene of chaos ere creation; the winds cut the hissing wave-tops off as though invisible giant swords flashed across the ghostly ocean darkness. Then another sea came over, crash! right over the galley. The cook was washed through the door, still clutching the pots that he had been trying to keep on the galley stove. His rapid exit knocked us over as he was washed by, and we all clutched each other and bravely held on, each to the other, to save our own lives. The man at the wheel was washed from the poop and joined us; the skipper took his place. No one was lost; some miracle saved the boat and all of us; the wind howled and rushed away as quickly as it arrived.

The skipper was a good sort; he had sailed in the black-birding days with cargoes of natives to the Isles of Mystery. Now he gave us rum, and we were the happiest crew on the high seas in our new lease of life, for that is how we all felt. Only experience could paint to you the wildness of a South Sea hurricane, and what we sailors felt as we slid along the vessel's deck holding on to each other's legs and hair to prevent ourselves being clutched and torn away into the infinite waters.

We put into Palmyra Isle and made things ship-shape, and then left for Apia and Fiji, where I left the boat and took a steamer for New South Wales.

CHAPTER XXVII

My England—Its Chief Stronghold—The Island Race—Barbaric Customs—Their Code of Morals—A Tribalistic Clash—An English Spring

THIS chapter is written for the benefit of those natives who may come across my book in the South Sea Islands and elsewhere. Of course I know England well, because I am an Englishman. I escaped from my birthplace at an early age, shipped before the mast of a sailing ship and roamed the world. England is always the dear old Homeland to me, and so it might interest my readers if I include reminiscences of my own country in this book.

My England is an island surrounded by open sea and Channel. The climate is variable; Atlantic winds blow over it and copious rains drench the population at frequent intervals. The "survival of the fittest" theory is finely illustrated by the athletic appearance of the native stock; the climate kills all weaklings at birth.

London is the chief stronghold; battalions of pale-faced native warriors tramp the tracks that divide the mighty forests of gloomy walls. They are a brave tribe, and ever on the warpath as they glide along, passing under historic arches and over the bridges that rib their old river, which is called the Thames. At night, when the stars are out and the moon is high in the sky, you can stand on those bridges and see the monuments that have been erected to commemorate old tribal heroes. The spires of the vast city for miles and miles point to the heavens, under the pale, glittering stars, like outstretched fingers on the vast hands of Pride.

The island race is a happy one, and hope springs eternal in the native breast. If no sun shines this summer, still they hope on till the next summer.

The common papalangi or serf class are warrior-like and cheerful folk, and not unlike the South Sea Island races in their habits. On tribal holidays they go off to various resorts, drink toddy and do war dances; many appear next morning before the high chiefs, who hear with solemn countenance of their misdeeds as they lean on the official war-club and fine them five dollars.

The aristocrats are similar to Fijian and Solomon Islanders of royal blood, for they are cannibalistic; they do not eat human flesh, but they live on the blue blood that runs in their veins and on the vigour of the flesh of the common natives. Their ancestry is similar to that of the South Sea Islanders—through some mighty deed, that when tested by the code of morals appears dubious, their line is famous for ever. They have a *Peerage* and *Who's Who*, which are genealogical and tell of the first high chief in the family, what he did and what they do now. Their chief aim is to forget all else and produce sons, so as to keep the tribal name going. The camp fires have disappeared and the tribal den is now a mighty residence made of stone; on the walls hang ancestral weapons. These grandees sit beneath them, eat and drink well and no longer dye their bodies with woad.

They have a dreadful inquisition called *respectability*; once in its clutches the common natives lose their intellectual equilibrium, become hollow-throated and cough with a windy soullessness.

Old tribal customs are fast disappearing, and the high chiefs losing their power and influence over the natives, who are becoming well educated and will soon own the country. Human nature will still be the same, so there will be sixty or seventy million kings, as many kings as the population amounts to, and only God knows what will happen then.

The native women are white and have beautiful blue eyes, like the blue of your skies. They wear ridis that reach to their ankles. Their morals are excellent, but, like their sisters in the far South Seas, some of them still retain the old instincts and fall before the temptation of the white man, and the fallen maid takes all the blame.

If one stops a chief or his wife on the forest track and says, "Aloha! Mitai Chipi," and grasps their hand in true friendship, one is liable to be taken before the high chief and fined five hundred dollars.

The forest idols are gone, but the natives still kneel in amphitheatres, before stone images, where they hold festivals, and their old high priest accepts confessional bribes and then forgives them their sins—which are many.

The old-time convivial spirit has passed away; you cannot jump in the island lagoons unless fully dressed. Many of the old barbaric customs are still in vogue, but are practised in secret. They have wild festivals, still play tom-toms, big drums and reeds, and whirl round and round in the old tribalistic Siva dance, clinging to each other's bodies and gazing lasciviously into each other's blue eyes. Their *fantoes*,[17] instead of being carried on their mothers' backs in the old primitive basket, are wheeled along in vehicles to an advanced age; and dominate the native villages and the lives of the chiefs. There is no camping out now; free dens have disappeared. For camping in the forest as of old, one is liable to get fastened up between stone walls for six months. One cannot pick coco-nuts, yams and bread-fruit if one is hungry.

17. Children.

There is an organization for starving natives, presided over by high chiefs with cheerless, glassy eyes. The elder natives have to apologise for being old when they go there; but most of them when they are hungry run for their lives, and starve to death sooner than approach the organization's cave kindness. The poor-class natives drink a mysterious concoction made from a herb called the hop, and the high chiefs drink stuff called kava, or whisky. When those high chiefs are sober, they become solemn; and hold councils for putting down the drinking of hop-toddy. All the native girls aspire to marry chiefs. The code of morals is so peculiar that thousands of them die childless and mateless.

They are withal a brave, warrior-like race; and at present are engaged in one of their old tribalistic clashes with another tribe, of a group that lies not far from their own isle; a bloodthirsty race that are at heart still cannibalistic. The king of this other tribe is somewhat like old Thakambau, the late Fijian Emperor of the Cannibal Isles; he pretends to have embraced Christianity, but his real god is the high chief Krupp. I feel sorry for him, for the islanders are sure to get hold of him and he will wish he had embraced their creed. Several other warrior tribes are crashing away with the island natives; they charge well and sing fine old war-songs. It is much safer at present to live in the Solomon Isles.

The island country is very beautiful. In the springtime the landscapes and valleys are dotted with yellow things called primroses; other wild flowers grow on the hedgerow banks. Little birds sing in old trees to the sunsets; the grass grows, and grows high ere they cut it down. The woods smell of peat; the native homesteads in the villages burn wood, and you can smell its delightful odour along the lanes as you tramp by. It is a beautiful country; but violin-playing, music and poetry are not appreciated by the natives as they are appreciated in the South Seas.

But still I love the memory of the hedgerows, wild flowers and far-off hills, and the remains of the old forests wherein long ago their ancestors camped; by old hills where the young lambs bleat in the springtime and wild birds sing in leafy woods and hollows. I hope in the end I shall be buried somewhere near where the wind and the wild blackbird sing; and not very far from the shores of the sea, where their ships go down Channel with sailors outbound for distant lands.

Milton Keynes UK
Ingram Content Group UK Ltd.
UKHW040831071024
449371UK00007B/725